# WARS AND SOLDIERS IN THE EARLY REIGN OF LOUIS XIV

Volume 7 – Armies of the German States 1655-1690 Part 3

**Text and Illustrations by Bruno Mugnai**

'This is the Century of the Soldier', Fulvio Testi, Poet, 1641

HELION & COMPANY

Helion & Company Limited
Unit 8 Amherst Business Centre
Budbrooke Road
Warwick
CV34 5WE
England
Tel. 01926 499 619
Email: info@helion.co.uk
Website: www.helion.co.uk
Twitter: @helionbooks
Visit our blog http://blog.helion.co.uk/

Published by Helion & Company 2025
Designed and typeset by Mary Woolley, Battlefield Design (www.battlefield-design.co.uk)
Cover designed by Paul Hewitt, Battlefield Design (www.battlefield-design.co.uk)

Text © Bruno Mugnai 2024
Photographs and illustrations © as individually credited
Maps by George Anderson © Helion and Company 2024
Colour artwork by Bruno Mugnai © Helion & Company 2024

Every reasonable effort has been made to trace copyright holders and to obtain their permission for the use of copyright material. The author and publisher apologize for any errors or omissions in this work and would be grateful if notified of any corrections that should be incorporated in future reprints or editions of this book.

ISBN 978-1-804517-49-9

British Library Cataloguing-in-Publication Data.
A catalogue record for this book is available from the British Library.

All rights reserved. No part of this publication may be reproduced, stored in a retrieval system, or transmitted, in any form, or by any means, electronic, mechanical, photocopying, recording or otherwise, without the express written consent of Helion & Company Limited.

For details of other military history titles published by Helion & Company Limited contact the above address or visit our website: http://www.helion.co.uk.

We always welcome receiving book proposals from prospective authors.

# Contents

| | | |
|---|---|---|
| 1 | Introduction: Military Labour and Recruitment in Germany | 5 |
| 2 | The Armed States | 9 |
| 3 | Imperial Free Cities | 56 |
| 4 | The Duchy of Lorraine | 78 |
| 5 | Wars and Factions in Germany (1653–1689) | 103 |

| | | |
|---|---|---|
| Colour Plate Commentaries | | 121 |

Appendices:

| | | |
|---|---|---|
| I | Orders of Battle and Tabular Data | 133 |
| II | German Regiments, Squadrons and Companies – 1657–1690 | 160 |

# 1

# Introduction: Military Labour and Recruitment in Germany

*'As things are, the army must inevitably consist of the scum of the people, and of all those for whom society has no use.'*
(Comte de St Germain, War Minister of France)

As focused on by authoritative historians, the second half of the seventeenth century saw significant changes in the 'Military' of Western Europe. Collectively, these changes are most commonly labelled as 'the introduction of standing armies'. The changes certainly had a deep impact on the terms as well as the conditions of military labour, since armies typically ranked as the largest single employer within states, and soldiers constituted the most numerous 'unified' labour force within Europe. In this scenario, historians debate whether this development should be understood as a transformation of the armies, putting military labour into a typology of its own, or whether it is more appropriate to investigate the aspects of continuity and place these changes in a general framework of servile labour in the modern age: a topic that promises to be interesting and full of surprises.[1]

Though the most obvious expression of the changes was inevitably connected with the number of professional troops, it does not consist simply of significant growth of many European armies. Although figures illustrate the extent of this growth, it is often impossible to determine the exact strength of these armies, due to the discrepancies between 'on paper' figures and the reality, and because the numbers are often the result of a more or less rough estimate. Therefore, they cannot offer more than an impression of the quantitative aspect of armies. To get an idea of the overall level of military mobilisation in Western Europe, historians would have to include the forces of several of the medium-size powers of Germany. Such an investigation would include not only Brandenburg, Bavaria, Saxony (and Münster) but also Celle, Hannover, Hessen Kassel, Württemberg as well as others such as

---

1 On this topic, see Michael Sikora, 'Change and Continuity in Mercenary Armies: Central Europe, 1650–1750' in E. J. Zürcher (editor), *Fighting for a Living. A Comparative Study of Military Labour 1500–2000* (Amsterdam: Amsterdam University Press, 2013), pp.201–242.

some Saxon Duchies and the Free Imperial Cities, where the relationship between the number of professional troops and population level offers is an extremely varied scenario.

Throughout Germany, as a result of this establishment of professional armies, the demand for recruits increased dramatically. Indeed, the growth in absolute numbers was fuelled by the continuous need for replacements in order to maintain the permanent force as well as for the trade of soldiers with foreign powers. Since the 1650s, the business of recruitment met challenges of a new dimension, forcing recruitment methods to change significantly. By the sixteenth century, Germany had a well-established tradition of military recruitment, often managed by local warlords such as Frundsberg, Berlichingen, Sickingen, Waldburg and Fugger as well as many others. To fill the ranks of their armies, early modern governments made use of a variety of methods of recruitment, which stood on a spectrum of anywhere between voluntary and involuntary. Standing somewhere between voluntary and involuntary forms of recruitment was what might best be termed the quasi-feudal system. The socio-cultural identity of the nobility remained bound up with military endeavour, and the medieval notion that nobles had a feudal obligation to fight for their ruler retained some vigour. Governments also forcibly drafted men whom they regarded as harmful to society or otherwise useless, and this was not a novel expedient. However, the enlistment of dissolute persons should not be exaggerated and probably looms lesser in the historiography than is narrated. Moreover, rogues, vagabonds, and criminals made bad soldiers, and commanders were reluctant to have too many in their forces, and it was generally agreed that volunteers made better soldiers than pressed men.

The typical German method of voluntary recruitment – the *Bestallung* – involved negotiating an agreement with a military contractor for the delivery of a specified number of troops at an agreed time and place. These contract troops developed a reputation for being assertive in defence of their rights, refusing to fight if they were not paid, and usually they were not cheap. However, they comprised a high proportion of veterans, came ready trained and equipped, and acquitted themselves so well on the battlefield that few states dared do without them. This opened up the potential for a novel form of contracting that historians designate as 'general contracting'.[2] Since rulers lacked the necessary native manpower, the administrative structures, and the liquid cash to recruit and supply the soldiers themselves, they turned to the services of general contractors, who undertook the provision of whole regiments and even armies. This system reached a peak during the Thirty Years' War.[3]

---

2 Fritz Redlich, *The German Military Enterpriser and His Workforce: a Study in European Economic and Social History* (Wiesbaden: Franz Steiner Verlag, 1965).

3 Frank Tallet, 'Soldiers in Western Europe, *c.* 1500–1790' in E. J. Zürcher (ed.), *Fighting for a Living. A Comparative Study of Military Labour 1500–2000* (Amsterdam: Amsterdam University Press, 2013), p.141. The contractor made agreements with financiers and bankers, merchants, arms manufacturers, and others to supply the army with food, clothing, munitions, equipment, and pay. Accordingly, regiments or armies such as those raised by Ernst von Mansfeld, Bernhard of Saxe-Weimar, Albrecht von Wallenstein, and others represented the

## INTRODUCTION: MILITARY LABOUR AND RECRUITMENT IN GERMANY

From the second half of the seventeenth century, methods of recruitment changed in a number of significant ways. In the first major development, states made greater use of involuntary recruitment. They continued to draft criminals, vagrants and uprooted, but in larger numbers than before. More importantly, states developed the obligation to perform military service to draft men into militias. Of the great powers, it was France under Louis XIV that led the way. Many German states made even greater use of the militia. In Brandenburg, Bavaria, Mecklenburg, and Württemberg by the 1660s, militia formations were already being raised and then drafted into the regular army as the need arose. Elsewhere, such as in Saxony, Mainz, and Würzburg, the intermediate militia stage was omitted and men on the militia lists were taken straight into the army.[4]

The second major development concerned the system of military contracting. This did not end altogether after 1650, but it changed markedly. The general contractors who had figured so prominently in the Thirty Years' War disappeared from the scene, and military contracting in its classical sense was substantially modified. Accordingly, the use of general contractors was phased out and the role of the private entrepreneur was diminished. For a while, the market for contract troops was left to the younger sons of German Princes who had no personal patrimony or hope of royal succession. However, from the late seventeenth century, a substantial number of Princes began to rent out their armies to foreign employers. The states concerned in this soldier-trade were principally German.[5]

As well as relying on impressed men, militias, and hired forces, states also developed their systems for finding volunteers. Although the old feudal system of recruitment was in decline, nobles nevertheless continued to associate their social status with military virtues and service in the army. Rulers made use of this to engage their social and political elites in the recruitment and maintenance of their forces. Many nobles were prepared to put themselves and their private fortunes at the disposal of monarchs in the expectation of gaining prestige but also because this was what was expected of them. One way of encouraging nobles to do so was by formally implementing a system of venality under which officers purchased their commissions. Venality gave officers ownership of their office and not of their men, but in practice they were still expected to recruit their companies and regiments. They did so by public appeal to volunteers, by using their influence over dependants, and by deploying their private retinues – in those instances where they still maintained them. Moreover, nobles were expected to use their own resources

---

    accumulation of venture capital on a huge scale, and the commander presided over a group of stakeholders who all expected a return on their investment, whether that investment be financial or purely military, with massive implications for the relationship between soldier and employer.

4    The matter is summarised by Peter H. Wilson, *War, State and Society in Württemberg* (Cambridge: Cambridge University Press, 1995), pp.79–81; Charles Ingrao, *The Hessian Mercenary State* (Cambridge: Cambridge University Press, 2003); and Christopher Duffy, *The Army of Frederick the Great* (Warwick: Helion & Company, 2020), pp.54–57.

5    Tallet, 'Soldiers in Western Europe', p.143. Significantly, many of the troops who were hired had been forcibly drafted into the army with implications for scholars seeking to construct a taxonomy of army types.

to equip, pay, and feed their men when state funding ran out, as it invariably did. Venality gave officers an incentive to invest their personal resources in the recruitment and maintenance of their units. Even where venality was not introduced, nobles could still be lured into accepting a commission and acting as a recruiting agent by the expectation of making a profit.[6]

These systems reflected the nature of the early modern state, and in particular the relative fiscal and administrative weakness of central authority. Governments relied upon the use of mercenaries, including general contractors for a time, as well as upon their social and political elites to recruit and maintain armies. Even when the use of general contractors was phased out, states still found it easier to hire troops rather than raise them, and the dependence of rulers upon the cooperation of their nobilities, who served as intermediate agents of government, remained very considerable. This features increased of importance within German armies, and became integral to the process of raising and maintaining military forces.

---

6   This was the so called *Kompaniewirtschaft*, the system whereby captains made money from administering the finances of a company of soldiers.

# 2

# The Armed States

## Pfalz-Neuburg

In the mid-1600s, this Catholic branch of the Palatine-Wittelsbach family ruled territories bizarrely scattered between the Upper Palatinate, the Danube and the Rhineland as the result of dynastic inheritances throughout the centuries. Pfalz-Neuburg held pre-eminence over the other branches, having received the primogeniture status, a factor that had important consequences in 1685 when the line of Neuburg inherited the Electorate of the Palatinate. As immediate Princes of the Empire, the Dukes were members of the Bavarian and Westphalian Circles. The latter territories were key locations lying on both the banks of the Rhine, a circumstance that became a cause of the bloodless Cow's War of 1651 against Brandenburg. Consequently, the greatest attention was paid to the two Rhine duchies, in which the most modern fortresses were located.

Due to the separation of their domains, the Dukes had established two residences: one in Neuburg, in the southern part of the state, and the other in Düsseldorf, in the Rhine region.

The description of the Duchy at the end of the 1660s by Galeazzo Gualdo Priorato also contains data concerning regular soldiers and militia. According to him, Düsseldorf quartered a garrison of 100 cavalry and 800 infantry. Additionally, the city and the countryside could gather 5,000 militia of the *Landausschuss*.[1] Düsseldorf was the most modern fortress of the state with five strong bastions, a ditch, and some updated external works.[2]

Other strategic places were Jülich and Düren, both lying on the left bank of the Rhine and bordering the Spanish Low Countries. Jülich could quarter the same garrison as Düsseldorf, and 1,000 militiamen.

---

1  Galeazzo Gualdo Priorato, *Relatione degli Stati del Serenissimo Filippo Guglielmo Duca di Juliers, Neuburg, ecc.* (Cologne, 1668), p.6.
2  Gualdo Priorato, *Relatione degli Stati del Serenissimo Filippo Guglielmo Duca di Juliers, Neuburg, etc.* (Cologne: 1668), p.25.

Neuburg an der Donau, in a print dating to 1687 after an engraving by Christoph Riegel (Author's archive).

Duke Wolfgang Wilhelm (r. 1614–1653) was actually the founder of the Pfalz-Neuburg's standing army. In 1651, to meet the Brandenburg threat, he assembled a considerable force of professional soldiers by means of recruitment in his states and of foreign mercenaries directly enlisted or hired from abroad. In this period, the cavalry and the infantry received their first stable organisation. A cavalry company was to be of 1 *Rittermeister*, 1 *Leutnant*, 1 *Cornet*, 1 *Quartiermeister*, 1 *Musterschreiber*, 1 *Feldscherer*, 3 *Corporalen*, 2 *Trompeten* but an undefined number of troopers. The infantry company was to be 1 *Hauptmann*, 1 *Leutnant*, 1 *Fahnrich*, 1 *Feldweibel*, 1 *Führer*, 1 *Fourier*, 1 *Musterschreiber*, 1 *Feldscherer*, 4 *Corporalen* and 2 *Spielleueten*, again the number of privates remained undetermined. A general command for infantry and cavalry regiments was also set out with 1 *Obrist*, 1 *Oberstleutnant*, 1 *Obrist Wachtmeister*, 1 *Regiments Quartier Mesister*, 1 *Adjutant*, 1 *Schultheissen* (auditor), 1 *Capelan*, 1 *Regiments Secretario* and 1 *Profoss*.[3]

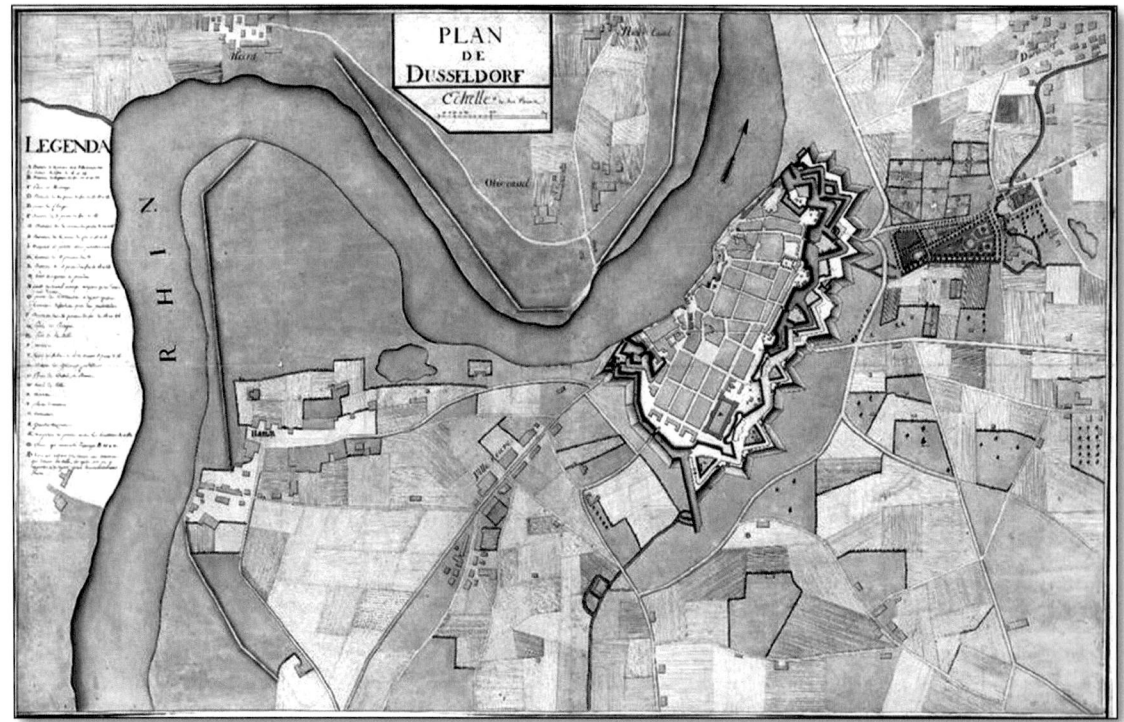

Plan of Dusseldorf in a print dating to the first half of the eighteenth century. (Author's collection) The original five bastions are still recognisable, while the ditch mentioned by Galeazzo Gualdo Priorato has been replaced by the external works built after 1668.

---

3   Bezzel, *Geschichte des kurpfälzischen Heeres von seinen Anfängen bis zur Vereinigung von Kurpfalz und Kurbayern*, vol. I (Munich, 1925), *Anlagen*, pp.22–23: *Ordinanz. Was für dess*

# THE ARMED STATES

At the peak of the tension, more than 12,000 soldiers were quartered in the Duchies of Jülich and Berg.[4] This burden required a considerable economic effort that, however, was rejected by the estates. On 20 March 1653, Wolfgang Wilhelm died, leaving to his son Philipp Wilhelm (r. 1653–1690) a country exhausted and with few soldiers. As occurred in other German principalities, the Estates influenced the expenditure of the new Duke. He, nevertheless, cleverly exploited the geopolitical circumstances to conduct a dynamic military policy, although the results were often below expectations.

In 1658, Philipp Wilhelm entered the Rhenish Alliance alongside his Protestant cousins of Pfalz-Zweibrücken, whose line of Kleeburg had received the Swedish throne in 1654. The new ruler devoted a great deal of resources to strengthening the defence of his states. Within the limits imposed by the meagre budget, he increased the number of the professional troops and commissioned a cannon foundry in Cologne to produce modern artillery. In 1656 the first four cannons were transferred to Düsseldorf. The Duke appointed *General* Baron Virmund, Governor of Düsseldorf, as supervisor for the improvement of the fortifications to make the city the main fortress of the Rhine territories. Then, he recruited technicians in the Dutch Republic and in France, and also hired Germany's leading fortification specialist, engineer Albrecht Faulhaber.[5] To keep costs down as far as possible, the soldiers were employed in the works and, in additional, all vagrants and homeless were called upon to carry out work on the fortifications. These improvements continued for almost 10 years, and in 1671, a new arsenal was built, entrusted to the *Zeug und Rüstmeister* Schwab and *Zeug Director* Nicola Adami, who had held this position since 1660. Düsseldorf arsenal joined the *Zeug-und-Rüsthaus* of Neuburg in the production of weapons. In the same period, a new cavalry barracks was built close to the old curtains.[6] After Düsseldorf,

Duke Wolfgang Wilhelm of Pfalz-Neuburg (1578–1653), portrait by Johannes Spielberg. (Stadtmuseum Düsseldorf) Skilful and shrewd, Wolfgang Wilhelm faced Brandenburg's claim over Jülich and did not hesitate to raise a considerable army to defend his rights. The Duke personally travelled to Prague to seek the Emperor's support. He also tried to gain the alliance of France and England. With the achievement of the Jülich succession, Wolfgang Wilhelm not only had more territory but could also enrich the Neuburg economy.

---

*Durchleuchtigsten Fürsten und Herrn / Herrn Wolfgang Wilhelm / Pfalzgraf bey Rhein / in Bayern / zu Jülich, Cleve und Berg* ...., dating to 30 August 1651.

4   Gualdo Priorato, *Relatione degli Stati del Serenissimo Filippo Guglielmo Duca di Juliers, Neuburg, etc.* (Cologne: 1668), p.5.

5   Oskar Bezzel, *Geschichte des kurpfälzischen Heeres von seinen Anfängen bis zur Vereinigung von Kurpfalz und Kurbayern*, vol. I (Munich, 1925), p.149. They were the Dutch engineer Khal and the Frenchman De Roy; Faulhaber was dismissed shortly afterwards because he was a Protestant.

6   Oskar Bezzel, *Geschichte des Kurpfälzischen Heeres von Seinen Anfängen bis zur Vereinigung von Kurpfalz und Kurbayern* (Munich: Lindauer LTR-Verl, 1925), Band I, p.149.

by 1673 Jülich defences were updated with a wide curtain wall and additional works at the gates.

Military involvement occurred in 1663, when the Emperor called on the German princes to support him against the Ottomans in Hungary. As a member of the Rhenish League, Pfalz-Neuburg sent a regiment of 1,000 foot, divided into seven companies, to Hungary, and to which an eighth company raised by Paflz-Zweibrücken was added. The regiment was under *Obrist* Gerhard Wilhelm von Hochstätten, a member of the family of a veteran commander from Jülich. The cavalry company, with 110 rank and file, was under *Rittmeister* Eynatten. On 21 October 1663, the contingent, together with Commissar Hautenstein and with two cannon, left Neuburg to reach Krems via the Danube. Here it was attached to the *Deutsche Allianz* corps under *Generalleutnant* Julius von Hohenlohe. However, the Duke still provided 50 horse and 200 foot for the Westphalian Circle regiments.[7] From Vienna, after a strenuous march through the Styrian mountains and a stop in Pettau, the German troops arrived at the joint assembly point near Zriniyvár, on the Muhr River, on 20 January 1664. The next day, the Allies advanced towards Pécs, which surrendered after a short bombardment. In February, the infantry regiment still had 900 men and the cavalry company was merged with the Lower Saxony *Kreisregiment* Rauchaupt.[8] On 7 February, in an engagement near Szigetvár, the Pfalz-Neuburg cavalry suffered 17 wounded including the captain. In June, the infantry participated at the siege of Kanisza, while the cavalry fought at Szentgotthárd on 1 August.[9]

The recruitment of troops for the Hungarian campaign had provided Philipp Wilhelm with a favourable opportunity to strengthen his army beyond the maximum number allowed by the Estates. In February 1664, he established an office for the direction of the troops, appointing Governor Virmund as general 'of our present and future militia'.[10] Two years later, Philipp Wilhelm devoted his attention to what was happening in the Brandenburg territories of Cleves and Mark, and every movement of troops on the borders of the Pfalz-Neuburg territories was a cause for concern. In the summer of 1666, the presence of a strong contingent of Brandenburg troops in Cleves was interpreted as a sign of an imminent resumption of hostilities. The Duke responded with a threat of war, and to increase his army he made arrangements with the Prince-Bishop of Münster to hire four infantry regiments. The conflict was limited to these showdowns and on 9 September 1666, the agreement of Cleves closed half a century of disputes and quarrels.[11]

---

7   Georg Tessin, *Die Regimenter der Europäischen Staaten im Ancien Régime des XVI bis XVIII Jahrhunderts* (Osnabrück: Biblio Verlag, 1986), Teil 1, p.274.

8   See Bruno Mugnai, *Wars and Soldiers in the Early Reign of Louis XIV, volume 2: The Imperial Army 1657–1687* (Warwick: Helion & Company, 2019), p.288.

9   Oskar Bezzel, *Geschichte des Kurpfälzischen Heeres von Seinen Anfängen bis zur Vereinigung von Kurpfalz und Kurbayern* (Munich: Lindauer LTR-Verl, 1925), Band I, p.152.

10  Kurt Peball, 'Die Schlacht bei St. Gotthard-Mogersdorf 1664', in *Militärhistorische Schriftenreihe*, III–1964.

11  J. R. Beitelrock, *Geschichte der Herzogtum Neuburg oder der jungen Pfalz* (Aschaffenburg: Wailandt, 1866–67), p.45.

# THE ARMED STATES

The insecure scenario favoured the signing of the alliance with Electoral Cologne and the Bishopric of Strasbourg in 1667, in order to secure the middle Rhine from the French presence in Flanders. According to the terms of the 'armed neutrality', he was obliged to provide 1,600 horse and 3,000 foot of his own troops.[12] Philipp Wilhelm exploited the agreement to increase his army, and three years later, he used this force to resolve the long-lasting dispute over Siegburg with the local abbot. On the night of 4/5 February 1670, *Feldmarschall* Virmund seized the town, which surrendered after a feeble defence and was then garrisoned by 200 infantry from Neuburg.[13]

The alliance concluded with the ecclesiastical princes of Strasbourg and Cologne had led to the formation of two cavalry regiments, which were completed in July 1671. A month later, however, due to the shortage of funds both regiments had to be reduced from 10 to 7 companies, 1,330 men in all, including the mounted *Leibgarde* of 190 men in two companies quartered in Düsseldorf and Neuburg. Once again, the Duke's ambitions for the creation of a permanent army were frustrated by the resistance of the Estates, which would not authorise new taxes for the financial requirement. This became an insurmountable problem and forced Virmund to advance large sums from his own funds to complete the recruitment of the infantry.[14] On 30 August 1671, 11 infantry companies with 2,276 men were registered at a muster, but a few weeks later, the soldiers deserted in large numbers due to the lack of food to the point that Virmund felt compelled to impose forced

The town and castle of Siegburg in a print dating to the early seventeenth century. This fief was located in the south of the Duchy of Berg, and enjoyed the rights of an immediate Imperial territory governed by an abbot. Since 1609, Duke Wolfgang Wilhelm had claimed possession. In 1655, an agreement was signed under the patronage of the Emperor, but this did not leave Duke Philipp Wilhelm satisfied. Now the opportunity was right to settle the issue once and for all.

12 Oskar Bezzel, *Geschichte des Kurpfälzischen Heeres von Seinen Anfängen bis zur Vereinigung von Kurpfalz und Kurbayern* (Munich: Lindauer LTR-Verl, 1925), Band I, p.153.
13 Oskar Bezzel, *Geschichte des Kurpfälzischen Heeres von Seinen Anfängen bis zur Vereinigung von Kurpfalz und Kurbayern* (Munich: Lindauer LTR-Verl, 1925), Band I, p.156.
14 Oskar Bezzel, *Geschichte des Kurpfälzischen Heeres von Seinen Anfängen bis zur Vereinigung von Kurpfalz und Kurbayern* (Munich: Lindauer LTR-Verl, 1925), Band I, p.156.

labour at the arsenal and even death sentences.[15] As before, the Estates and the subjects complained about recruitment, new taxes and the behaviour of soldiers who, without pay and food, retaliated against civilians with extortion and violence; they demanded a reduction in troop numbers. The grievances were examined by a 'special war council' convened in Düsseldorf at the end of September 1671 under the chairmanship of Virmund. This time, however, the Elector of Cologne and the Bishop of Strasbourg proved to be more powerful than the Estates, insisting on the treaty strength of 1,600 horse and 3,000 foot. At the end of October, Virmund proposed to recruit a new eighth company of cavalry, and to reinforce the existing 7 companies with 10 additional men to 100 men per company, and also to use the 2,000 men currently recruited in Neuburg to garrison the fortresses of Jülich and Berg in addition to the 3,000 foot to be made available to the allies.[16] The latter proposal, however, could not be put into practice because of the opposition of the Estates. Before the end of the year, one regiment of infantry under *Obrist* Johann Emmanuel Waldbott von Bassenheim (PnI-3), of 8 companies each of 250 men, had been completed, although equipment and weapons were still incomplete.[17]

From Neuburg, the first company to march was that of *Obristleutnant* Neuland in February 1672. On the way to Wertheim, where it was embarked and transported to Frankfurt am Mein, it passed through the territories of several states and aroused the protests of the local authorities. In particular, the Margraves of Ansbach-Bayreuth and Bayreuth-Kulmbach complained about looting and robbery by the soldiers, and their undisciplined behaviour in Frankfurt was the subject of further protests.[18] In April, five companies arrived on the middle Rhine; the last two companies only reached Jülich later. The *Leibcompagnie* also included 10 *Trabanten*, while two other companies each had 10 artillerymen. However, before the end of the year, the regiment was disbanded and the companies assigned to garrisons in Jülich and Berg.[19]

---

15 'In this affair, the interference of the Catholic clergy manifested itself, who in several cases not only prevented the execution of death sentences and imposed new trials, but also refused to hand over soldiers who had taken refuge in monasteries, without the government daring to take action against these inconveniences, which certainly did not help its reputation.' Oskar Bezzel, *Geschichte des Kurpfälzischen Heeres von Seinen Anfängen bis zur Vereinigung von Kurpfalz und Kurbayern* (Munich: Lindauer LTR-Verl, 1925), Band I, p.157:

16 Oskar Bezzel, *Geschichte des Kurpfälzischen Heeres von Seinen Anfängen bis zur Vereinigung von Kurpfalz und Kurbayern* (Munich: Lindauer LTR-Verl, 1925), Band I, p.157.

17 Oskar Bezzel, *Geschichte des Kurpfälzischen Heeres von Seinen Anfängen bis zur Vereinigung von Kurpfalz und Kurbayern* (Munich: Lindauer LTR-Verl, 1925), Band I, p.157: 'The regiment required 1,232 muskets of the same calibre, 96 short muskets for the NCOS and lieutenants, and pikes for the other private soldiers.'

18 The protests were met with surprise, as the reports sent to the Duke by Virmund stated that 'the ensign is a young knight fresh out of pageboy status, and the soldiers are mostly untrained but still good people'. As a consequence, the *Obristlieutnant* was arrested and temporarily suspended from the command of his company. Oskar Bezzel, *Geschichte des Kurpfälzischen Heeres von Seinen Anfängen bis zur Vereinigung von Kurpfalz und Kurbayern* (Munich: Lindauer LTR-Verl, 1925), Band I, p.157.

19 Oskar Bezzel, *Geschichte des Kurpfälzischen Heeres von Seinen Anfängen bis zur Vereinigung von Kurpfalz und Kurbayern* (Munich: Lindauer LTR-Verl, 1925), Band I, p.158. Colonel Waldbott was appointed commander of the Westphalian *Kreisregiment* of infantry quartered in Cologne.

In 1672, the Palatinate-Neuburg also provided a *Kreiscompagnie* assigned to the Free Imperial City of Cologne.[20]

On the eve of the Franco-Dutch War, Philipp Wilhelm had been opposed by Austria in the recent Polish Royal election and so was inclined to be more sympathetic to France, but still wanted to avoid direct involvement in a conflict that would inevitably have adverse repercussions for his own lands, given their proximity to the United Provinces. To further strengthen his position, Philipp Wilhelm promoted a scheme that, however, could turn into a major problem. Exploiting the strategic importance of his possessions on the Rhine, his influence in Westphalia, dynastic connections, and apparent readiness to treat with Louis XIV, the Duke pursued his plan. However, he refused to accept French domination as the price for neutrality and pursued his own attempts at mediation when war broke out in April 1672. As a first step he agreed a treaty of neutrality with Louis XIV at Zeist on 24 July 1672. This was also based on the principle of a Third Party, which the Duke hoped to form by calling on his Wittelsbach relations in Sweden, Bavaria and the Palatinate. He was compromised from the beginning by the Treaty of Zeist and his receipt of French subsidies between December 1672 and March 1675 in return for allowing transit of Turenne's army. He achieved a diplomatic success when he contributed to the Peace of Vossem, by which Brandenburg temporarily withdrew from the war in 1673. Emboldened, he continued his negotiations for a Wittelsbach dynastic union to be enlarged by the inclusion of Cologne, and other German pro-French principalities to create a group powerful enough to impose peace on the warring parties. Since virtually all the proposed members of the Duke's Third Party were French clients, the whole thing became automatically suspect to both the Dutch and the Emperor.[21]

In early 1673, while the war between France and the Dutch Republic was being fought, Pfalz-Neuburg remained anchored to its insecure neutrality entrusted to 6 cavalry companies, of which three were quartered in the Duchy of Neuburg, and 19 infantry companies. To these, the Duke could add his mounted *Leibgarde*, now consisting of three companies: the 'old' and 'new' of Düsseldorf and the 'old' of Neuburg, each with 140 men.[22] The condition of the troops, however, was very bad; besides salaries being paid late, rations were often insufficient. Some infantry companies were housed in makeshift quarters and others were even in cellars and stables, and consequently soldiers deserted in large numbers.[23]

Ultimately, Philipp Wilhelm's hopes proved illusory, and he found himself manipulated by French diplomats to secure German non-intervention in

---

20  Georg Tessin, *Die Regimenter der Europäischen Staaten im Ancien Régime des XVI bis XVIII Jahrhunderts* (Osnabrück: Biblio Verlag, 1986), Teil 1, p.274.
21  Peter H. Wilson, *German Armies. War and German Politics, 1648–1806* (London: UCL Press, 1998), p.178.
22  Oskar Bezzel, *Geschichte des Kurpfälzischen Heeres von Seinen Anfängen bis zur Vereinigung von Kurpfalz und Kurbayern* (Munich: Lindauer LTR-Verl, 1925), Band I, p.158. The *Leibgarde* had one captain-lieutenant and one standard for the whole corps.
23  Oskar Bezzel, *Geschichte des Kurpfälzischen Heeres von Seinen Anfängen bis zur Vereinigung von Kurpfalz und Kurbayern* (Munich: Lindauer LTR-Verl, 1925), Band I, p.159.

their master's dismemberment of the Spanish Low Countries. In the course of the year, looking with concern at the risks of a war in Germany, and fearing the seizure of his lands threatened by the Emperor, Philipp Wilhelm tried to reinforce his position by any means. A lot of time was spent on maintaining the fortresses, increasing the number of cannons and accumulating ammunition in the arsenals, especially in Düsseldorf and Jülich. The militia was called to arms and the *Landsreiterei* also joined the regular cavalry in guarding the borders. In the summer of 1673, French and Allied parties that crossed the borders occasionally requested the intervention of the Pfalz-Neuburg's troops, but in September all the cavalry was put in readiness when Turenne moved to meet the Imperial and Brandenburg troops marching to the Rhine.

The pact of armed neutrality that bound him to the Elector of Cologne, who sided with France, could no longer be exploited to keep his territories safe from military operations when, in November 1673, the Elector Maximilian Heinrich was forced to sign a truce with the Allies. Now the risks of being involved in the war became dramatically real. The Duke only once derogated from the neutrality he had imposed on himself, by adhering to the Diet's request for the *Reichskrieg* against Sweden, hiring a cavalry regiment to Brandenburg in March 1675, after breaking relations with France.[24] In the following months, troop movements across the border increased and caused damage in the territories of Berg and Jülich. Events should have induced the Duke to abandon his policy of neutrality, to which the foreign troops paid no heed, and every time the entry of foreign soldiers into the country was accompanied by looting and plundering despite the Duke's protests. The passage of the Celle, Dutch, Lorrainer and French troops in July 1675 forced the population of the countryside to flee. In other circumstances, the Duke showed his gratitude by granting generous funds and help, as he did with the troops of Münster who passed through his lands in order and disciplined, and with the Spanish commander to whom he gave a gold necklace for sparing the countryside from violence and forced contributions.[25]

Formally, the neutrality of Paflz-Neuburg continued until January 1676. Intrigued by the events and prospects offered by the market in soldiers, Philipp Wilhelm signed an agreement with the Dutch-Spanish to hire a corps of mercenary troops and thereby gain political prominence. The plan to turn Pfalz-Neuburg into an armed state committed the Duke to provide the considerable figure of 8,500 soldiers in exchange for subsidies to be paid, half at the signing of the contract and the balance at the troop review scheduled for July. The contingent would serve all together, and the Duke insisted with the allies that priority be given to the reconquest of Maastricht, whose proximity to the Duchy's borders was considered to be the greatest danger. The contingent was to comprise 2,500 cavalrymen and artillery, and 6,000 infantrymen, but as early as February the Estates' resistance to supplying the resources to recruit such a large number of soldiers changed

---

24 Ernst Friedrich Christian Müsebeck, *Die Feldzüge des Grossen Kurfürsten in Pommern 1675–1677* (Hamburg: von der Ropp,1897), p.66.
25 Oskar Bezzel, *Geschichte des Kurpfälzischen Heeres von Seinen Anfängen bis zur Vereinigung von Kurpfalz und Kurbayern* (Munich: Lindauer LTR-Verl, 1925), Band I, p.160.

# THE ARMED STATES

Painting celebrating the marriage between Leopold I Habsburg and Eleonore Magdalena of Pfalz-Neuburg, daughter of Duke Philipp Wilhelm. In the centre, the bride and groom are represented as gods, surrounded by German princes. The union between the Imperial House and that of Pfalz-Neuburg was another decisive step towards Pfalz-Neuburg joining the side of the Allies. The wedding took place in Passau on 14 December 1676 and was the third and last marriage of Leopold I. Painting by Jakob Heybel. (Königsfeld Castle, Alteglofsheim)

the ambitious plan and the formation of the contingent therefore faced many difficulties. An extension was granted, decreasing the number of soldiers to 1,500 cavalry and 4,000 infantry for July. The Duke appointed a new Commander-in-Chief, Count Franz of Schellart, to take command of the contingent, relieving the elder Virmond of this task. *Obrist Inhaber*'s licences were granted to four officers, one of them Walloon, for the formation of four infantry regiments each of 1,000 men, divided in 10 companies. Two more regiments had to be raised from July and a seventh before the end of the year, to provide soldiers for the garrisons of the duchy. In addition to these troops, two cavalry and one dragoon regiment were to be raised and equipped, each with 6 companies, 500 men in all.[26]

Although recruitment proceeded slowly, *Musterkommissär* Terlahn, managed to recruit the troops and lead them to Venlo where they arrived between 4 and 6 July 1676. Only the infantry regiments *Schellart* (PnI-4), *Spee* (PnI-5), and *Waldenberg* (PnI-8) were at the establishment strength,

---

26 Oskar Bezzel, *Geschichte des Kurpfälzischen Heeres von Seinen Anfängen bis zur Vereinigung von Kurpfalz und Kurbayern* (Munich: Lindauer LTR-Verl, 1925), Band I, pp.161–162. They were infantry regiments Schellart, Saint-Paul, Waldenberg, Spee; cavalry regiments Schellart, Franckenberg, and Manderscheid dragoons. Before the end of the year infantry regiments Manderscheid, Boisbernard and Neuland were also raised.

while regiment *Saint-Paul* (PnI-6) only had 434 men divided into 3 veteran companies and 7 newly recruited companies. As for the mounted troops, the *Manderscheid Dragoner* (PnD-1) had 6 companies with 464 men. Thanks to the payment received for this first contingent, recruitment was intensified and by August a fifth infantry regiment was ready to march under the Walloon *Obrist* Elss de Boisbernard (PnI-9). The enlistment ended on 21 August in Düsseldorf with the arrival of the cavalry regiment *Schellart*, which consisted of 3 companies from Neuburg and 3 companies recruited in the Duchy of Berg.[27]

William of Orange actually employed the Paflz-Neuburg contingent for the planned siege of Maastricht and asked the Duke to prepare Düsseldorf as a logistics base for the campaign. Düsseldorf had to provide artillery, ammunition, pioneers, wagons and food, and many difficulties were to be expected, but in the end the resolute attitude of the Prince prevailed and the plan for the siege of Maastricht was agreed between the allies after long and unpleasant negotiations. On 7 July 1676, the Prince of Orange arrived before Maastricht with the vanguard which included the *Manderscheid Dragoner*. On 2 July, the infantry also arrived, comprising the regiments Saint-Paul, Waldenberg, Boisbernard and the newly raised *Neuland zu Fuss* (PnI-10). *Generalwachtmeister* Waldenberg held the command of the infantry. Each regiment formed a grenadier company of about 50 men under a captain. However, this new organisation was only temporary, while the presence of 100 *Schnapphahnen* in each infantry regiment represents the beginning of a gradual rearming of the infantry with more modern weapons.[28]

From the opening phase of the siege, *General* Waldenberg informed the Duke about the bad treatment received by the troops. Throughout the siege, relations between Waldenberg and the Allies were strained and negatively affected operations. In a report to the Duke, Waldenberg considered that many losses were due to the unfair attitude of the Dutch-Spanish commanders and emphasised his opinion by stating: 'General Louvigny, who led the attack on the external works, does not appreciate the service of His Serene Highness's troops, and employs them with little care for their lives.' The Duke's complaints sent to the Prince of Orange, drew the attention of the Commander-in-Chief and, for a moment, were successful.[29]

However, the controversy resumed. According to Waldenberg, the greatest losses were caused by the poor diet that encouraged desertion. Added to this were the delayed payment of wages, poor discipline and the high incidence of illnesses such as dysentery caused by the consumption of rotten fruit and vegetables, all of which contributed to the poorer performance of the troops. Relations between Waldenberg and the Allied commanders deteriorated further when the latter complained about the poor work in the approach

---

27  Oskar Bezzel, *Geschichte des Kurpfälzischen Heeres von Seinen Anfängen bis zur Vereinigung von Kurpfalz und Kurbayern* (Munich: Lindauer LTR-Verl, 1925), Band I, p.162.
28  Oskar Bezzel, *Geschichte des Kurpfälzischen Heeres von Seinen Anfängen bis zur Vereinigung von Kurpfalz und Kurbayern* (Munich: Lindauer LTR-Verl, 1925), Band I, p.168.
29  Oskar Bezzel, *Geschichte des Kurpfälzischen Heeres von Seinen Anfängen bis zur Vereinigung von Kurpfalz und Kurbayern* (Munich: Lindauer LTR-Verl, 1925), Band I, p.165: '*dass seine Leute zu hart gestrapaziert würden.*'

# THE ARMED STATES

trenches, entrusted to pioneers who were hastily recruited peasants from Pfalz-Neuburg. To make the situation even more heated, Waldenberg was assigned to command a Dutch siege section and thus separated from his troops contrary to the agreements. At the end of July, the situation became unsustainable but the commissioner arrived with the money for the troops, although the officers were outraged when they learned that the payment was conditional on an inspection of the companies. The colonels, whose rights they felt had been infringed by this order, objected and turned to *Feldmarshall* Schellart, arguing that a regular review was impossible under the present circumstances, 'in which two regiments stand in the trenches every day and the others serve in the perimeter.'[30]

Desertion and disease hit hard, and in early August, the *Saint-Paul* and *Waldenberg* regiments had only 300 men each.[31] On 18 August, a

Dutch print of the siege of Maastricht in July-August 1676. (Author's collection)
The campaign for retaking Maastricht was carefully planned by Prince William of Orange and his generals, but the stubborn resistance of the French garrison and the arrival of a relief force caused the siege to be raised. The role played by the Pfalz-Neuburg troops in the siege of Maastricht is known in detail up to mid-August. After the assault on 30 July on the outer works of the Dauphin Bastion, in which the *Saint-Paul* regiment took part, on 4 August an attempt was made to take this position, the Liège Gate and the outer horn-works at the same time. The operation took place with heavy losses for the regiments involved in the action. The *Saint-Paul* and *Neuland* regiments formed the assault column against the Liège Gate. The former lost its commander, the son of the colonel proprietor, as well as 18 dead and 9 wounded, while Neuland suffered the loss of only 3 dead and 8 wounded. As for the *Waldenberg* regiment, 14 men were killed and 38 wounded in the attack on the outer works. Of the 24 veteran soldiers who formed the head of the assault column, only 8 were unhurt. The casualties of the *Boisbernard* regiment in the assault on the horn-work were 2 killed and 39 wounded. Further losses followed in the following days in the trenches and in the digging of mines.

---

30   Oskar Bezzel, *Geschichte des Kurpfälzischen Heeres von Seinen Anfängen bis zur Vereinigung von Kurpfalz und Kurbayern* (Munich: Lindauer LTR-Verl, 1925), Band I, p.165.
31   Oskar Bezzel, *Geschichte des Kurpfälzischen Heeres von Seinen Anfängen bis zur Vereinigung von Kurpfalz und Kurbayern* (Munich: Lindauer LTR-Verl, 1925), Band I, p.166. Regiment Waldenberg had lost one captain during the first attack on the night of 11 August and several officers and a large number of men were wounded. The assaults performed on the nights of 18–19 and 19–20 August had some effect, but the French responded with a fierce sortie on the night of 21 August. The regiments Saint-Paul and Waldenberg suffered a severe blow on the night of 25 August, when the premature explosion of two mines under the counterscarp caused great damage and confusion among the attackers and the progress of the previous days was lost

reconnaissance reported the approach of a French relief force under *General* Schömberg, which persuaded Prince William to lift the siege. The retreat was so precipitous that the troops of Pfalz-Neuburg had to leave most of their heavy artillery behind due to the lack of draught animals. What remained of the contingent was sent into winter quarters in the Spanish Low Countries. Regiments *Schellart* and *Spee* were quartered in and around Brussels along with the corps under Villa Hermosa, but were later transferred to Bruges. Due to the poor conditions of the barracks, the troops suffered greatly from the cold; the *Schellart* regiment lost 68 men in two weeks alone.[32]

In March 1677, the infantry returned to Pflaz-Neuburg. The contingent had fallen to less than half of the original strength and the Dutch-Spanish representatives asked the Duke to fulfil the contract by completing the regiments with new recruits. In April, Philipp Wilhelm tried to reassure the Allies by reforming the regiment *Schellart*, which took the name *Erbprinz Leibregiment zu Fuss*, and which was completed with recruits enlisted at the expense of the *Kronprinz* Johann Wilhelm. The regiment had soon to face many hardships. At the end of May, the companies were transferred from Düsseldorf to Dordrecht and embarked on the Rhine. The journey proceeded very slowly, and due to inconveniences and mishaps, food supplies arrived erratically. With the exception of a bread distribution in Antwerp, which soon ran out, no further provisions were made to meet the food needs of the soldiers crammed onto the boats, causing many of them to starve to death.[33] In June, Prince Johann Wilhelm made money available to enlist further soldiers.

At the end of August 1677, the recruits left Düsseldorf for the Spanish Low Countries, where the regiment was mustered and quartered near Brussels from 2 to 14 September. The muster recorded 1,094 men in 14 companies.[34] However, the situation did not improve. Unhealthy quarters, cold and hunger caused many deaths. In October, the Colonel stated the loss of 390 men in just one month; regiment *Avila* (former *Spee zu Fuss*) suffered the same problem and numbered 800 men in 10 companies.[35] Before the end of the year, the regiment was transferred to Düsseldorf due to its poor condition, where it was completed again reaching a strength of 12 companies with recruits from Neuburg and completed with soldiers from the disbanded infantry regiment Waldenberg. The *Leibregiment* was increased by two companies, probably from the regiment *Manderscheid zu Fuss*.[36]

32 Oskar Bezzel, *Geschichte des Kurpfälzischen Heeres von Seinen Anfängen bis zur Vereinigung von Kurpfalz und Kurbayern* (Munich: Lindauer LTR-Verl, 1925), Band I, p.166.
33 Oskar Bezzel, *Geschichte des Kurpfälzischen Heeres von Seinen Anfängen bis zur Vereinigung von Kurpfalz und Kurbayern* (Munich: Lindauer LTR-Verl, 1925), Band I, p.167.
34 Oskar Bezzel, *Geschichte des Kurpfälzischen Heeres von Seinen Anfängen bis zur Vereinigung von Kurpfalz und Kurbayern* (Munich: Lindauer LTR-Verl, 1925), Band I, p.167.
35 Oskar Bezzel, *Geschichte des Kurpfälzischen Heeres von Seinen Anfängen bis zur Vereinigung von Kurpfalz und Kurbayern* (Munich: Lindauer LTR-Verl, 1925), Band I, p.167. Baron Spee had been appointed *Generalkriegscommissär*.
36 49 men of the *Leibregiment* remained in Berg with 250 others from the free companies in Düsseldorf. In Jülich were four companies with 500 men in all. In the other garrisons were men of the Franckenberg and Schellart cavalry regiments and the incomplete Manderscheid infantry regiment, and finally three more free companies. The *Kreiskompagnie* was in Cologne, and was

Internal disputes within the senior officers caused problems and mutual mistrust. Saint-Paul, appointed as Governor of Düsseldorf, had become a favourite of the Duke and the Crown Prince. He openly favoured all the Walloons serving in the army and for this, he was accused of injustice and incompetence. Some colonels demanded his dismissal because of the constant disputes with the general 'who practised the Walloon method and custom.'[37] For the 1678 campaign, Pfalz-Neuburg assembled approximately 5,500 horse and foot. On 11 June, a part of these troops joined the Dutch-Spanish armies along with the other German auxiliary troops in Roermond. *Schellart zu Pferd* and *Manderscheid Dragoner*, *Leibregimnt* and *Avila zu Fuss* fought at Saint-Denis on 14 August 1678. The Peace of Nijmegen, signed four days before the battle, left Pfalz-Neuburg alone with the forts of Sittard, Heinsberg, Linnich, Düren and part of the Duchy of Jülich under French occupation. During the negotiations, which continued until February 1679, Louis XIV's delegates demanded the almost prohibitive payment of 1,046,319 *livres* to return the territories.[38]

The size of the payment, although made in instalments, was the prelude to the demobilisation of the troops. In September 1678, Count Schellart asked for Waldenberg's foot regiment to be disbanded and incorporated into his cavalry regiment, as well as for Manderscheid's dragoons to be merged into the foot regiment under the same colonel.[39] Between October 1678 and May 1679 all the infantry regiments were disbanded except *Avila zu Fuss* and the *Leibregiment*. In April this latter, still deployed 12 companies with 716 men fit and 31 sick. In May, a further 'reduction' reduced the *Leibregiment* to 9 companies. On 19 May the strength was 1,000 foot, but a few weeks later it had fallen to 876 men. Additionally, 12 independent companies were also disbanded. The garrison of Düsseldorf numbered 800 infantry divided into independent companies of 100 men each, supported by 2,000 militia on paper, although effectively only 600.[40] On 10 November, the *Leibregiment* was reduced to six companies with a total 600 men in all. The same number of companies formed the Infantry Regiment *Avila*, assigned to the garrisons in the Duchy of Jülich. The regiment received muskets to replace the pikes, which were 'more convenient for the defence of a fortress' but in July, the

---

    reduced by half in September and then quartered in Düsseldorf. Their quarters were so bad that people were almost exposed to death, especially since there was a contagious disease in the city. In Düsseldorf there were also 200 *Landeschützen* (militia) assigned to guard the city's gates. Oskar Bezzel, *Geschichte des Kurpfälzischen Heeres von Seinen Anfängen bis zur Vereinigung von Kurpfalz und Kurbayern* (Munich: Lindauer LTR-Verl, 1925), Band I, p.168.

37 'The elderly *Obrist* Neuland also joined the protests and resigned because of the favour given to another foreign officer, the younger *Generalwachtmeister* Boisbernard, who was appointed Governor of the fortress of Düren.' Oskar Bezzel, *Geschichte des Kurpfälzischen Heeres von Seinen Anfängen bis zur Vereinigung von Kurpfalz und Kurbayern* (Munich: Lindauer LTR-Verl, 1925), Band I, p.168.

38 J. R. Beitelrock, *Geschichte der Herzogtum Neuburg oder der jungen Pfalz* (Aschaffenburg: Wailandt, 1866–67), p.78.

39 Oskar Bezzel, *Geschichte des Kurpfälzischen Heeres von Seinen Anfängen bis zur Vereinigung von Kurpfalz und Kurbayern* (Munich: Lindauer LTR-Verl, 1925), band I, p.170: 'However, it seems that the proposal regarding the dragoons was not implemented.'

40 Oskar Bezzel, *Geschichte des Kurpfälzischen Heeres von Seinen Anfängen bis zur Vereinigung von Kurpfalz und Kurbayern* (Munich: Lindauer LTR-Verl, 1925), Band I, p.170.

Print after an engraving by Romeyn de Hooghe, illustrating French soldiers looting a village during the Franco-Dutch War (Collection of the Rijksmuseum, Amsterdam).
In 1676 and 1677, Pfalz-Neuburg suffered French retaliation in the Rhine territories. The outcome was dramatic, as people fled the area in terror and conditions returned to those experienced during the Thirty Years' War.

regiment again received pikes, 'which make a much better impression on parade', but with the condition that the companies had to be trained at the same time with muskets.[41] Before the summer of 1679, the cavalry regiments and dragoons, numbering about 800, were also disbanded.

Once again, the treatment of the soldiers in the garrisons was very poor, and to meet the troops demands, a loan from the Crown Prince was finally used to pay half a month's wages.[42] However, the Duke continued to trade in soldiers, although on a reduced scale. In early 1679 he enlisted four companies of dragoons dismissed by Würzburg and numbering 130 rank and file, of which only 20 were regularly equipped and mounted. They were quartered in Düsseldorf, but after a few weeks all the companies were transferred and then disbanded because their lack of discipline had caused fear among the

---

41  Oskar Bezzel, *Geschichte des Kurpfälzischen Heeres von Seinen Anfängen bis zur Vereinigung von Kurpfalz und Kurbayern* (Munich: Lindauer LTR-Verl, 1925), Band I, p.173.
42  'The people were dying of hunger and disease, it was feared that the city would be sacked …. Burgsdorff reported that 250 soldiers are sick in Düsseldorf, and the best deserted every day. The sick lie without fire, many without beds or laid on bare straw, and receive only bread and water. The officers have no resources left for the diseased soldiers. All lieutenants and ensigns are completely without funds for their subsistence.' Oskar Bezzel, *Geschichte des Kurpfälzischen Heeres von Seinen Anfängen bis zur Vereinigung von Kurpfalz und Kurbayern* (Munich: Lindauer LTR-Verl, 1925), Band I, p.173.

population of the countryside.[43] The only mounted troops who still remained in service were the *Leibgarden*, who in August 1679 formed a new company, denominated *Leibgarde des Erbprinzen*. The company was established to a strength of 160 men under Franz von Schellart, with the best troopers of his regiments. But the *Leibgarde*, at such a strong force was destined to be short-lived. On 21 November, 100 troopers were dismissed for lack of funds to pay them, and in compensation they received horses and equipment.[44]

A modest reinforcement took place in 1682 and was based on the Imperial Diet's resolutions of 1681. The assembly of the Westphalian Circle established the *miles perpetuus* of 2,708 infantry and 1,321 cavalry and dragoons, to which Pfalz-Neuburg had to contribute with 92.6 horsemen, 191.5 dragoons and 253 footmen.[45] The Estates agreed the fund to recruit this force. The duke considered these concessions a favourable opportunity to make up for the reduction of troops that occurred in 1679. He also believed that he would find the Estates more willing to authorise the necessary funds, given the danger posed by the persistent French presence threatening the Rhenish territories. After difficult negotiations with the Estates, Philipp Wilhelm' proposals were finally approved. Colonel Heinrich Ferdinand von Bernsau recruited two infantry companies in addition to the battalion he was completing, in order to form a new regiment in Neuburg. The lieutenant-captain of the Horse Guards, Florentin de Monceau, received the order to raise a cavalry regiment in Düsseldorf of which he was to become the commander, and at the end of 1682 he actually held the command of the new *Leibregiment* with a strength of 12 companies. Further recruitments for the cavalry regiment were in progress, while another foot regiment was to be raised under colonel d'Avila, newly appointed as *Generalwachtmeister* and Governor of Jülich, with 10 companies. A free cavalry company under *Rittmeister* Nagel was also raised. Fortress improvements also started and in 1683 the reconstruction of the Düsseldorf curtain according to Vauban's model was even initiated. Before the end of the year, a new infantry regiment was also raised in Neuburg.[46]

No contingent from Pfalz-Neuburg joined the relief force for Vienna in 1683, because the Duke, as with other German princes, expressed his concern about the French pressure on the Rhine. In April 1684, the Duke sent a cavalry company under *Rittmeister* Hamilton to join the *Reichsarmee* in Hungary. In May 1685, Philipp Wilhelm became Elector of the Palatinate. At this time, all the troops serving in the garrison on the Lower Rhine under his son were merged into the Electoral Army.[47]

---

43   Oskar Bezzel, *Geschichte des Kurpfälzischen Heeres von Seinen Anfängen bis zur Vereinigung von Kurpfalz und Kurbayern* (Munich: Lindauer LTR-Verl, 1925), Band I, p.171.
44   Oskar Bezzel, *Geschichte des Kurpfälzischen Heeres von Seinen Anfängen bis zur Vereinigung von Kurpfalz und Kurbayern* (Munich: Lindauer LTR-Verl, 1925), Band I, p.171. In December 1679, the *Leibgarden* consisted of only 60 horsemen under *Kapitänlieutenant* Hamilton.
45   Oskar Bezzel, *Geschichte des Kurpfälzischen Heeres von Seinen Anfängen bis zur Vereinigung von Kurpfalz und Kurbayern* (Munich: Lindauer LTR-Verl, 1925), Band I, p.176.
46   Oskar Bezzel, *Geschichte des Kurpfälzischen Heeres von Seinen Anfängen bis zur Vereinigung von Kurpfalz und Kurbayern* (Munich: Lindauer LTR-Verl, 1925), Band I, p.177.
47   Oskar Bezzel, *Geschichte des Kurpfälzischen Heeres von Seinen Anfängen bis zur Vereinigung von Kurpfalz und Kurbayern* (Munich: Lindauer LTR-Verl, 1925), Band I, p.178.

## Reuss

By the mid-1600s, the small principality of Upper Saxony was ruled in condominium by four branches. Apart from their position on the border between the territories of Upper Saxony and those of Franconia, none of the counties held any noteworthy strategic relevance. Furthermore, none of them had the resources for maintaining regular standing troops. Nevertheless, some princes served as field commanders and raised troops for other German armies in exchange for subsidies. From 1664 to 1682, there were Reuss members serving as colonel proprietor in Saxony, Brandenburg, and Austria. In 1672, the young and resourceful Count Heinrich VI of Reuss-Pleuen entered the business of mercenaries raising a regiment of cavalry and two regiments of infantry for the Prince-Bishop of Münster. The agreement committed Heinrich to raise 540 horse and 2,000 foot. In December 1672, after he had failed to provide the established contingent, the Count

Prince Ludwig Anton of Pfalz-Neuburg (1660–1694). The House of Pfalz-Neuburg obtained prestigious political recognition in various forms, including religious and military careers. Ludwig Anton was the third son of Duke Philipp Wilhelm. In 1664, he and his elder brother Wolfgang Georg, aged five, were initiated into a religious career. His father applied for Ludwig Anton to be admitted to the *Teutsche Order* (the Teutonic Order), where Ludwig Anton held the rank of *Koadjutor* of the *Hoch und Deutschmeister* (Grand Master) in 1679. After his travels to Vienna in 1681, Ludwig Anton entered the Imperial service as colonel proprietor of the regiment *Neuburg zu Fuss*. He contributed personally for completing the regiment. In 1683, the Duchy of Pfalz-Neuburg did not contribute to the formation of the *Kreiskontingent* for the relief of Vienna, but in 1684, Philipp Wilhelm contributed to raise a company for the regiment of his son. In 1685, Ludwig Anton was elected *Hoch und Deutschmeister* and promoted to *Feldmarschall Leutnant* by the Emperor. In 1686, he held a command post during the siege of Buda. In 1689, he fought at the siege of Mainz, where he was wounded, and after the fall of the city became Imperial Governor. At the same time, Ludwig Anton pursued a religious career. In August 1689, he was elected assistant to the Prince-Provost of Ellwangen Abbey and two years after became Coadjutor-Archbishop of Mainz. In June 1693, the cathedral chapter of Worms Cathedral elected him as Prince-Bishop of Worms, and in January 1694 he was finally ordained as a priest by Anselm Franz von Ingelheim, Elector of Mainz. He was a candidate to become Prince-Bishop of Liège, but he died on 4 May 1694 before the election was finalised.

## THE ARMED STATES

abandoned Münster and in 1673 passed over to the Allied side.[48] In June, Count Heinrich pledged to recruit one infantry regiment for the Emperor and to send it on the Rhine. The regiment had been capitulated for a strength of 1,000 men in 8 companies. The muster carried out in October 1673 recorded 980 rank and file, but when the regiment arrived at its destination, the strength had decreased to just 324 men.[49] In early 1674, what remained of the regiment entered the Imperial Army.[50] However, this failure did not close the attempts to gain the status of an armed state through the trade of soldiers, and by the next century, in association with Schwarzburg, Reuss hired troops to the Franconian Circle.

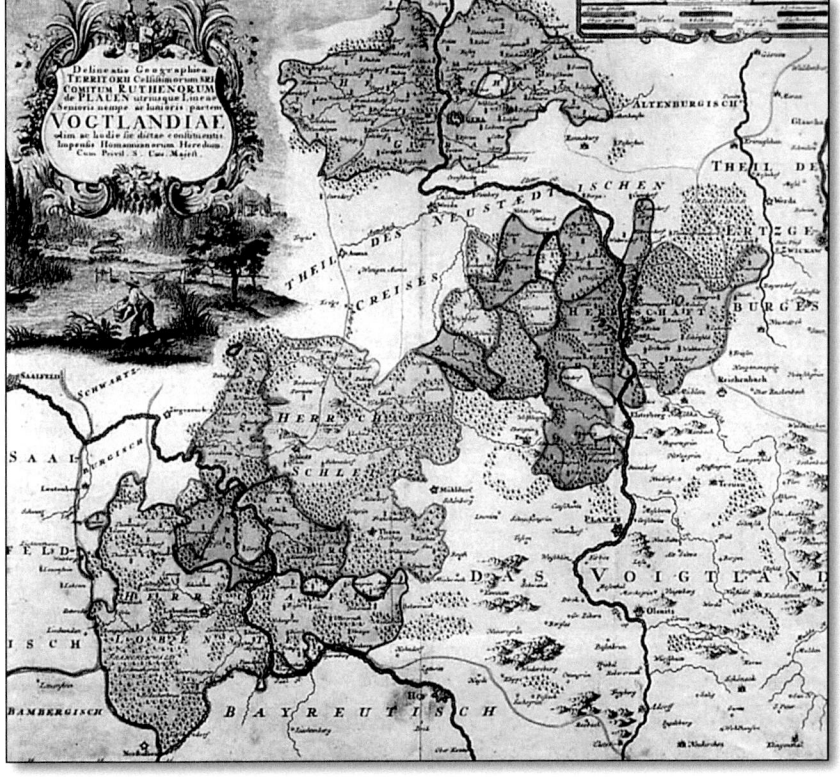

The territories of Reuss in a map dating to the 1650s. (Author's collection) In 1663, as members of the Upper Saxony Circle, the Counts were to provide *in simplum* 3 horse and 15 foot to the *Reichsarmee*. This quota increased to 5 and 24 respectively in 1681.

---

48  Georg Tessin, 'Beiträge zur Formationsgeschichte des Münsterischen Militärs', in *Westfälische Forschungen. Mitteilungen des Provinzialinstituts für Westfälische Landes- und Volksforschung des Landschaftsverband Westfalen-Lippe*, vol. 32 (Münster: Aschendorffsche Verlagsbuchhandlung, 1982), p.95. There is no reliable information on the actual number of infantry, while in the cavalry regiment, only the *Leibkompanie* numbered 82 men, while the other seven companies had between 23 and 62 men.

49  Anton Marr, 'Der Feldzüg im Jahre 1675 in Deutschland. Nach österreichischen Originalquellen' in *Österreichische Militärische Zeitschrift* (Vienna: Kaiserl. Koenigli und Hof und Staatsdruckerei 1839), Band III, p.283.

50  Bruno Mugnai, *Wars and Soldiers in the Early Reign of Louis XIV, volume 2: The Imperial Army 1657–1687* (Warwick: Helion & Company, 2019), p.83.

## The Saxon Duchies

The fragmentation of the Ernestine-Wettin domains into numerous small Thuringian territories began in 1572, as a result of the old German succession law that divided inheritances among all sons. Additionally, every prince inherited the title of Duke in order to establish no precedence over the others, as a result, brothers sometimes ruled the territory inherited from their father jointly, but sometimes they divided it. After the Peace of Westphalia, four lines with the rank of immediate Princes of the Empire ruled the Duchies. These were Saxe-Weimar, Saxe-Gotha, Saxe-Coburg, and Saxe-Altenburg. At the time, two main lines emerged, the House of Saxe-Weimar and the House of Saxe-Gotha. While the former had only a few collateral lines, the Houses of Gotha and Coburg counted a great many collateral lines, most of which ruled over their own lands as cadet branches. Saxe-Eisenach was established in 1662 for the heir of duke Wilhelm of Saxe-Weimar, while Saxe-Marksuhl went to the other duke's cadet son, Johann Georg, who in 1672 inherited Saxe-Eisenach and joined both duchies. In the same year Saxe-Altenburg was inherited by Saxe-Gotha and by 1672, the denomination Saxe-Gotha-Altenburg became common, while Johann Ernst II of Saxe-Weimar (r.1662–83) also established the duchy of Saxe-Jena for his younger brother Bernhard II (r.1662–78), whose line became extinct in 1690.

In 1675, five new principalities were created by Duke Ernst I of Saxe-Gotha (r.1640–75): Saxe-Meiningen, Saxe-Saalfeld, Sachsen-Hildburghausen, Saxe-Röhmild, and Saxe-Eisenberg, established for his cadet sons, who ruled as vassals of the elder brother Friedrich I, Saxe-Gotha (r.1675–91).

Additionally, there were further duchies that had been established in 1654 by Prince-Elector Johann Georg I. These were Saxe-Weissenfels, Saxe-Merseburg and Saxe-Zeitz, whose princes enjoyed limited rights since they were vassals of Electoral Saxony.[51] As the aforementioned cadet lines of Thuringia, they had no seats in the Empire's Diet. Finally, the Duchy of Saxe-Lauenburg, located in Lower Saxony and held by the Ascanien line, had lost all ties with the relatives of Thuringia and Saxony, and since the 1650s had strong relations with Sweden.

All the duchies of the Ernestine line belonged to the Upper Saxon Circle and, as long as there was a convergence of interests between the member states, they regularly contributed with their contingents to the *Reichsarmee*. Following the military tradition drawn up by Bernhard of Saxe-Weimar, each family prided itself on training officers of both cavalry and infantry who served abroad. Saxony and Brandenburg were the easiest destinations, but the Emperor also welcomed many captains from the Saxon Duchies.[52]

---

51  See also Bruno Mugnai, *Wars and Soldiers in the Early Reign of Louis XIV, volume 7, German Armies 1655–1690: part 1* (Warwick: Helion & Co., 2024), p.186.

52  In 1690, a member of the Saxe-Hildburghausen House entered the service of Württemberg as colonel proprietor of an infantry regiment; see Tessin, *Die Regimenter der Europäischen Staaten im Ancien Régime*, p.325.

# THE ARMED STATES

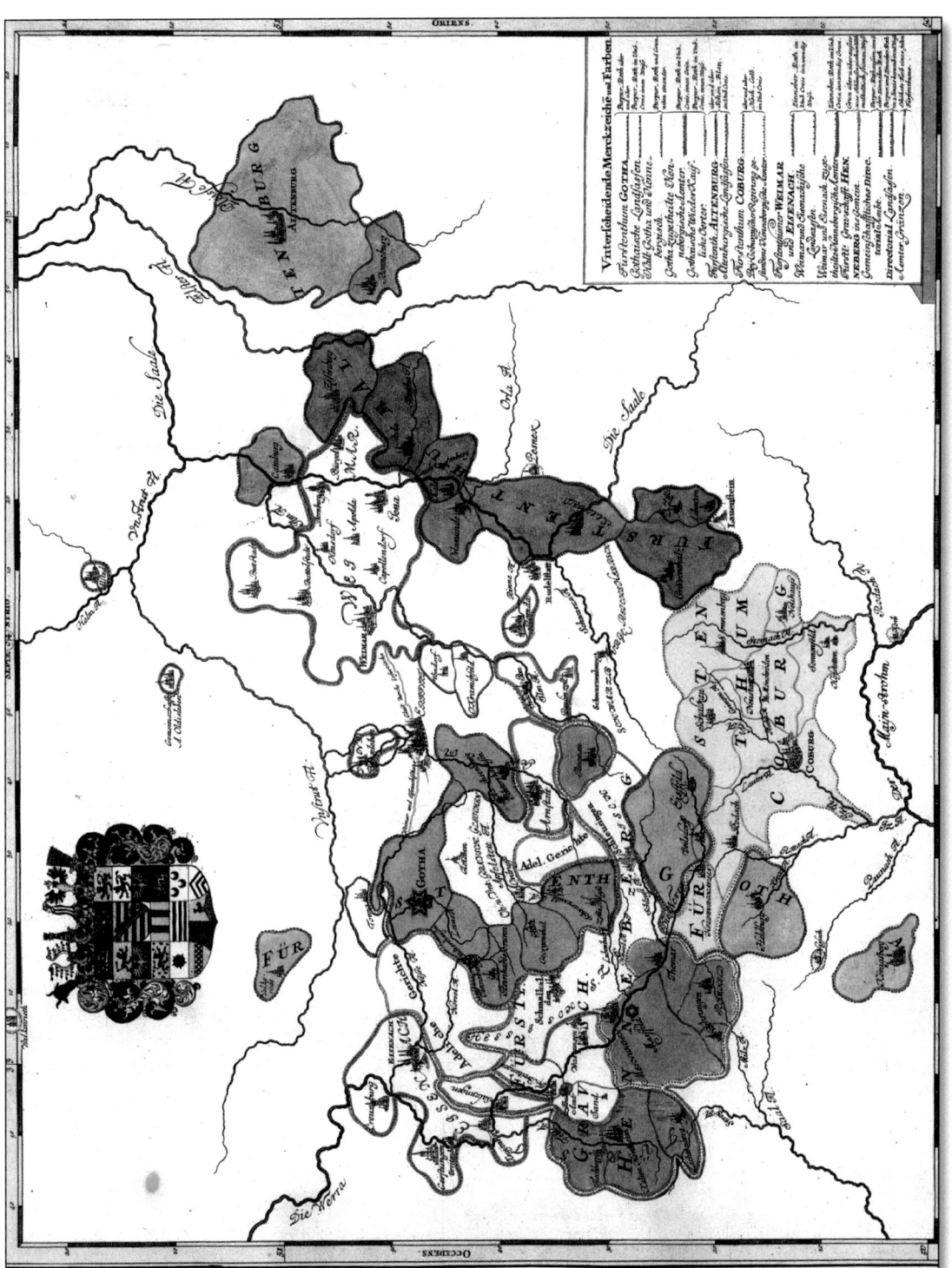

The Ernestine Duchies of Saxe, map by Friedrich Zollmann. (author's collection)

Ernst I, Duke of Saxe-Gotha and Altenburg (1601–1675) in a contemporary print. (Author's collection)
Contemporaries praised the duke as 'father and saviour of his people.' His life was simple and industrious, regulated on all sides by religious exercises. He was an active defender of Protestantism and his efforts were not limited to his own land. He tried to intercede with the Emperor for his Austrian co-religionists, and wanted to establish them in Gotha. He became a benefactor to the Evangelical Lutheran Church of the Germans in Moscow, and entered into friendly relations with the tsar. He even sent an embassy to introduce Lutheranism into Abyssinia, but this failed to accomplish its purpose. His rule of his family is a miniature of his government of his land; the strictest discipline prevailed at court. Oliver Cromwell counted him among the most sagacious of German princes.

Between 1659 and 1700, six Ernestine-Wettin princes served as *feldmarschälle* in the Imperial Army.[53]

In the duchies, there were only autonomous companies of professional troops forming the garrisons, and until the 1670s there were no regimental sized units. In case of an emergency, the peasant and town militias could be called to arms. The size of the respective forces obliged the Saxon Duchies to cooperate, but though vital, this was extremely problematic. Ernst I of Saxe-Gotha made the first attempt in response to the Ottoman threat of 1663 by promoting the idea of a common army. Keen to establish leadership not only within the Upper Saxon Circle but directly over the Ernestine Duchies as well, Elector of Saxony Johann Georg II took up the project in 1669–1670 by proposing a common 'Saxon army' that could fulfil the region's obligations to the Empire. Ernst of Saxe-Gotha agreed but was overruled by Johann Ernst of Saxe-Weimar (r. 1662–83), who feared a loss of autonomy. However, he was unable to carry his younger brothers in Jena and Eisenach with him during the Franco-Dutch War, as his alternative based on a territorial defence militia proved incapable of preserving their lands from billeting and transit during 1674–1677. After 1672, both Saxe-Eisenach and Saxe-Jena joined Gotha in seeking a substitute for the Upper Saxon Circle which was paralysed by the conflicting ambitions of the Electors of Saxony and Brandenburg.[54]

Consequently, like other German princes, Johann Georg I of Saxe-Eisenach (r. 1671–86) chose the armed princes' route, signing a bilateral treaty with Vienna in 1674 to provide 1,000 men in return for exemption from billeting. The regiment served with the Imperial Army on the Upper Rhine until November 1676, when it was joined with the corps raised by Duke Friedrich I of Saxe-Gotha (r. 1672–1691) for a further 2,000 men in exchange for subsidies from Vienna.

---

53 Antonio Schmid-Brentano, *Kaiserliche und k.k. Generale, 1618–1815* (Vienna-Munich: Österreichisches Staatsarchiv, 2006), pp.85–86.
54 Peter H. Wilson, *German Armies. War and German Politics, 1648–1806* (London: UCL Press, 1998), p.159.

# THE ARMED STATES

Duke Julius Franz of Saxe-Lauenburg (1641–1689), print by an unknown engraver (Public domain)

During the Franco-Dutch War, the Duchy contributed an infantry company to the Lower Saxony Circle's contingent. As a result of late payment of wages and poor food treatment, the company mutinied in summer 1675 along with Mecklenburg's contingent. The company consisted of musketeers and pikemen, respectively two-thirds and one-third of the strength, all dressed in green (the dynastic colour of the House). Julius Franz was the last Duke of Saxe-Lauenburg, leaving no son and no acknowledged male heir, only two daughters, Anna Maria and Sibylle. The Duchy followed the Salic Law, but Julius Franz decided to nominate his elder daughter as his heir and proclaimed laws permitting female succession in his Duchy. This self-serving innovation was not accepted by the senior members of his dynasty – the other potential successors – and a succession crisis ensued with the occupation of the principality by Duke Georg Wilhelm of Celle. The succession dispute lasted until 1728, when Emperor Carl VI finally legitimised and awarded Georg Wilhelm's grandson, George II of Great Britain, who was also Elector of Hanover, with the Duchy of Saxe-Lauenburg. The Hoause of Saxe-Lauenburg also maintained strong relations with Sweden, where Prince Franz Erdmann held command of two German regiments in 1655-57.

They served with the Imperial Army until February 1679. In the following years, Saxe-Gotha achieved major military status among the Duchies. In 1683, Erzhog Friedrich I recruited an infantry regiment as a contingent of the Upper Saxony Circle combining with four companies from Gotha, one from Meiningen and one from Coburg. By the treaty of 15 May 1689, the duke also raised a cavalry regiment of 425 men for the Dutch Republic that served in the Spanish Low Countries during the War of The League of Augsburg.[55] In the same year, he also added one horse and two foot regiments to the contingent sent by the Elector of Saxony on the Rhine. In 1690, Friedrich I offered the Emperor two regiments of cavalry, two of dragoons and four of infantry, 6,000 men in all, of which the aforementioned three were already with the allied army on the Rhine. By the time of his death in 1691, Friedrich had a professional force of 10,000 men: a burden that ruined the economy of the Duchy. Saxe-Coburg too raised an infantry regiment of 1,800 men in 1689, which entered Imperial service before the end of the year, while in 1690, Saxe-Weimar formed an infantry regiment for the *Reichsarmee*.[56]

Further initiative in the military trade of soldiers involved the cadet lines. In 1687, Erzhog Bernhard I of Saxe-Meiningen (r.1675–1706) raised a company of 100 infantry in association with the Landgrave of Hessen-Darmstadt for gathering one regiment of 1,000 men for the Republic of Venice.[57] In 1690, Prince Ernst Ludwig of Saxe-Meiningen entered the army of the Palatinate as general and colonel of infantry.

---

55  Peter H. Wilson, *German Armies. War and German Politics, 1648–1806* (London: UCL Press, 1998), p.53.
56  Georg Tessin, *Die Regimenter der Europäischen Staaten im Ancien Régime des XVI bis XVIII Jahrhunderts* (Osnabrück: Biblio Verlag, 1986), Teil 1, p.291.
57  See also Chapter 5: 'The Two Hessen.'

Duke Friedrich I of Saxe-Gotha-Altenburg (1646–1691), in a print after the engraving of Jacob von Sandrart. (Author's collection)
Friedrich continued the work of his father, Erzhog Ernst I. In order to prevent future disputes between his descendants, he established primogeniture for his House in 1685. In 1683, he took part in the Great Turkish War and in 1689 in the War of the Grand Alliance against France. He was also an avid diary writer; these diaries have become one of the most important resources for the period. However, passion for theatre and military involvement nearly ruined the finances of his small duchy.

## Salzburg

The history of the Prince-Archbishopric goes back to the late Roman Empire, becoming an immediate Imperial principality in 1213. In the mid-seventeenth century, the territory was roughly congruent with the present-day Austrian district. The long reign of Archbishop Paris Lodron (r. 1619–1653) is regarded as the Golden Age of Salzburg.

Not only did he manage to keep the state safe from devastation during the Thirty Years' War, but he established a university and improved the economy, introducing new technology for mining, agriculture and breeding. In military matters, Lodron hired the Italian architect and engineer Santino Solari, who designed and directed the construction of a new curtain at Salzburg, with five large bastions in the most updated style of the *trace italienne*.[58]

After Lodron, three bishops succeeded before 1700: Guidobald von Thun (r. 1654–1668), Maximilian Gandolph von Kuenburg (r. 1668–1687) and Johann Ernst von Thun (r. 1687–1709). In this period, Salzburg was often connected with the Bishopric of Passau, which between 1664 and 1673 was ruled by a member of the Thun family. Although the Bishops were all natives of Austria, Salzburg did not always support the Habsburgs. In 1667, Guidobald von Thun headed the strong pro-French party that opposed the Empire's involvement in the War of Devolution.

The Bishopric did not have a modern military, and except for the company of *Trabanten* as palace guard, the only regular troops consisted

---

58 Solari's works gave to Salzburg its modern aspect. The *Müllner Schanze* protected the old town on the left bank. The fortress of Hohensalzburg was also considerably expanded in line with the new defence technology, and the outworks in particular were reinforced (Author's note).

of the garrison of Salzburg that numbered less than 400 men in the 1660s. In 1664, Salzburg and Passau sent a battalion to the Emperor as a subsidy regiment. Formally, it was neither part of the *Reichsarmee* nor of the *Deutsche Allianz*, and fought at Zrínyivár under Hohenlohe. From 1674 to 1678, a battalion of 600 foot recruited in Salzburg manned the garrison of Cologne as a contingent of the Bavarian Circle.[59] In 1683, one infantry regiment of 1,000 men was raised for the relief corps for Vienna. At the Battle of Kahlenberg, the regiment was deployed alongside the Electoral Bavarian infantry. The regiment served in Hungary until 1688, when it was recalled to the Rhine.[60] In the following years, Salzburg and Passau provided the largest part of the Bavarian Circle's contingent.

## Waldeck-Pyrmont

The Upper Rhine principality held a relevant politic role in the Empire notwithstanding its small extent. The man who managed this achievement was Prince, later Count, Georg Friedrich (r. 1664–1692). As already discussed, he earned a considerable reputation serving as a mercenary officer in the armies of Brandenburg, and Sweden, both as field commander and as a military entrepreneur. As an undisputed authority in the soldier market, Georg Friedrich acted as adviser and partner of some European states, notably the Dutch Republic. He extended his net of relationships in Germany, holding the office of military consultant to the Duke Georg Wilhelm of Celle from 1665 to 1671.[61] From the 1650s, the prince had been a resolute opponent of the Austrian Habsburgs but after 1678 he turned to the Imperial party as principal organiser of the military contingent of the Western Circles of the Empire: an action that, more or less consciously, favoured Vienna. Other members of the House served in Brandenburg, Celle, Brunswick, Electoral Cologne and Venice.

Prince-Archbishop Paris Lodron (1586–1653), in a print after the engraving of Johannes Jenet (Universitätsbibliothek Salzburg). Coming from an Italian family of Trento, in 1619 Lodron succeeded Markus Sittich von Hohenems as ecclesiastical Prince of Salzburg. He was able to keep the principality out of the Thirty Years' War and concentrate on improvements to his domain. Despite the military and political problems of his time, Lodron was able to complete many projects begun but unfinished by his predecessor, including the restoration of Salzburg Cathedral.

---

59  Peter H. Wilson, *German Armies. War and German Politics, 1648–1806* (London: UCL Press, 1998), p.48.
60  Georg Tessin, *Die Regimenter der Europäischen Staaten im Ancien Régime des XVI bis XVIII Jahrhunderts* (Osnabrück: Biblio Verlag, 1986), Teil 1, p.303.
61  See also Chapter 3: 'The Three Brunswicks'.

# WARS AND SOLDIERS IN THE EARLY REIGN OF LOUIS XIV – VOLUME 7 PART 3

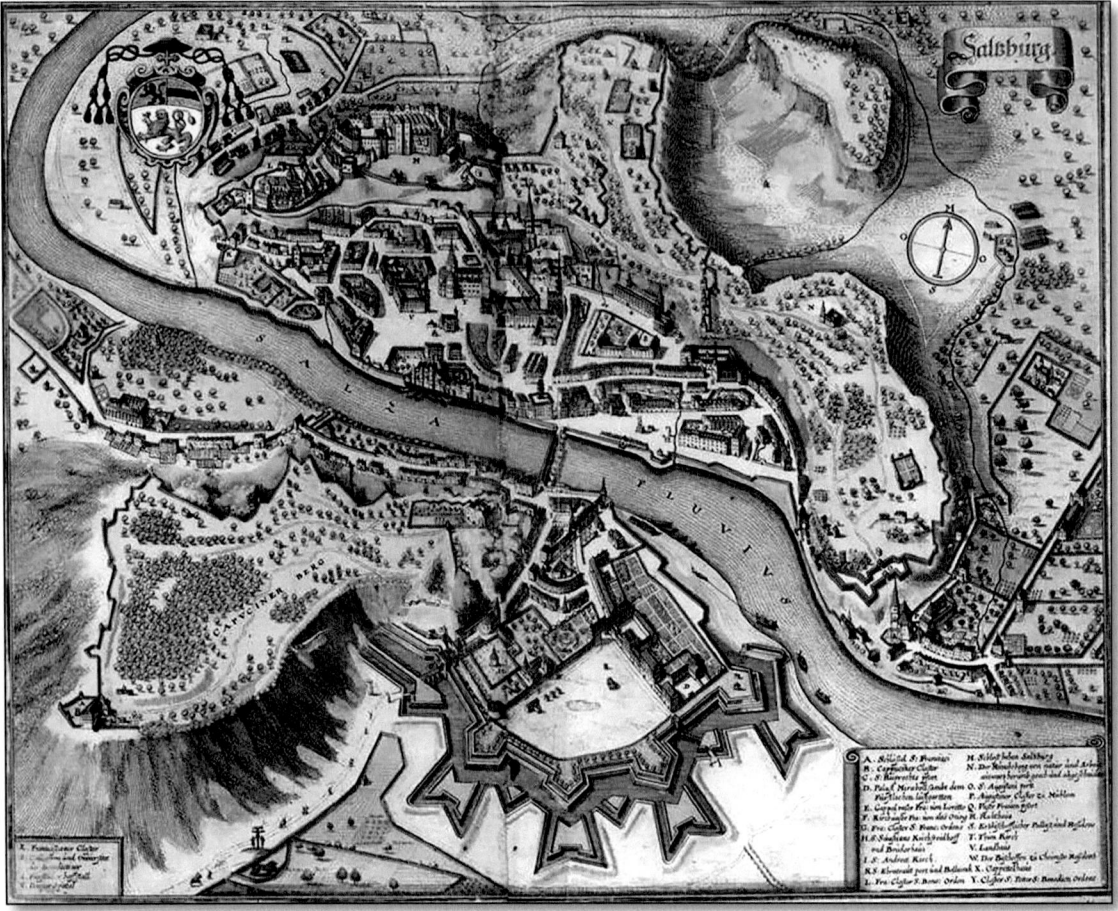

Plan of Salzburg showing the fortifications designed by Santino Solari, print by Matthäus Merian the Elder, 1650. The Italian architect devised a defensive ring with five large bastions around the new town, which stretched from the Linzertoren over the Franz-Josef-Straße area to the former Mirabell Gate. In the Old Town, the rock of the Mönchsberg was excavated all round, levelled and smoothed, and thus made usable as natural defensive walls. The *Müllner Schanze* formed the end of the Old Town on the left bank in the north. The Hohensalzburg Fort was also considerably expanded in line with the modern design, and the outworks, in particular Nonnbergbasteien, Hasengrabenbastei, and Katzen were considerably reinforced.

The exuberant personality of the Prince has often overshadowed the 'military' of the principality. Located between Hessen-Kassel and the Westphalian possessions of the Electorate of Cologne, the principality also comprised small enclaves in the Empire ruled in condominium by the branches of Waldeck-Eisenberg and Waldeck-Wildungen.[62]

Apart from the Kassel claims for the allegiance as a Hessian fief, the principality was an active member in the Upper Rhine Circle, retaining a status that was cleverly exploited by its rulers. Because of the military involvements of the rulers, the principality gathered a significant number of veteran native officers and soldiers who had served in the foreign armies. The first regimental sized unit raised in Waldeck were the 600 horse in 8

---

62   The branches joined in 1692.

companies who entered the Swedish army under the agreement of July 1655.[63] Another regiment of horse was recruited for Brandenburg in the same year. In 1663, an infantry regiment was raised with Electoral Cologne under *Obrist* Josias von Waldeck as a contingent for the Rhenish League for the war against the Ottomans. In 1666, another infantry regiment under *Obrist Lieutenant* Degenfeld took part in the relief of Bremen.

In 1672, a regiment of cavalry of 4 companies, of 390 men, was raised for Brandenburg under *Obrist* Friedrich of Waldeck-Wildungen, which served on the Lower Rhine until 1673. The principality provided troops for the Upper Rhine contingent during the Franco-Dutch War, and in June 1674 was among the states that negotiated the new *Armatur* for the *Reichskrieg*

Map of the county of Waldeck-Pyrmont, from Willem Janszoon Blaeu, *Theatrum Orbis Terrarum, Sive Atlas Novus in quo Tabulæ et Descriptiones Omnium Regionum* (Amsterdam: 1645).

---

63 Georg Tessin, *Die Deutschen Regimenter der Krone Schweden, 1660–1718* (Cologne-Graz: Böhlau, 1967), Teil II, p.34.

against France and its allies.⁶⁴ The results achieved by this association of states were disappointing, and in 1677, participation came to a halt due to lack of resources for maintaining the troops. However, Waldeck and other Upper Rhine territories continued to suffer until 1679 from the billeting and depredations of the armed states, notably Münster. Georg Friedrich was able to summon the Upper Rhine Diet to face the threat and succeeded in raising a contingent for guarding the unarmed territories against foreign intrusions.⁶⁵ In 1680, the princes retained two half companies of professional infantry as garrisons in Waldeck and Aarolsen. In 1685, troops from Waldeck joined the Upper Rhine contingent marching to Hungary as a part of the cavalry and infantry regiments raised by the Circle. The war against the Ottomans fuelled the business for the trade in soldiers. In January 1688, after two years of negotiation, Count Friedrich of Waldeck-Wildungen agreed with the Republic of Venice to recruit an infantry regiment of 1,000 men for service in Greece. This unfortunate regiment received its baptism of fire in the terrible campaign of Negroponte, suffering the loss of 782 men from June to November.⁶⁶ A second infantry regiment for Venice was raised in 1692 by Count Christian Ludwig.⁶⁷

## Württemberg

At the end of the Thirty Years' War, the Duchy of Württemberg was in a miserable state, comparable to that of other German territories that had suffered most during the conflict. In 1655, the population was just 40 percent of that before the 'painful occupation of the lands' between 1634 and 1635, which had caused the flight of inhabitants.⁶⁸ In the post-war years,

---

64  Theo Schüler, 'Die Nassauer unter den Truppen des Oberrheinischen Kreises im Reichskrieg gegen Frankreich 1674–79', in *Alt-Nassau*, VII, 87 (1917), pp.20–21. The Circle's Diet met in Friedberg and agreed to form an initial contingent of troops from only the northern states, namely Hessen-Kassel, Hessen-Darmstadt, Nassau-Idstein, Nassau-Usingen, Nassau-Weilburg, Hanau-Münzenberg, Solms, Isenburg, Leiningen-Westerburg, Wittgenstein, Waldeck, the abbey of Fulda and the Imperial Cities of Frankfurt am Main, Friedberg and Wetzlar. The contingent mustered 700 horse and 1,400 foot, under Count Moritz of Solms. The result was less than hoped, because the Landgraves of Hessen-Kassel and Hessen-Darmstadt did not send their troops. See Bruno Mugnai, *Wars and Soldiers in the Early Reign of Louis XIV, volume 2: The Imperial Army 1657–1687* (Warwick: Helion & Company, 2019), pp.116–117.

65  Otto Münter, 'Die Waldeckische Truppen von 1681–1750', in *Geschichtsblätter für Waldeck*, 71 (1983), p.179. Waldeck-Pyrmont raised one infantry company comprising 1 *Hauptmann*, 1 *Leutnant*, 1 *Fähnrich*, 2 *Feldwebel*, 1 *Fourier*, 3 corporals, 9 lance corporals and 75 privates, one-third armed with pikes and the other two-thirds with muskets.

66  Georg Tessin, 'Die Deutschen Regimenter der Republik Venedig', in *Zeitschrift für Heereskunde*, X – 1982, p.24.

67  With this agreement, a durable bond was established by Venice and Waldeck-Pyrmont, and in 1716 two infantry regiments were raised for the garrison defending Corfu. Further reading: A.Prelli and B. Mugnai, *L'Ultima Vittoria della Serenissima. L'Assedio di Corfù, 1716* (Bassano del Grappa: Itinera Progetti, 2016).

68  Wolfgang von Hippel, *Wirtschafts- und Sozialgeschichte* in: *Handbuch der Baden-Württembergischen Geschichte* (Stuttgart: Klett-Cotta, 2007), p.333. Most people did not die as a result of direct acts of war, but mainly from epidemics and hunger. It was not until the middle of the eighteenth century that the population loss was evened out again. Nevertheless, Wolfgang

the Duchy's lack of resources, and its over-indebtedness was immense. Duke Eberhard III (r. 1633–1674), reinstated in his territories in 1638, until the 1660s focused primarily on restoring the administration and strengthening the economy and finances. In the following decades, he devoted much effort on a cultural revival in the state and on politic matters, including diplomacy and foreign affairs.

Württemberg's geographical position meant that its relations with the Emperor had to be worked out within the context of its ties to the Swabian Circle and, increasingly, also its attitude towards France. This scenario became increasingly unsafe for all the Swabian principalities, of which there were 92 in all, and none of a size to compete with their powerful neighbours.[69] The Duke held one of the two executive posts in the Swabian Circle's *Direktorium*. Periodic rivalry with the much smaller Margraviate of Baden-Durlach prevented Württemberg from exercising exclusive leadership of the Protestant members, but in the 1660s the Duke assisted the Catholic Bishop of Constance to retain his executive position, and tried to reduce the confessional division along the Swabian states. In 1667, the Duke negotiated with Bavaria for a general pacification of Southern Germany, but unlike the Elector, he did not adhere to a bilateral alliance with France. In 1673, the elderly but still energetic Eberhard met Philipp Wilhelm of Pfalz-Neuburg in the plan for imposing a peace on the warring parties involved in the Franco-Dutch War.[70]

Though his achievements in government and foreign policy had increased his authority, the Duke was fully aware that he ruled a weak state. Württemberg covered nearly one-third of the Circle's area, but it was virtually indefensible because of the poor geographical barriers. Moreover, all fortresses were in need of radical improvements. In 1650, the capital, Stuttgart, still had a medieval curtain with towers and a ditch along the whole perimeter. The other major towns, such as Marbach, Heidenheim and Tübingen, also needed to update their fortifications.

Württemberg had already established a core of professional troops in the 1620s, however, their trial in the field was not promising. On 6 September 1634, Duke Eberhard sided with Horn and Saxe-Weimar at the Battle of Nördlingen, but lost all his troops, and after the defeat he was forced into exile. Once re-installed as legitimate ruler, his military policy was for a long time affected by the country's economic constraints as well as opposition from the Estates. Nevertheless, Eberhard managed to create an autonomous model for the defence of the state, and established an organisation well ahead of its time. The House of Württemberg also enjoyed the contribution of other ducal branches that provided several skilled military officers. These were

---

    von Hippel's surveys showed that after the war, the supply of food to the people was better than before the war due to the large population losses and despite numerous deserted fields.
69  The Emperor also kept alive the idea of the medieval 'Duchy of Swabia' as an Austrian possession. In 1699 a rumour that he was trying to re-establish this greatly alarmed the Swabian princes. See Peter H. Wilson, *War, State and Society in Württemberg, 1677–1793* (Cambridge: Cambridge University Press, 1995), p.106.
70  Peter H. Wilson, *German Armies. War and German Politics, 1648–1806* (London: UCL Press, 1998), p.178.

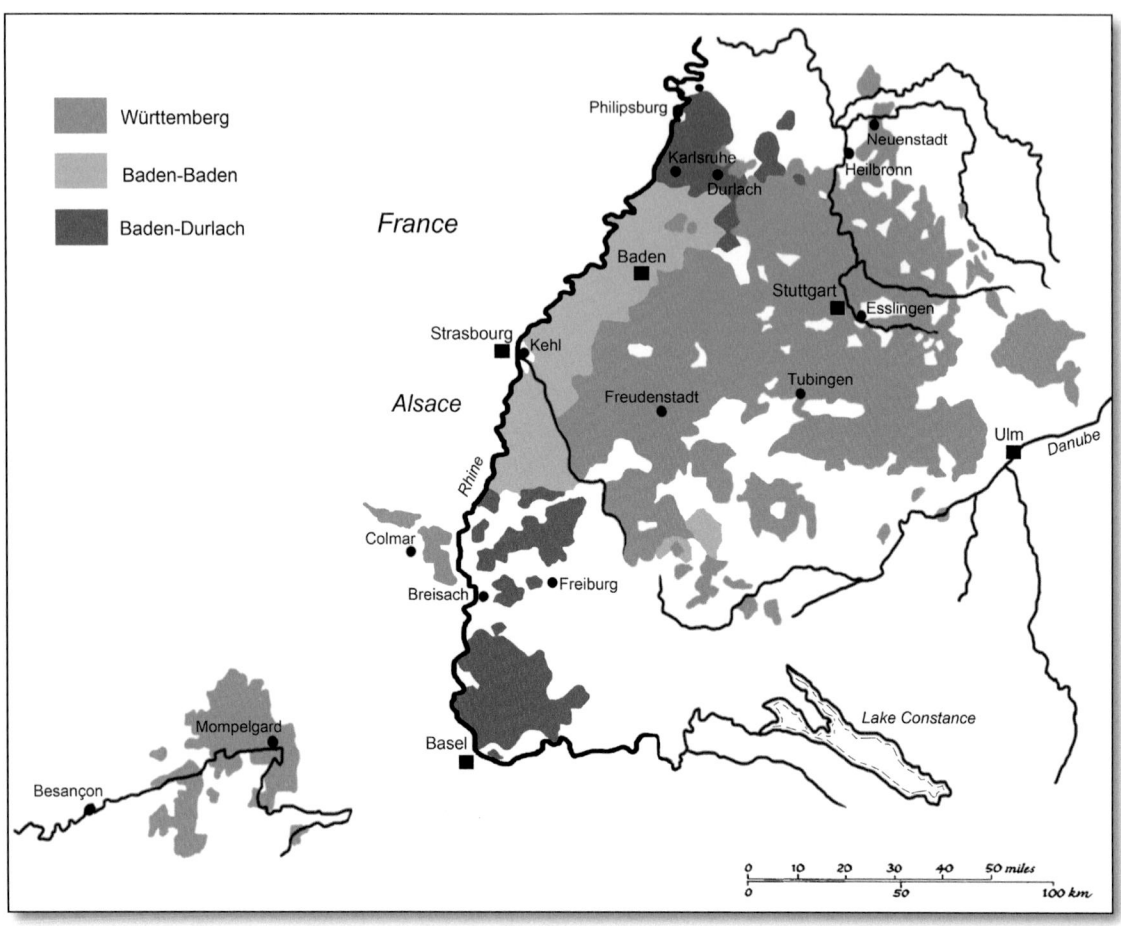

The Duchy of Württemberg and the Margraviates of Baden after 1648. The Duchy of Württemberg was reinstated after long negotiations during in the Peace of Westphalia. The effects of war, poverty, hunger and the bubonic plague had reduced the population from 350,000 in 1618 to 120,000 in 1648.

Württemberg-Mömpelgard (1608–1723), Württemberg-Stuttgart (1608–1693), Württemberg-Weiltingen (1617–1708), Württemberg-Oels (1648–1792), Württemberg-Neuenstadt (1649–1742), Württemberg-Neuenbürg (1651–1671). A further branch, Württemberg-Winnental, was established in 1674 for the younger son of Eberhard, Friedrich Carl, whose lineage survived until 1733. Along with the *Privater Rat* (private council), in 1651 the duke also established a *Geheimrat* (secret council), and a *Kriegsrat* (war council), the latter becoming a permanent office in the 1660s. For this latter council, the Duke chose each member from those who had knowledge on matters relating to troops and fortifications, appointing as secretary the veteran *Feldzuegmeister* Georg Friedrich von Holz.[71]

In 1651, the Duke formed a life guard of 180 foot, which, along with 24 *Trabanten* of the palace guard, remained the only professional military force

---

71  Leo Ignaz Stadlinger, *Geschichte des Württembergischen Kriegswesens von der frühesten bis zur neuesten Zeit* (Stuttgart: Druck und Verlag der K. Hofbuchdruckerei zu Guttenberg 1856), p.312. On 10 July 1673, the duke ordered that everything relating to the state's defence was to be discussed collegially in the council of war, and that this was to deal with the conscription registers, the musters, weapons and training sessions. The council was also in charge of the maintenance of the fortifications, and in particular of ensuring the supply of food and ammunition to the garrisons.

Duke Eberhard III of Württemberg (1614–1674), portrait by Johann Andreas Thill (Landesmuseum Württemberg, Stuttgart).
In 1633, Eberhard was declared of legal age at which point he assumed full rule of the Duchy at a very difficult time. Following a major defeat of his troops at the Battle of Nördlingen on 6 September 1634, Württemberg was severely looted and plundered. Eberhard fled to Strasbourg, returning to Württemberg four years later after long negotiations with Emperor Ferdinand III. By this time many territories had already been passed on by the Emperor to other parties to push forward Catholicism in the region. Eberhard held a view of sovereignty quite different from that implied by his later image, and his reign too was filled with disputes with the Estates over the establishment of a small permanent army, the attempt to fortify some strategic place, his disorderly personal life and his various mercantilist schemes. However, 'in tone and style' he had remained a traditional German prince, who earned the title *der Grosse* from his contemporaries.

until 1660. In Württemberg, as in other German principalities, the Estates were reluctant to contribute to the maintenance of troops for the 'particular service of a prince', but recognised that subjects were obliged to assist the sovereign in the event of war, and therefore they agreed to contribute to raise the contingent for the Circle when this had been decided and established. The first result in the raising of a corps of professional troops, albeit belonging to an association of states, had been achieved. The Swabian Diet began to deal with this matter in 1654, but on 18 September 1652 the duke had issued the *Generalrescript* for the state's militia, the *Landesdefension*.[72] In return for special concessions and the reduction of taxes on their property, the Duke extended service in the militia to his subjects by inviting them to apply for non-commissioned officer posts as well. Officers were granted complete freedom from labour; however, they had to pay the charges from their property like other subjects. In 1655 there were four mixed regiments, which together numbered 17 companies of horse and 34 companies of foot, distributed between 35 garrisons. The *Oberinspection* over the militia was entrusted to the *Feldzeugmeister* Holz, who in April 1651 had been

---

72 Leo Ignaz Stadlinger, *Geschichte des Württembergischen Kriegswesens von der frühesten bis zur neuesten Zeit* (Stuttgart: Druck und Verlag der K. Hofbuchdruckerei zu Guttenberg 1856), p.310.

appointed as Commander-in-Chief; he was to conduct a general muster of the companies every year with the colonels.

Exploiting the outcome of the acceptance of the request made by the college of princes to the Emperor at the Diet of 1657, which obliged the subjects to provide manpower and free labour for the defence of the Empire, the Duke drew up a plan to improve the fortifications of his state.[73] Instead, the project to build new defences was opposed by the Estates, who rejected the plan to protect the western border with a modern fortress at Freudenstadt.[74]

The City of Stuttgart in a print by Mattäus Merian the Elder's *Theatrum Europeum* dating to 1650.

---

73  Leo Ignaz Stadlinger, *Geschichte des Württembergischen Kriegswesens von der frühesten bis zur neuesten Zeit* (Stuttgart: Druck und Verlag der K. Hofbuchdruckerei zu Guttenberg 1856), p.310. The college of princes requested that the Emperor grant the following addition to the Imperial order issued in 165, 'The landowners, citizens and subjects are also obliged to manage and respect the pacts covenants of their sovereigns, dominions and authorities which do not contradict the Peace of Westphalia, and they must provide the necessary means for maintaining fortresses and their garrisons and for the satisfaction of necessary needs, whereby no privileges and no freedoms, whatever their name and the time when they were obtained, shall be granted to them'. The Emperor, however, considering the last point unfair, and refused, after long negotiations, to authorise the concession, although not its application.

74  In vain, the ducal plenipotentiaries endeavoured to convince the Estates on the great value of this fortress, thanks to which the whole country could expect 'greater protection and salvation, and to which the rulers and subjects could retreat in case of necessity and save what was dear to them in temporal goods'. It was explained that the fortress could be built at any time and without causing inconvenience to the population, but the Estates insisted that the expense was unsustainable and that the subjects were not in favour. Leo Ignaz Stadlinger, *Geschichte des Württembergischen Kriegswesens von der frühesten bis zur neuesten Zeit* (Stuttgart: Druck und Verlag der K. Hofbuchdruckerei zu Guttenberg 1856), p.312.

# THE ARMED STATES

Plan of the fortress of Freudenstadt in a contemporary print (Hauptstadtsarchiv Stuttgart). (public domain)

In 1659, Duke Eberhard III decided to build a modern fortress, examined several proposals and decided to build it at Freudenstadt. In the opinion of his advisers, the location was particularly suitable for a fortress, as it barred the Kniebis Pass, and also because 'the air here was salubrious, there was a sufficient supply of water and the supply was also easy to manage.' The fortress was to be in the form a regular octagon, and a citadel with a castle and a covered passage was to be built on a nearby hill.

The works began in 1661, because the opposition of the Estates delayed the project. According to them, the final cost would be too high. The construction proceeded slowly, and after a great deal of money had already been spent, it was stopped completely in 1674. However, in May, Duke Wilhelm Ludwig took into his service *Obristlieutenant* Kieser from Frankfurt as military adviser, artillery officer and inspector of fortifications, and sent him to Freudenstadt to inspect the construction. He declared that the location was completely unsuitable for a fortress, mainly due to the nearby mountains. The project was abandoned within a few days.

In the meantime, the Duke's attention was turning to other affairs. Between 1657 and 1660, Württemberg was involved in negotiations for the formation of the *Deutsche Allianz*. Eberhard hesitated for a long time because his advisers and his own brother, Prince Friedrich, were against the alliance, as it would inevitably irritate the Emperor, and the Estates also strongly advised against. Eventually, on 25 January 1660, the Duke joined the alliance, because in his opinion there was no better means to protect the state and its people from invasion. He pledged to provide 100 horse and 200 foot for the *Allianz*. The infantry was the *Leibwache*, and consisted of half musketeers and half pikemen,[75] while the cavalry was to be provided by a new unit recruited with the help of the 104 aristocratic families of the Duchy.[76] Consequently, on 8 February 1660, the Duke ordered the commander of the Foot Guards, *Obristleutnant* Klenck, to select 174 horsemen who would form the company of the mounted life guard. Klenck was entrusted with the command of both units, the only ones formed by professional soldiers. The Duke appointed the cavalry Captain Eyb as commander of the contingent for the *Allianz*, which headed to Hungary with 100 cavalry, and 250 infantry under *Hauptmann* Hoff. In addition to the financial resources for the enlistment of recruits, the

---

75  Leo Ignaz Stadlinger, *Geschichte des Württembergischen Kriegswesens von der frühesten bis zur neuesten Zeit* (Stuttgart: Druck und Verlag der K. Hofbuchdruckerei zu Guttenberg 1856), p.322. The percentage of pikemen decreased to a third of the total in 1673.

76  Leo Ignaz Stadlinger, *Geschichte des Württembergischen Kriegswesens von der frühesten bis zur neuesten Zeit* (Stuttgart: Druck und Verlag der K. Hofbuchdruckerei zu Guttenberg 1856), p.313.

Detail of plate 16 of Leo Ignaz Stadlinger's *Geschichte des Württembergischen Kriegswesens von der Frühesten bis zur Neuesten Zeit* (Stuttgart: Druck und Verlag der K. Hofbuchdruckerei zu Guttenberg 1856). (Public domain) According to the author, the Württemberg cavalry wore metal armour until the 1670s, which was later replaced by leather waistcoats as worn by the man on the right. He wears coat and breaches of grey-bluish cloth, which could be artistic licence by the artist, but the same colour is also attributed to the infantry of Württemberg in 1710 by Richard Knötel in plate II / 21 of *Grosse Uniformenkunde* (Berlin: Max Babenzien, 1891)

Estates also authorised an extraordinary contribution for the maintenance of the troops on campaign.

The idea of increasing the professional military force was revived at the end of 1663, when the Diet of the Circle set troop quotas for the contingent to be sent as part of the *Reichsarmee* to Hungary. Although he had joined the Rhenish Alliance, Eberhard decided to also contribute to the Swabian Circle's contingent, managing to obtain the resources from the Estates to recruit one company of horse and one of foot.[77] In May 1664, 70 horse under *Rittermeister* Roth, and 200 infantry under *Hauptmannleutnant* Barthels followed as reinforcements, joining the Swabian regiments assembled near Ulm, where Duke Ulrich of Württemberg-Neuenbürg was gathering the cavalry.[78]

Thus at the Battle of Szentgotthárd, the Duke deployed troops in two corps into two different political alliances. At the end of the campaign, the ducal contingent took the road home. The troops suffered greatly from poor provisions; they received no bread for five days and had to resort to mouldy flour that was mostly unusable.[79] In November 1664, the troops of the Rhine Alliance returned home, and on 28 February 1665, those of the Swabian Circle, to whom Emperor Leopold sent

---

77  Georg Tessin, *Die Regimenter der Europäischen Staaten im Ancien Régime des XVI bis XVIII Jahrhunderts* (Osnabrück: Biblio Verlag, 1986), Teil 1, p.323. In 1664, the *Leibgarde zu Ross* was merged into the regiment *Birkenfeld zu Fuss*, while the second company joined the other Swabian regiment *Fürstenberg zu Pferd*. See Bruno Mugnai, *Wars and Soldiers in the Early Reign of Louis XIV, volume 2: The Imperial Army 1657–1687* (Warwick: Helion & Company, 2019), p.285.

78  Adolph von Schempp, *Der Feldzug 1664 in Ungarn unter Besonderer Berücksichtigung der Herzoglichen Württembergischen Allianz- und schwâbischen Kreistruppen* (Stuttgart, 1909), p.92. At Ulm, the infantry was embarked and sailed to Vienna via the Danube. Margrave Hermann of Baden led the troops through Dedenburg and Radkersburg and into Hungary where they joined the main army of *Feldmarschall* Montecuccoli. The cavalry, under Erzhog Ulrich von Württemberg-Neuenbürg marched towards Ungarisch-Altenburg (Mosonmagyaróvár).

79  Leo Ignaz Stadlinger, *Geschichte des Württembergischen Kriegswesens von der frühesten bis zur neuesten Zeit* (Stuttgart: Druck und Verlag der K. Hofbuchdruckerei zu Guttenberg 1856), p.315.

his satisfaction in writing, stating that they had behaved well and bravely against their enemies 'to their eternal glory and to his most welcome pleasure.'[80] The Duke declared that his troops had proved to be as disciplined inside as outside the country, and that his cavalry, mostly composed of good and experienced officers, should not be dismissed, at the risk of losing the best and most loyal among them. His wish, however, had to be negotiated, as always, with the Estates. They granted the money on the condition that the professional troops be 'well quartered and fed so that they do not disturb the inhabitants.' With the troops returned from Hungary, the Duke could reform them into one life guard of horse and one of foot.[81]

Perhaps, the most decisive episode for Württemberg's military policy occurred in 1663, when the Duke ordered a census of the adult male population of the state. Probably inspired by the Swedish model, he wanted to introduce a form of compulsory conscription consistent with the condition of his state. The census recorded a figure of 58,376 males aged between 17 and 55, of whom 33,685 were declared eligible for military service. From this number, 9,000 men were to be drawn for actual service in the *ausschuss*, to be assembled into 18 cavalry and dragoon companies, and 4 infantry regiments; the Duke appointed colonels and all the officers with a special patent. Great care was taken in the administration of the units, including the distribution of uniform clothing and colours, whose hue gave the infantry regiments their names. At the end of the year, the 'black regiment' numbered 1,799 men, the 'blue regiment' 1,852, the 'red regiment' 1,800, the 'yellow regiment' 1,851; the cavalry and dragoons comprised 1,690 troopers, for a total of 8,992 horse and foot.[82] To prevent the pool of recruits from shrinking, bans on enlistment in the foreign armies were issued, following the similar bans of 1644 and 1657.[83]

Duke Ulrich of Württemberg-Neuenbürg (1617–1671), portrait by an unknown artist. (Author's collection)
The most famous of the Württemberg captains of his generation, Ulrich was a soldier of fortune who served between 1639 and 1659 for Venice, Denmark, Bavaria, Austria, Spain and France. In the last years of his life, he was stricken by increasingly serious illnesses, including an eye disease that cost him his sight, which forced him to give up serving as a general in the Circle of Swabia.

---

80  Schempp, *Der Feldzug 1664 in Ungarn*, p.121.
81  Leo Ignaz Stadlinger, *Geschichte des Württembergischen Kriegswesens von der frühesten bis zur neuesten Zeit* (Stuttgart: Druck und Verlag der K. Hofbuchdruckerei zu Guttenberg 1856), p.316.
82  Leo Ignaz Stadlinger, *Geschichte des Württembergischen Kriegswesens von der frühesten bis zur neuesten Zeit* (Stuttgart: Druck und Verlag der K. Hofbuchdruckerei zu Guttenberg 1856), p.314.
83  Leo Ignaz Stadlinger, *Geschichte des Württembergischen Kriegswesens von der frühesten bis zur neuesten Zeit* (Stuttgart: Druck und Verlag der K. Hofbuchdruckerei zu Guttenberg 1856), p.312.

The Duke convened the Estates again in early 1668 for discussing military matters. He expressed his concern about the ongoing war between France and Spain in the Low Countries, and requested additional resources to increase the regular troops.[84] The Estates replied that:

> …because of the great poverty of the subjects, the recruitment of more mercenaries was not possible, as it has not been necessary up to now, and, moreover, would not bring any benefit, but only harm, because the troops recruited would be of no help in the event of a greater danger, while the well-trained militia was sufficient to prevent acts of violence by foreign armies.[85]

The negotiations lasted until March, and when the Duke highlighted the example of other German princes who had recruited professional troops in addition to militia, he obtained funding to recruit further mercenaries.[86] However, the emergency ended with the signing of the Peace of Aix-La-Chapelle on 2 May 1668 which ended the war between France and Spain, and the resources were set aside for possible future needs.

The Duke did not stop in his concern with the militia and its improvement, showing great zeal and interest in the introduction of new regulations. Availing himself of the commander of the *Landesdefensionsvölker*, the skilled *Generalleutnant* Friederich Moser von Filsed, and the war council, the Duke received an accurate report on the condition of the militia. On 11 June 1668, he issued a 16-point *Rescript* in which he stated that, except for a few shortcomings, 'our national defence is now in such a state that it can survive with divine help for the protection and security of the country.'[87]

---

84  In his speech to the Estates, the Duke declared that: 'The dangerous conjunctures taking place inside and outside the German Empire are such that the national contingent (the militia) is no longer sufficient to defend and secure the borders, and for its reinforcement, more cavalry and infantry must be recruited, for which the country is obliged to provide the means.' Leo Ignaz Stadlinger, *Geschichte des Württembergischen Kriegswesens von der frühesten bis zur neuesten Zeit* (Stuttgart: Druck und Verlag der K. Hofbuchdruckerei zu Guttenberg 1856), p.317.

85  Leo Ignaz Stadlinger, *Geschichte des Württembergischen Kriegswesens von der frühesten bis zur neuesten Zeit* (Stuttgart: Druck und Verlag der K. Hofbuchdruckerei zu Guttenberg 1856), p.317.

86  'However, the Estates did not want to contribute to the costs of recruiting and equipping the new troops and declared that this contribution was made only of their own free will, in violation of provincial treaties, and that therefore no consequences should be drawn for the future.' Leo Ignaz Stadlinger, *Geschichte des Württembergischen Kriegswesens von der frühesten bis zur neuesten Zeit* (Stuttgart: Druck und Verlag der K. Hofbuchdruckerei zu Guttenberg 1856), p.317.

87  Point two stated: 'In order to maintain the order that has now been introduced, annual inspections of the militia must take place, particularly for the cavalry in companies, in the spring and at the end of the year after the completion of the autumn trades and jobs, in a location particularly suitable for this purpose. In addition to the company commander, an officer with a clerk must always be present to record defects, and then send a report and ensure that the defects are rectified as soon as possible.' Point 14 was dedicated to officers in financial difficulties, 'who must be supported by the state for their equipment.' Point 16 established for horsemen the exemption of half of the taxes, 'and they may sell their horse only if they purchase another suitable one within the prescribed time.' Leo Ignaz Stadlinger, *Geschichte des Württembergischen Kriegswesens von der frühesten bis zur neuesten Zeit* (Stuttgart: Druck und Verlag der K. Hofbuchdruckerei zu Guttenberg 1856), p.317.

# THE ARMED STATES

The document was written in tones of, perhaps exaggerated, optimism, but the general conditions of the militia must have been very satisfactory. Any regular troops were enlisted in the following years, and those still in service were the horse of the two companies of the *Leibgarde*, the first of which now reduced to 86 men, and the 150 foot of the *Leibwache*.[88]

In the spring of 1672, the news of the Franco-Dutch War caused new concerns. The Duke met the request of the Diet of the Swabian Circle to provide 100 cavalry and 200 infantry and thus turned to the Estates to provide the necessary funds for their maintenance: '…in accordance with the content of the Imperial constitution and agreements with our Estates.'[89] However, a new Diet was convened in February 1673 because the situation had become increasingly alarming. This time, the Duke asked the Estates for the necessary contributions to raise 600 horse and 2,000 foot and to mobilise the militia extending its service to guard the borders. Eberhard III used his tested tactics of persuading the Estates each time to make one last grant towards the upkeep of the troops, promising that they would then be disbanded, but again the answer was negative. The Estates declared that such a considerable contribution was a 'sheer impossibility' and it was only after a long negotiation that the parties agreed a compromise. The Estates agreed to pay for the extraordinary service of the militia and the recruitment of 300 horse and 1,000 foot of professional troops.[90]

Preparations were intensified to put the militia into a state of full efficiency, and 500 volunteers were drawn from it for the regular troops in exchange for tax exemption and a generous engagement bonus. In

Württemberg *Leibgarde*, plate 7 of Leo Ignaz Stadlinger, *Geschichte des Württembergischen Kriegswesens von der Frühesten bis zur Neuesten Zeit* (Stuttgart: Druck und Verlag der K. Hofbuchdruckerei zu Guttenberg 1856). (Public domain)
According to Stadlinger's work, the back and breast and helmet marked the difference between the companies of the *Leibgarde*: those of the company of the Duke were natural metal, and the company of the Crown Prince had the same items in black polished metal. Again according to Stadlinger, in the early 1670s the other two cavalry companies wore a red coat, had a red saddle cover edged in white, and yellow and black standards.

---

88 Leo Ignaz Stadlinger, *Geschichte des Württembergischen Kriegswesens von der frühesten bis zur neuesten Zeit* (Stuttgart: Druck und Verlag der K. Hofbuchdruckerei zu Guttenberg 1856), p.319.

89 Leo Ignaz Stadlinger, *Geschichte des Württembergischen Kriegswesens von der frühesten bis zur neuesten Zeit* (Stuttgart: Druck und Verlag der K. Hofbuchdruckerei zu Guttenberg 1856), p.319.

90 Leo Ignaz Stadlinger, *Geschichte des Württembergischen Kriegswesens von der frühesten bis zur neuesten Zeit* (Stuttgart: Druck und Verlag der K. Hofbuchdruckerei zu Guttenberg 1856), p.319. As for the maintenance of these troops, it was agreed that the Estates would have to contribute until 1 March 1674, while the duke would take over the entire supply of hulled fodder, but only a third of the raw fodder.

June 1673, an infantry regiment of 1,000 men in 10 companies had been recruited under *Obrist* Cronhjorst (WüI-1); the Foot Guards formed the *Leibcompagnie*. The professional cavalry consisted of 4 companies, two of the *Leibgarde* and two others newly raised, which could be combined into a field regiment for tactical needs. On 6 November 1673, regular troops and militia were assembled at Feurbach for a joint exercise, and to greet the arrival of the *Kronprinz* with his wife, *Prinzessin* Magdalena Sibylle of Hessen. They were 7,224 men in all, including 100 artillerymen.[91]

A few days later, *Prinz* Wilhelm Ludwig inherited the title of Duke, also receiving from his father a well-organised army and militia, which managed to secure the neutrality of the state, at least in the first year. Without abdicating his duties as immediate prince of the Empire, the new Duke continued to collaborate in the common defence of the Swabian Circle but, like his father, opposed the union of the Circle's troops with those of the Emperor. However, he could not prevent the Imperial troops from crossing his territories in 1674, nor having to provide billets and winter quarters that put a considerable burden on the economy of the countryside.

The situation worsened in the following years. After repelling a French attempt to cross the border in August 1675, in the following winter both regulars and militia were unable to prevent the entry of foreign troops, which caused severe damage in the countryside. Further contributions had to be made to the Imperialists and their allies for winter quarters. In February 1676, the duke negotiated with the Emperor for his participation in the war against France in return for exemption from winter quarters and billeting. He agreed to transfer the Circle regiments under the Imperial command, and provided artillery and ammunition for the siege of Philippsburg. In April 1677, Württemberg, as well as the other states of Swabia and Franconia, withdrew its troops from the war in protest against the billeting of Imperial troops in the Circles' territories. Württemberg remained under threat, especially when the campaigns moved to Swabia in 1677–1678. Consequently, the Duke retained in service the troops from the disbanded Swabian regiments until 1679, after the signing of the Peace of Nijmegen.[92]

However, Wilhelm Ludwig would not live to see peace. He died on 23 June 1677 and his younger brother Friedrich Carl assumed the regency until Crown Prince Eberhard Ludwig (r. 1693–1733) came of age.

Friedrich Carl belonged to the cadet branch of Württemberg-Winnental family, and was reputed a valiant soldier. He was colonel proprietor of a Swabian cavalry regiment from 1674 to 1677, and was distinguished as much by courage as by his tireless activity, but his particular skill had yet to be revealed. Although nominally obliged to share power with the privy

---

91　Leo Ignaz Stadlinger, *Geschichte des Württembergischen Kriegswesens von der frühesten bis zur neuesten Zeit* (Stuttgart: Druck und Verlag der K. Hofbuchdruckerei zu Guttenberg 1856), p.321.

92　'Even after the Peace of Nijmegen in 1679, marauders crossed the Duchy, plundering and robbing until professional troops and militia managed to chase the stragglers out of the towns and the border passes were manned by strong corps.' Leo Ignaz Stadlinger, *Geschichte des Württembergischen Kriegswesens von der frühesten bis zur neuesten Zeit* (Stuttgart: Druck und Verlag der K. Hofbuchdruckerei zu Guttenberg 1856), p.323.

council and with Eberhard Ludwig's mother, he soon seized the reins of government for himself.[93] His dual role as Regent and prince of the junior Winnenthal line conferred special characteristics to his rule. On the one hand, he realised that his nephew Eberhard Ludwig would one day become the reigning duke and he would once again he reduced to the relative obscurity of prince of a junior line. He therefore tried to extract maximum advantage for himself and his lineage while his power lasted. On the other hand, owing to the length of his rule – Eberhard Ludwig was scarcely a year old when Friedrich Carl became Regent on 27 November 1677 and under Württemberg law could not become duke before his eighteenth birthday in 1694 – he developed attributes of a reigning duke, and he therefore interfered in the internal structure of the duchy.[94] Friedrich Carl was determined to turn the tables and profit from the fact that both France and the Emperor needed his help, and might therefore each be induced to provide protection against retaliation from the other. This was nonetheless a dangerous policy as, quite apart from the possibility of retaliation, the duke ran the risk of merely exchanging dependence on one power for dependence on the other.

In 1678, he assumed the title of *Herzog-Administrator* (Duke Administrator), and among his first government actions he dealt with the army. In February 1679, the Estates not only demanded the disbanding of the professional troops, but even that the militia should be

Duke and Regent Friedrich Carl of Württemberg-Winnenthal (1652–1698), in a portrait by an unknown artist. (Author's collection) Friedrich Carl was the archetypal German prince and military entrepreneur of the second half of the seventeenth century. Although nineteenth century historians condemned his unscrupulous conduct in the trade of human lives, the economic and material resources in Germany after 1648 were scarce and offered few alternatives to the lower classes in matter of employment. By sending thousands of young Germans into military service abroad, the rest of society could face the economic situation that would otherwise have been impossible. As far as foreign affairs were concerned, Friedrich Carl's policy of divide and rule was to prove its worth, as he attempted to free Württemberg from Imperial domination by taking advantage of the rise of France.

---

93 'His ruthless determination to establish himself as absolute ruler overshadowed all previous attempts by Württemberg Dukes in that direction, so that, by the time of his death, the Estates looked back to the spirit of cooperation and good-natured compromise of the reign of his father, Eberhard III, as a golden age.' Peter H. Wilson, *War, State and Society in Württemberg, 1677–1793* (Cambridge: Cambridge University Press, 1995), p.97.

94 'By the appointment of Friedrich Carl, who was already serving in the Army of the Empire, the Emperor hoped to have a man at Stuttgart through whom he could control Württemberg policy. However, to be doubly sure of this control and to prevent Friedrich Carl from becoming too independent, the Emperor confirmed the rights of two of the other claimants to the regency, namely Magdalene Sibylle and the privy council. This was a wise move.' As for foreign policy, the Emperor had other options: 'If the duke bowed to pressure to cooperate with France, he ran the risk of provoking Austria. Through his claims to the Duchy and his position as head of the *Reich*, the Emperor was in a good position to sequestrate Württemberg as punishment for such 'treacherous' collaboration. The Duke had, therefore, to tread carefully when entering into an agreement with either France or the Emperor.' Peter Wilson, *War, State and Society in Württemberg, 1677–1793* (Cambridge: Cambridge University Press, 1995), pp.107–108:

reduced, since the money had been granted until the danger had ceased.⁹⁵ The *Herzog-Administrator* called the war council for advice and swiftly took his decision. He decreed the reduction of the *Landwehr* cavalry to a mixed regiment of 800 horse and 200 dragoons, with the task of patrolling and guarding roads and countryside, escorting convoys and escorting the mail when necessary. The foot militia was divided into two classes. The first group, the permanent defence militia, was to comprise the most able-bodied individuals aged between 18 and 30, to form 4 regiments of 4 companies, each of 246 men including NCOs and officers. The second class, consisting of men between 31 and 55, was to be called up only in emergencies and used exclusively for garrison duties. The foot regiments numbered 984 men, of which one-third were pikemen; the second group was established to 3,274 men. Together with the cavalry and dragoons the new *Landesdefension* consisted of 8,210 men. Friedrich Carl established a *Generals-Stab* to direct the troops on the field, and also a *Regiments-Stab* for each infantry regiment. As for the professional troops, he retained 3 companies of infantry, including the Foot Guards *Leibwache*, a total of 624 men in all; the only cavalry unit still in service was the life guard of the Duke with 75 men. The overall figure totalled 5,635 men, not including the militia of the second class.⁹⁶

Reducing the military force beyond a certain number was not part of the plan of the *Herzog-Administrator*. An opportunity for reversing this trend appeared in 1680 with the development of renewed tension between the Emperor and France. The former was still smarting from his failure in the Franco-Dutch War, and hoped to mobilise the German states for a new war against France. The latter wanted to consolidate its new gains on the eastern frontier by reactivating old claims to other territories through the *Réunions*. To win support for this policy and prevent the Emperor intervening, Louis XIV launched a diplomatic offensive. Friedrich Carl hoped to profit from this situation by seeking on the one hand a closer cooperation with France, while on the other keeping the back door open should things go wrong and the need arise to call upon the Emperor for support.⁹⁷ In 1680 the Parliament of Besançon proclaimed Mompelgard (today Montbeliard in France) and its dependent territories to be a Burgundian fief and therefore now under French sovereignty. French troops moved in to make good these claims, causing the Württemberg-Mompelgard family to flee to their relatives in Oels where they remained until 1698. Friedrich Carl realised he had to act quickly or the possessions would be lost to the family for good. Despite protests from his Mompelgard relations, he recognised French overlordship on 18 February 1681 on their behalf in order to recover actual possession for

---

95 Leo Ignaz Stadlinger, *Geschichte des Württembergischen Kriegswesens von der frühesten bis zur neuesten Zeit* (Stuttgart: Druck und Verlag der K. Hofbuchdruckerei zu Guttenberg 1856), p.323.

96 Leo Ignaz Stadlinger, *Geschichte des Württembergischen Kriegswesens von der frühesten bis zur neuesten Zeit* (Stuttgart: Druck und Verlag der K. Hofbuchdruckerei zu Guttenberg 1856), p.323.

97 Peter Wilson, *War, State and Society in Württemberg, 1677–1793* (Cambridge: Cambridge University Press, 1995), p.93–94. In moving towards France, Friedrich Carl was really recognising the balance of power on the Upper Rhine.

Leopold Eberhard (1670–1723), who succeeded as Duke in 1699. Although he had by now also aroused the hostility of his councils, Friedrich Carl continued his pro-French course and was one of the few German princes to recognise the French annexation of the Imperial City of Strasbourg later that year.

However, when in May 1681, the Diet of the Empire issued the new *matricel* for each Circle, Friedrich Carl summoned the Estates to obtain the funds to recruit the troops established for Württemberg. As had been the case nine years earlier, the Estates agreed to finance the formation of a contingent for the Circle, and this enabled Friedrich Carl to raise one company of horse and one of dragoons, each of 100 men, alongside four infantry companies to a total of 840 men at all.[98] Then, on 21 March 1683 a restricted council approved additional funds in view of the fact that the Ottomans were marching towards the Austrian borders. The common appeal of Diet and Emperor had just been issued, and Friedrich Carl immediately ordered two companies of cavalry and four companies of infantry to prepare to march alongside the troops of the Swabian Circle. The Württemberg contingents passed Regensburg on 21 August and joined the Allied Army under Sobiesky and Lorraine on 7 September. They served in the subsequent campaigns in Hungary until 1688 as a part of the Swabian Circle's contingent. The almost continuous warfare following 1683 prevented the Estates from finding areas on which to disband the professional troops.[99] Friedrich Carl clearly intended to use these new forces to improve his position within the Duchy. In 1683 he wanted to shake off Imperial domination by openly allying with France. With French protection, he planned to expand his army by confiscating the church property, *Kirchengut*, and then to intimidate the Estates. The plan fell through, as most of the privy councillors simply refused to cooperate with the Duke-Regent, while the troops sent to Hungary with the Swabian contingent deprived him of the main instrument of power.[100]

The setback he received in 1683 caused Friedrich Carl to look more closely to the trade in soldiers. Every year, contingents had to be replenished and the reinforcements sent to Hungary and other fronts. After a few years the shortage of recruits was such that some German princes turned to recruiting volunteers in other states. Friedrich Carl realised that this could be exploited for substantial profits. In 1687, he entered the scene initially as a sub-contractor for Hannover, hoping to create appropriate employment

---

98 Leo Ignaz Stadlinger, *Geschichte des Württembergischen Kriegswesens von der frühesten bis zur neuesten Zeit* (Stuttgart: Druck und Verlag der K. Hofbuchdruckerei zu Guttenberg 1856), p.324.
99 Peter Wilson, *War, State and Society in Württemberg, 1677–1793* (Cambridge: Cambridge University Press, 1995), p.108.
100 'For the moment, the Regent had to bide his time, but he returned to his project again in the late 1680s. That he was planning such a military putsch is clear from the comments to the French envoy in 1687. He made it plain that he intended to use the troops he had just raised for Venice, once they returned, to overthrow the Estates and make his nephew Eberhard Ludwig absolute ruler. He also claimed that he would have done this if he had been born sovereign Duke himself. It appears that he was hoping thereby to make himself indispensable so that he could continue to direct affairs once Eberhard Ludwig had achieved his majority.' Peter Wilson, *War, State and Society in Württemberg, 1677–1793* (Cambridge: Cambridge University Press, 1995), p.110.

for his growing family and to turn the regiments on the Duchy when they returned.[101] On 13 January, the Duke concluded an agreement with Ernst August of Hannover for the supply of one infantry company of 150 men under Prince Carl Rudolph of Württemberg-Neuenstadt to join the troops serving in Greece for Venice.[102] Shortly afterwards, however, Venice extended the Treaty of Lüneburg demanding an entire regiment from Württemberg. In a short time, Friedrich Carl recruited 1,000 men, formed as two companies of grenadiers and eight of musketeers, divided into two battalions, and after four months they were ready start their march through the Tyrol to Italy under Prince Carl Rudolph as colonel proprietor (WüI-2). Service for Venice was established for the duration of two years.[103]

At the beginning of June, the regiment was embarked at the Lido of Venice and transported to the island of Santa Maura (today Lefkada in Greece). Carl Rudolph and his soldiers took part in the campaign of 1687 under Morosini and Königsmarck, participating in the landing of Patras, which opened to the opportunity for the sieges of Corinth and Athens. With the expiry of the contracts between Venice and the German princes who had provided mercenaries since 1684, Friedrich Carl took advantage of the void that had been created within the Venetian army for promoting his 'trade' and providing further regiments for Greece. On 20 November 1687, a new capitulation was signed. Friedrich Carl pledged 'out of special attachment to the Republic' to provide, in addition to the regiment already in service, a further 3,000 infantry, making 4,000 men in all, 'all of them good, strong, able-bodied and aged not less than 20 and not more than 50', in exchange for a subsidy, and to be employed in Greece.[104] Finding it difficult to meet his requirements, he also subcontracted the raising of a regiment to a prince in a position similar to him – Georg of Hessen-Darmstadt.[105] This agreement specified that the 3,000 men would form three regiments each divided into two battalions, each battalion with one company of grenadiers and four of

---

101 Ernst August of Hannover was obliged by the terms of the agreement with Friedich Carl to use his good offices with Venice to secure an annual pension for the three-year-old '*Obrist*' Carl Alexander. See Rudolph von Ander, 'Die Württembergischen Regimenter in Griechenland, 1687–89', in *Württembergische Vierteljahreshefte für Landesgeschichte* XXXI (1922/4), p.254.
102 'Initially, Ernst August requested only a company with the special stipulation that prince Carl Rudolph of Württemberg-Neuenstadt would be the commander, and that the soldiers should wear Brunswick uniform, a red coat with blue cuffs and lining.' Leo Ignaz Stadlinger, *Geschichte des Württembergischen Kriegswesens von der frühesten bis zur neuesten Zeit* (Stuttgart: Druck und Verlag der K. Hofbuchdruckerei zu Guttenberg 1856), p.325.
103 'The regiments were in effect his private army, though his position as Regent enabled him to make use of Württemberg government officials to help him with the recruiting. Financial affairs were handled by War Councillor Tobias Heller who was also responsible for the Duchy's *Kreistruppen*, and so was both government official and the Regent's private agent.' Peter Wilson, *War, State and Society in Württemberg, 1677–1793* (Cambridge: Cambridge University Press, 1995), p.112.
104 Leo Ignaz Stadlinger, *Geschichte des Württembergischen Kriegswesens von der frühesten bis zur neuesten Zeit* (Stuttgart: Druck und Verlag der K. Hofbuchdruckerei zu Guttenberg 1856), p.327.
105 See also Chapter 5: 'The Two Hessen.'

musketeers.[106] The regiments were to arrive at the Venice Lido accompanied by a commissioner from Württemberg, and assembled as soon as possible and no later than April 1688. The Republic would ask the Emperor for permission to transit the troops through the Tyrol. Two years after the regiments had entered the Venetian service, they were to be brought back to the Lido, completely re-equipped at the expense of the Republic and handed over to a commissioner from Württemberg together with two months' pay.[107]

The Commander-in-Chief was Prince Carl Rudolph, a colonel of the regiment that was already in Greece; under him, Count Carl Ludwig zu Pfalz commanded as *Generalleutnant*. The expedition suffered some delays and changes of programme. One of the newly formed regiments, the *Jung-Württemberg* (WüI-3), under Friedrich Carl's second son Heinrich Friedrich, arrived at Lido at the beginning of May 1688. A few days later, all the companies were embarked and on 29 May they arrived in Poros, where Captain General Morosini had assembled the troops returning from Athens. The second regiment, that under the command of *Obrist* Pilsen (WüI-4), together with the first battalion of the Riedesel regiment (WüI-5), only joined the Venetian field army in Negroponte in mid-August, while the second battalion arrived in Greece on 6 October.[108] The fourth regiment, recruited from Hessen-Darmstadt and Saxe-Meningen, arrived in Greece when the campaign was already over – which was very lucky for these soldiers, who had thus avoided the catastrophic siege of Negroponte.

While the infantry served in Greece, on 25 July 1688, Friedrich Carl signed an agreement with the Dutch Republic, to provide three cavalry regiments of 300 men each. Den Haag paid 60 thalers for each man provided with equipment and weapons, while the supply of horses was at the expense of the Republic. The patents were issued and recruitment soon began under the direction of the colonel-proprietors: Johann Eitel Truchsess von Wetzhausen, Prince Heinrich Friedrich of Württemberg, and Count Erffa. The Duke's life guard company joined Truchsess' regiment and the six companies were in Hasselt, not far from Maastricht, in June 1689 under the Dutch General Count of Nassau-Usingen; the overall number totalled 1,296 men.[109] In contrast to his Venetian enterprise, this agreement was an example

---

106 Peter Wilson, *War, State and Society in Württemberg, 1677–1793* (Cambridge: Cambridge University Press, 1995), p.112. Friedrich Carl also tried to persuade the Republic to hire a regiment of cavalry, appointing the three years old Prince Carl Alexander as colonel, but the attempt failed.
107 Leo Ignaz Stadlinger, *Geschichte des Württembergischen Kriegswesens von der frühesten bis zur neuesten Zeit* (Stuttgart: Druck und Verlag der K. Hofbuchdruckerei zu Guttenberg 1856), p.328.
108 Leo Ignaz Stadlinger, *Geschichte des Württembergischen Kriegswesens von der frühesten bis zur neuesten Zeit* (Stuttgart: Druck und Verlag der K. Hofbuchdruckerei zu Guttenberg 1856), p.329.
109 Leo Ignaz Stadlinger, *Geschichte des Württembergischen Kriegswesens von der frühesten bis zur neuesten Zeit* (Stuttgart: Druck und Verlag der K. Hofbuchdruckerei zu Guttenberg 1856), p.337.

Württemberg general from Leo Ignaz Stadlinger, *Geschichte des Württembergischen Kriegswesens von der Frühesten bis zur Neuesten Zeit*. (Public domain)
Natural steel armour, white cravat, red coat with gold lace, buttons and buttonholes; white breeches, red scarf, black broad-brimmed hat with white plumes and gold edge tape, black boots. The same author devotes several paragraphs to the first uniforms of the Württemberg army. Although much of the information on this subject from nineteenth century authors is unreliable, he does provide many details. In the 1670s, professional soldiers were dressed in yellow coats with different coloured cuffs and linings for each company. Clothing included natural leather breeches, striped stockings, shoes and hats trimmed with white braid. In 1663, half of a company still consisted of pikemen; by 1673, two-thirds were armed with muskets and only a third retained the pike. The muskets all had to be of the same calibre and were tested for firing a double charge. At the same time, the militia also received uniform clothing, consisting of a broad-brimmed hat, grey coats – probably a Pyerock – lined in white bay. Each regiment had facings – cuffs – according to the hue of the Colours and, in the cavalry according to the colour of the saddle cover. Thus infantry regiments were also called the yellow, black, blue or red regiment. The cavalry had back and breast plates painted black; the dragoons were dressed in blue with headgears edged in white.

of a second form of recruitment, whereby the contractor raised entire units which then passed directly into the service of the client.[110]

However, the unforeseen consequences of this agreement were dramatic for Württemberg. Louis XIV used the fact that the Duke was aiding his Dutch enemies as an excuse to invade the Duchy in December 1688. The real object of the invasion was to intimidate Friedrich Carl into siding with Louis XIV against the Emperor. As the Estates had rejected the Regent's plans in October to reorganise the duchy's *Landesdefension* territorial militia into an effective force, and as the *Kreistruppen* were still in Hungary, there were no troops left to oppose the French. The arrival of a small French invading party to levy contributions by force threw both the privy council and the Estates into a complete panic. As a consequence, the Dowager Duchess Magdalene Sibylle quickly gave in to French threats and surrendered the Duchy's fortresses. This capitulation naturally discredited the Württemberg elite in the eyes of the Emperor, who gave his full support to Friedrich Carl instead, as he was still prepared to fight.

On 24 December 1688, the Emperor issued a decree instructing all Württemberg military personnel to obey only the Regent and to no longer to accept orders from the privy council. Three days later Friedrich Carl

---

110 'Here the Regent secured both a generous fee for the recruitment and the appointment of his second son, Heinrich Friedrich as one of the colonels.' Peter Wilson, *War, State and Society in Württemberg, 1677–1793* (Cambridge: Cambridge University Press, 1995), p.113.

was appointed Imperial *Generalleutnant*. He could now resume his plan of creating an army to definitively overturn the Estates' resistance, achieving the succession as legitimate ruler to the Duchy. He had already tried to avoid negotiating with the Estates and where possible only called meetings of the restricted committee. To strengthen his hand against the Estates, Friedrich Carl did his best to please the Emperor by offering both him and his Anglo-Dutch allies troops for the new war against France. A few days after his appointment as Imperial *General*, Friedrich Carl agreed to sell one of the regiments that had just returned from Greece. Despite a lucrative offer from the Most Serene Republic for a renewal of the agreement for the regiments, Friedrich Carl recalled them once the contract expired in late 1689, and used them to bring the new Imperial regiment up to the required strength of 1,800 foot. Then, having at first rejected a Spanish request for troops at the beginning of 1690, he agreed to a second request and provided a further three infantry regiments totalling 2,364 men for the defence of Milan.[111] Further soldiers were recruited in Württemberg, and in early 1689, these latter numbered 350 cavalry and 777 infantry, while the militia totalled 6,015 men.[112]

The Emperor's backing that Friedrich Carl received enabled him to come closer than any previous duke into overturning the Duchy's constitution. Nevertheless, but for a single accident he might have succeeded in realising his plans completely. However, the circumstances of his downfall demonstrate that it was not yet possible for a prince to free himself from the system of checks and balances that made up the structure of the Holy Roman Empire.[113]

Ferdinand Wilhelm, Duke of Württemberg-Neuenstadt (1659–1701). (Author's collection)
Ferdinand Wilhelm was another Württemberg captain who served as a mercenary in foreign armies. He was the sixth child of Duke Friedrich of Württemberg-Neuenstadt. After service in the Imperial and Danish Armies, in 1689 he entered the Dutch Army, and in 1690 fought at the Battle of the Boyne and in 1692 at the Battle of Steenkerque. In 1693, Ferdinand Wilhelm was sent by William III with 16,000 men to raid Artois. The people of Artois eventually paid him 6 million guilders in contributions. Promoted *general* on 20 August 1693 after the Battle of Neerwinden, he became commander of the *Garde te Voet* as successor of Count Solms, who had been killed in the battle.

---

111 'He overcame his initial hesitation, because the Spanish had now requested that two of the regiments be of the more prestigious cavalry and because the Emperor urged him to agree.' Peter Wilson, *War, State and Society in Württemberg, 1677–1793* (Cambridge: Cambridge University Press, 1995), p.115.
112 Leo Ignaz Stadlinger, *Geschichte des Württembergischen Kriegswesens von der frühesten bis zur neuesten Zeit* (Stuttgart: Druck und Verlag der K. Hofbuchdruckerei zu Guttenberg 1856), p.337.
113 Peter Wilson, *War, State and Society in Württemberg, 1677–1793* (Cambridge: Cambridge University Press, 1995), p.115.

## Würzburg and Bamberg

After Salzburg, Würzburg was the largest ecclesiastical principality of Germany, and after Münster, the most heavily militarised Catholic Bishopric, making it an actual armed state.

The territories of Würzburg lay in the Franconian Circle, and as occurred in other Circles, religious factors were at work. The two Hohenzollern branches ruling Ansbach and Bayreuth alternately exercised a secular Protestant executive, while the Bishop of Bamberg held the Catholic position. The power of both executive princes was offset by the presence of the large Bishopric of Würzburg along with over 20 smaller territories sustaining regular assembly meetings. The prominence of Würzburg in the Circle increased when Bamberg was under the same ruler, as occurred between 1675 and 1683. Consequently, the principality contributed a larger quote of soldiers for the *Reichsarmee*.

This commitment affected the Bishopric's military policy, but the troops provided to the Circle were not the only ones, because Würzburg had raised its first professional army already in the 1550s and later, as a member of the

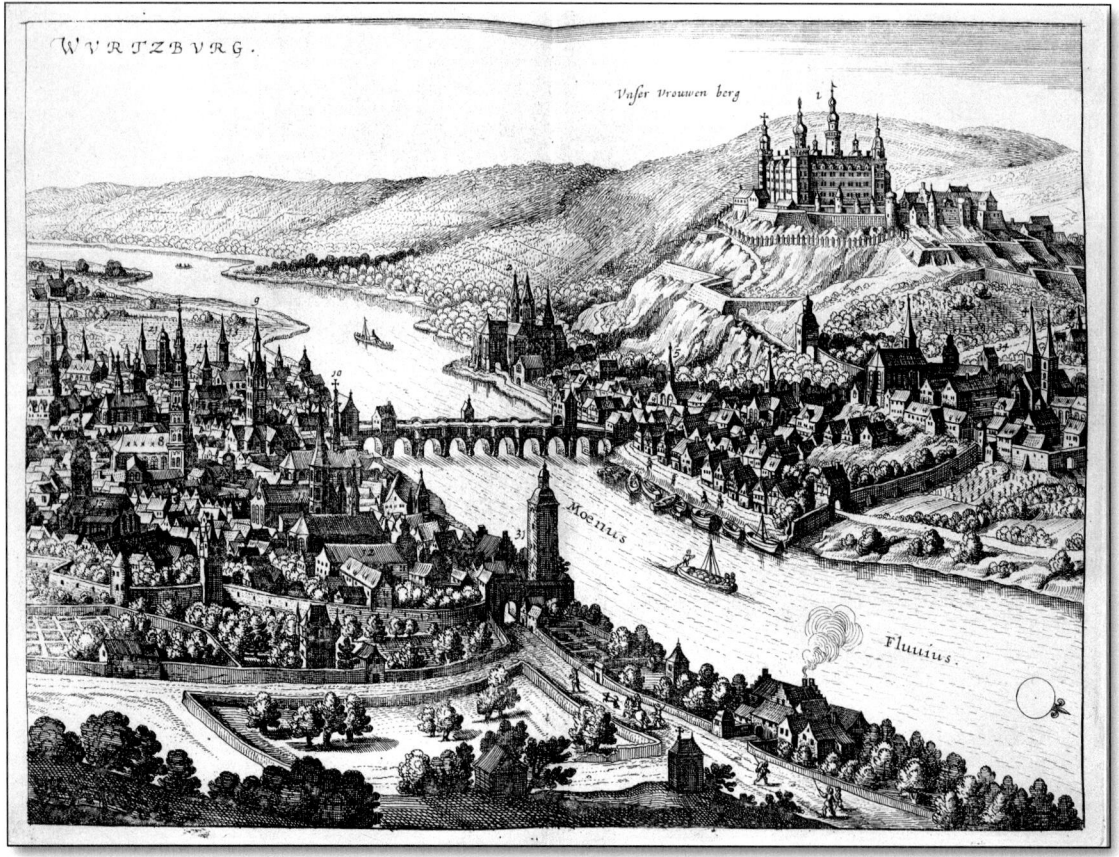

Panorama of Würzburg with the Castle of Marienberg by Matthäus Merian the Elder, after Cornelis Danckerts' *Historis* (Amsterdam: 1642). (Public domain)

Catholic League, between 1619 and 1639 the Bishopric raised four infantry regiments, a further six of cavalry and one of dragoons.[114]

The history of Würzburg in the second half of the seventeenth century coincides with the one of the Bishops who ruled the state. After the Peace of Westphalia, Würzburg was strongly linked with Mainz, because Johann Philipp von Schönborn held the rank of Bishop as well as local apostolic administrator until his death in 1673. Throughout this period, Würzburg was a major factor in raising Schönborn's political profile because it added significant resources and political weight to him. In September 1674, the Chapter elected Johann Hartmann von Rosenbach as Bishop, but he reigned for just seven months until his death in April 1675. The process of the

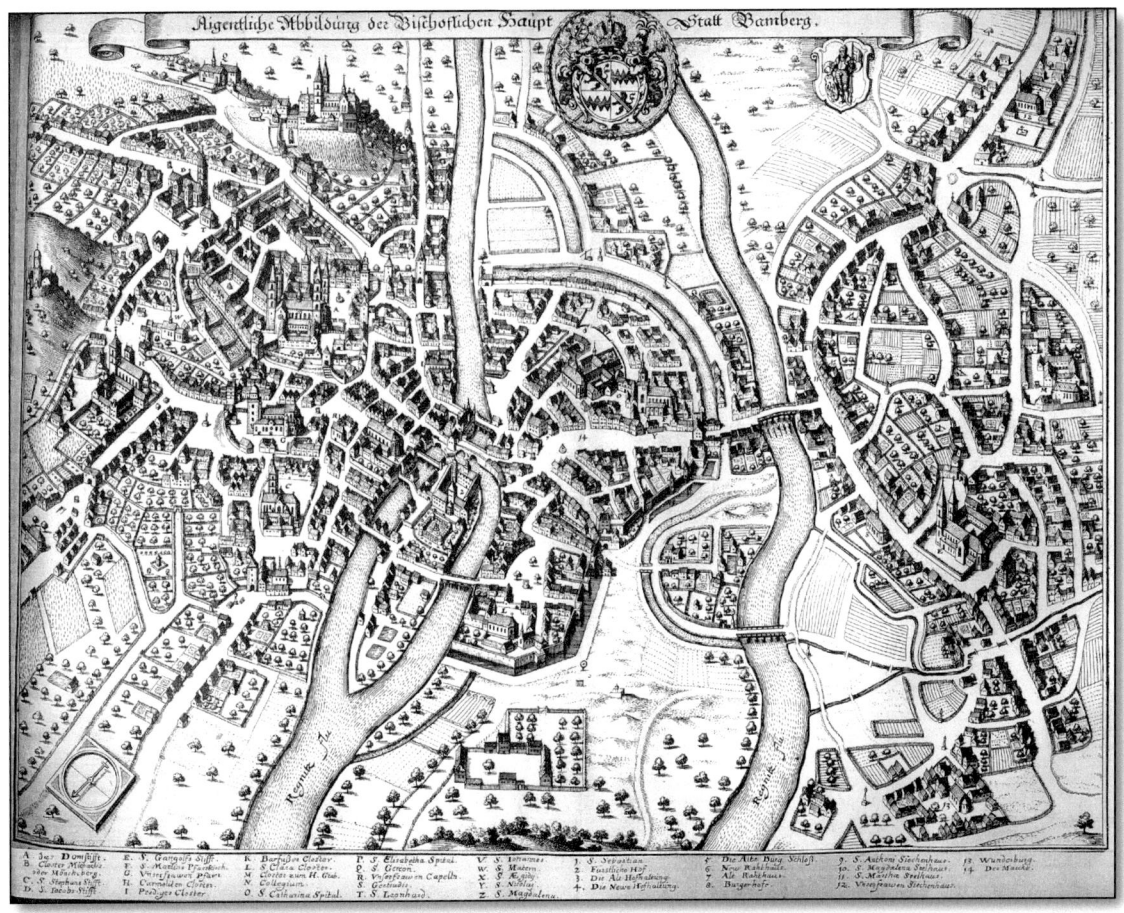

Bamberg in a print dating to 1648. (Author's collection)
Along with Würzburg, the Bishopric of Bamberg belonged to the Franconian Circle, and in 1664 it contributed 112 cavalry to the *Kreisregiment* Zobel and 200 infantry to the *Kreisregiment* Pleitner: an adjustment of the triple contingent. In 1681, the quote in *simplum* was established as 65 horse and 192 foot.

---

114 Georg Tessin, *Die Regimenter der Europäischen Staaten im Ancien Régime des XVI bis XVIII Jahrhunderts* (Osnabrück: Biblio Verlag, 1986), Teil 1, pp.330–331.

election of the new Bishop lasted until February 1676, when Peter Philipp von Dernbach, already Bishop of Bamberg since 1672, was appointed as the new ruler with the support of the Emperor. He ruled both bishoprics until 1683 and during his mandate he strongly supported the Imperial side against France. The sudden death of Dernbach in April 1683 resulted in the election of Konrad Wilhelm von Wernau (1683–1684), who was succeeded by Johann Gottfried von Guttenberg, elected in August 1686 after a vacancy of two years. Both the bishops maintained the principality on the side of Austrian Habsburgs, even at a moderate level.

A tireless chronicler, Galeazzo Gualdo Priorato provides an extensive description of the Bishopric in the 1660s, devoting many pages to the military matters. He describes the curtains of Würzburg with 14 bastions, three of which were 'in the modern style', and a large ditch provided by the River Main.[115] The Italian historian also mentions the Castle of Marienberg, the residence of the Bishops, located on the heights close to the city and described as the most imposing in Germany. The northern side was defended by inaccessible walls with *alla moderna* ramparts and numerous artillery.[116] He also refers to the arsenal, which was well-provided with portable cannons and ammunition in great quantity, and the quarter where the workforce had its residence. As for the lands, Gualdo Priorato describes 30 locations holding the status of Town. Finally, he refers to the permanent garrison of Würzburg, climbing to 300 men under a colonel, and the city militia with 53 companies comprising 1,500 armed bourgeoisie out of a population of 10,000 people.[117] Military matters were managed by the privy council of the bishop through a war secretary entrusted to a councillor. As a personal life guard, the bishop had eight *Trabanten* and 24 horse under a French officer.[118]

In 1663, the Empire's Diet established the quota of the *Reichskontingent*, to which Würzburg had to contribute 45 cavalry and 308 infantry *in simplum*.[119] However, being a Bishopric ruled by the Elector of Mainz, Johann Philipp of Schönborn, Würzburg did not provide troops to the circle. In 1661, one infantry regiment recruited in the Bishopric headed to Hungary and was then ceded to the Emperor before the end of the year, while in 1663, a mixed Mainz-Würzburg infantry regiment marched to Hungary as part of the auxiliary corps of the *Deutsche Allianz*. Even in the Franco-Dutch War, Würzburg did not join the Franconian contingent. On 21 February 1674, the Bishop agreed to provide one infantry regiment to the Emperor, and on 15 November 1675, he expanded this alliance to one cuirassier regiment, one dragoon regiment and two infantry regiments, 6,000 men in all. Alongside

---

115 Gualdo Priorato, Galeazzo, *Relatione .... del Vescovato e Principato di Herbipoli*, (Leyden, 1668), p.2.
116 Gualdo Priorato, Galeazzo, *Relatione .... del Vescovato e Principato di Herbipoli*, (Leyden, 1668), p.7.
117 Gualdo Priorato, Galeazzo, *Relatione .... del Vescovato e Principato di Herbipoli*, (Leyden, 1668), p.13.
118 Gualdo Priorato, Galeazzo, *Relatione .... del Vescovato e Principato di Herbipoli*, (Leyden, 1668), p.21.
119 *Verzeichnuß / Deß Heyl: Römischen Reichs / Teutscher Nation / Hochlöblichster: Hoch: und Wollöblicher Stände / nach den Zehen Reichs-Craissen* (Frankfurt am Main, 1663).

this force, Würzburg granted the Emperor permission to recruit soldiers within the Bishopric.[120] However, since Vienna defaulted on this subsidy and still assigned Imperial troops for winter quarter to Würzburg and Bamberg in 1676–77, Peter Philipp von Dernbach removed his contingent from the war as also did the Franconian Circle. This bitter experience persuaded the Bishop to join Georg Friedrich of Waldeck in his project, later known as the Laxenburg Alliance, which prepared the way for the permanent troops of the *Reichsarmee*.[121] After the death of Peter Phlipp von Dernbach, Bamberg and Würzburg maintained their military alliance despite the different Bishops, and in 1683 provided four companies of dragoons and two infantry regiments to the Emperor, which participated in the relief of Vienna. It was only in 1685 that both Bishoprics and their troops returned to association with the Circle, while the contingent serving in Hungary passed into the Imperial Army.[122] According to the *Matricel* of 1681, Würzburg contributed *in Triplum* with 320 horsemen and 1,002 infantrymen.

---

120 In 1679, the Imperial regiment *Stadl zu Fuss* recruited in Würzburg and Bamberg. See Bruno Mugnai, *Wars and Soldiers in the Early Reign of Louis XIV, volume 2: The Imperial Army 1657–1687* (Warwick: Helion & Company, 2019), p.77.
121 See also Chapter Two: 'The German Chessboard' and in Bruno Mugnai, *Wars and Soldiers in the Early Reign of Louis XIV, volume 2: The Imperial Army 1657-1687* (Warwick: Helion & Company, 2019), pp.121–123.
122 Georg Tessin, *Die Regimenter der Europäischen Staaten im Ancien Régime des XVI bis XVIII Jahrhunderts* (Osnabrück: Biblio Verlag, 1986), Teil 1, p.330.

3

# Imperial Free Cities

Often ignored, or at best marginalised, by the early modern age's historiography, the *Reichsstädte* (Free Imperial Cities), enjoyed a military tradition at least as old as that of many other German states.[1] Their apparent exit from history is due to the loss of political power in the Empire. After the flowering of the sixteenth century, the scenario changed decisively between 1618 and 1648, and with a few exceptions, the Free Imperial Cities became mere shadows of the past. The devastations of the Thirty Years' War led to a collapse of trade activity in Germany, and the process of recovery was very slow. This had strong repercussions for the Free Imperial Cities, which, unlike the principalities, could not rely on other significant income. It is true that the rise of Hamburg and Frankfurt am Main continued after 1648, and their political importance increased, but these cities were exceptional cases that merely emphasise the general stagnation. After the loss of the Alsatian cities to France in 1681–1682, the number of *Reichsstädte* fell to 51, the large majority situated in the south-west of Germany; this number is excluding the 45 small towns and villages, which retained the same status of Imperial Free territory. Most of them were very small and unable to hold their own in the struggle with the principalities that surrounded them. Even the more important cities like Augsburg, Nuremberg, Ulm, Rastatt in the south, and Cologne, Aachen, Bremen, and Lübeck in the north, found it difficult to adapt themselves to the changed conditions.

The South German towns were hard hit by the decline of the trade with Italy and the bankruptcies of the great banking houses of the Fuggers and the Welsers. The North German Towns suffered from overwhelming Dutch, and to a lesser extent English, competition. The Hanseatic towns had long declined under the double impact of foreign and internal competition. They no longer sent their own ships across the seas, but were satisfied if they

---

1   From the 1980s, several interesting works have enriched the existing historiography on this topic. These include Jürgen Kraus, *Das Militärwesen der Reichsstadt Augsburg 1548–1806* (Augsburg: Stadtarchiv, 1980); Thomas Schwark, *Lübecks Stadtmilitär im 17. und 18. Jahrhundert, Untersuchungen zur Sozialgeschichte einer reichsstädtischen Berufsgruppe. Veröffentlichungen zur Geschichte der Hansestadt Lübeck*, Reihe B. 18 (Lübeck: Schmidt-Röhmhild, 1990); Andree Brumshagen, *Das Bremer Stadtmilitär 1618–1810: zur Bedeutung und Funktion des Soldaten in der reichsstädtischen Gesellschaft* (Bremen: Staatsarchiv Bremen, 2010).

could act as intermediaries between foreign visitors and the hinterland. Additionally, Bremen and Cologne had to fight hard to preserve their status of Free Imperial Cities. Even the economic recovery of the last quarter of the seventeenth century did not lead to their revival. Generally worse hygiene conditions in the cities had an equally negative impact. The Great Plague marked the last of the big outbreaks in this period though it certainly did not disappear from Germany. Frankfurt for example, which had suffered considerably in the 1650s, suffered outbreaks again in 1664 and 1666.[2]

Even the nobility, the ruling class of the Imperial Cities, was declining and many had to seek offices and engagements outside. The rigid social structure of the Free Imperial Cities contributed to their decline. A wide gulf separated the nobility from the commoners, and this distinction was equally upheld by the urban patrician families. At Augsburg, Nuremberg, Frankfurt and Ulm, the noble families were strictly secluded from the burghers. At Nuremberg they considered it dishonourable to engage in commerce. At Frankfurt the nobility demanded from new members proof of eight noble ancestors and abstention from all commerce.[3]

In the second half of the seventeenth century, the power of the princes and the rise of the principalities made any progressive development of the Imperial Cities impossible: hemmed in on all sides they survived, undiminished in number, until 1803, but the days of their power and splendour were past. Only a relatively low number of Free Imperial Cities developed a modern 'military', but with some exceptions, most of them were unable to equip themselves with a number of professional troops quantitatively and structurally comparable to those of the dynastic states after 1648. Some historians have analysed this point in particular.[4] To the extent that absolutism proved inadequate for the Free Imperial Cities, their military system developed very differently from the princely states. The armies raised by the Free Imperial Cities contained organisation that could trace their origins to the late fifteenth century and combined heavy fortifications, paid professional garrison troops and bourgeois levies. These elements were primarily defensive, reflecting not only the inability of any city to maintain large, combat-ready field forces, but the deeply rooted belief that starting offensive wars was un-Christian.

---

2   'The worst affected regions lay along a line running across Germany south-west to north-east, roughly from Strasbourg to Stralsund. Average losses of about 50 percent have been estimated between 1650 and 1680. *New Cambridge Modern History*, 'The Ascendancy of France, 1648–1688' (Cambridge: Cambridge University Press, 1968), vol. V, p.20.

3   'Apart from these old noble families there were many recently ennobled ones: officers, officials and merchants, whose families engaged in ostentatious display. They drove round in gilded carriages, their wives would wear lace only from Paris or Venice, their houses were luxuriously furnished. Those whose patents of nobility dated from an earlier time looked down upon the newcomers.' 'The Ascendancy of France, 1648–1688' in *New Cambridge Modern History* (Cambridge University Press, 1968), vol. V, p.439.

4   Thomas Schwark, *Lübecks Stadtmilitär im 17. und 18. Jahrhundert, Untersuchungen zur Sozialgeschichte einer reichsstädtischen Berufsgruppe. Veröffentlichungen zur Geschichte der Hansestadt Lübeck*, Reihe B. 18 (Lübeck: Schmidt-Römhild, 1990), p.27.

# Augsburg

In 1583, the confirmation of the *Augsburger Reichs-und Religionsfrieden* (Imperial and Religious Peace of Augsburg), recognised in the city equal rights for both Catholic and Protestant citizens. The city acquired the title of *Paritätische Reichsstadt* (parity city) becoming a model of religious coexistence. Unfortunately, during the Thirty Years' War, Augsburg became a strategic goal of both sides. The Swedes occupied Augsburg in 1633, but after the defeat at Nördlingen, the city was surrounded and besieged by the Imperial and Bavarian troops in autumn 1634, with the intention of starving the Swedish garrison and the citizens into submission. All access routes were blocked and repeated attempts were made to cut off the water supply. At the end of the year, the city was hit by a famine of dramatic circumstances and 5,000 civilians died, after which only Protestant citizens were supplied. After the Swedish commander's attempts to secretly procure food from Ulm failed, the city capitulated on 13 March 1635: the population of Augsburg had fallen by two-thirds. Under the new commander Otto Heinrich Fugger, the original status of religious parity was restored. Over the next 12 years, Augsburg was spared from war but in September 1646, again became the target of a Franco-Swedish siege.

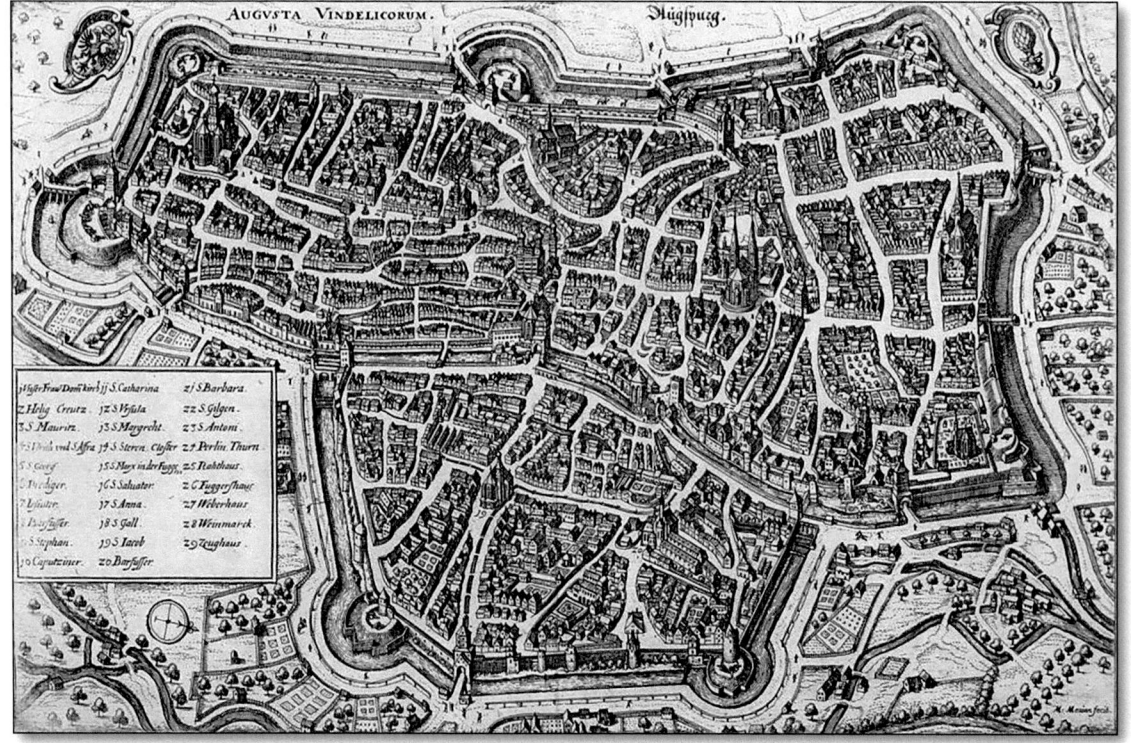

View of *Augusta Vindelicorum* (Augsburg) after Matthäus Merian the Elder, 1646. (author's collection)
According to Galeazzo Gualdo Priorato, the city did not have modern fortifications, but it had a well-stocked arsenal, capable of supplying the artillery with a large quantity of projectiles and ammunition.

However, the besiegers interrupted the operation when an Imperial-Bavarian relief army approached. After the Battle of Zusmarshausen, fought on 17 May 1648, Augsburg was swept-up by the events when the defeated Imperial and Bavarian troops retreated through the city and extorted heavy contributions from the Protestant inhabitants.

The Treaty of Westphalia recognised Augsburg's status as a bi-confessional city, but coexistence between the two communities continued to be uneasy, with the Catholic population remaining a minority. Religion also conditioned the military organisation of the city, with the *Burgermilitär* (city militia) divided between Catholic and Protestant units. Since all the city's offices were divided between the two religions, even the *Kriegsrat* and the *Kriegsdeputation* alternated Catholic and Protestant presidents and secretaries. These offices managed the defence of the city through a militia exclusively formed by residents from the three districts. The service was time-based and paid as a normal civic employment.

The chronicle of the year 1658 gives some interesting information on the strength of the militia. In summer, the newly elected Emperor Leopold I was offered a festive celebration for his arrival in Augsburg, and the City Council ceremoniously welcomed him with six companies of foot and four *standarten* of horse, as usual formed by militiamen from both confessions. On 16 August, a few days before the Emperor's arrival, the companies assembled

Portrait of a *Feldwebel* of the militia infantry of Augsburg, dating to 1680 (Stadtmuseum, Augsburg). Buff coat with red cloth sleeves and cuffs; a large black ribbon at the waist is partially concealed by the wide sword baldric, which is edged in gold. Along with the striking cravat, the clothing gives this NCO a slightly old-fashioned look, a common feature of the Free Imperial City's soldiers.

There is a variety of information regarding Augsburg's military colours dating back to the early seventeenth century, but the only known post 1648 ensign is the standard of the city militia cavalry company dating to 1677. Red silk background, black double-headed eagle with gold claws, beaks, sceptre, sphere, aureoles; silver fringes; the eagle carries the Coat of Arms of Augsburg: a green pinecone on a red (left) and white (right) field. (Augsburg City Museum, author's photograph)

for training in the field to the north of the city. This time, the districts fielded three Catholic and three Protestant infantry companies, but the Catholics had difficulty in raising the necessary men. The overall force numbered 306 horse and 1,619 foot.[5] After completing their service, the companies returned their weapons to the armoury on 30 August.

It was not until the 1670s that the permanent organisation of the militia into companies began. While the cavalry did not change its organisation and strength, the infantry was subject to several reforms. In 1673, under the pressure of the Diet for the *Reichskrieg* against France and with the military obligation as a member of the Swabian Circle, the citizens were minded to contribute to the defence of the city through service in the militia. The council also hoped that this would help to avoid an Imperial garrison in the town. However, the Catholics were not in favour of arming the citizens. The pretext was the unwillingness of the bourgeoisie to serve in the militia, and the danger posed by the distribution of arms to them. It was also feared that the weapons issued from the armoury would even be transferred to Jews.[6] The Protestants also rejected the proposal and therefore the matter was examined by the City Council. Because the majority of the Council did not want to quarter an Imperial garrison, a compromise was reached by diminishing the infantry companies to four. Each company comprised 2 officers, 9 *Feldwebel*, 1 *Captain d'Armes*, 1 *Leibschütz* (fourier-watchman), 4 drummers and 216 *Gemeine Musketieren*.[7] In January 1674, officers and NCOs were assigned to the new *Bürgerkompanien* and they all took the oath of allegiance and obedience. However, because the departure of the Circle contingent was now to be expected, this strength was far from sufficient to secure the city. In the following months, after a new selection of

---

5    Jürgen Kraus, *Das Militärwesen der Reichsstadt Augsburg 1548–1806* (Augsburg: Stadtarchiv, 1980), p.123. In detail these were: infantry company Imhoff (Catholic), 287; Koch (Protestants), 326; Schmidt (Catholic) 188; Miller (Protestant) 326; Schreiber (Catholic) 182; Zobel (Protestant) 310; cavalry company: Rehlingen (Catholic) 59; Böcklin (Protestant) 91; Ilsung (Catholic) 70; Schanternell (Protestant) 86.

6    Jürgen Kraus, *Das Militärwesen der Reichsstadt Augsburg 1548–1806* (Augsburg: Stadtarchiv, 1980), pp.123–124.

7    Jürgen Kraus, *Das Militärwesen der Reichsstadt Augsburg 1548–1806* (Augsburg: Stadtarchiv, 1980), p.124.

the available citizens, four more infantry companies were formed, and these entered service at the beginning of July 1674, all organised like the existing companies and divided according to their religion. Though the militiamen were to serve in rotation and each company had to remain in service with this strength, in the following year, the strength diminished to 240 private soldiers. However, the officers' staff now also comprised a *Fahnrich*, while the NCOs increased with one *Fürher*, one *Musterschreiber*, and one surgeon; 12 corporals and 48 *Gefreite* were also appointed.[8] Each company was divided in 12 *Corporalschaften*. The plan of the city authorities was to transform the militia into a semi-professional corps, similar to a modern national guard, and this concept was pursued by the formation of an artillery company, whose members received wages as a standing professional force. With this intention uniform clothing was distributed to the rank and file of all specialties.

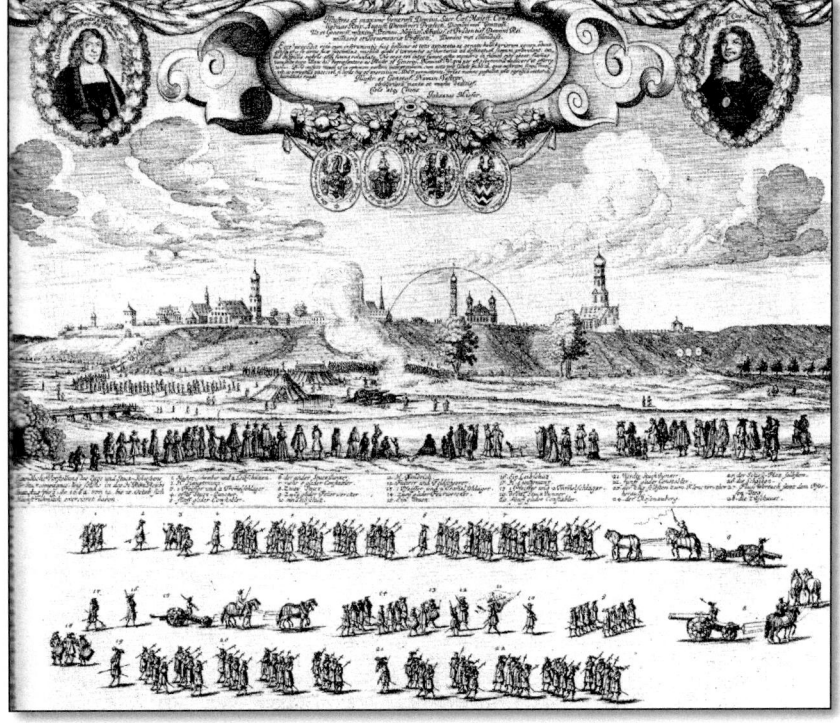

Officers, NCOs, drummers and private soldiers of the Augsburg artillery company in a print dating to 1682. (Author's collection) They wear coats with turned up cuffs and broad-brimmed hats, those of officers have plumes. Note the Colours with crossed cannon barrels. Unfortunately, the hue of the uniforms and Colours are not known.

In January 1681, one *Corporalschaft* in each infantry company was disbanded, and a second was disbanded in September 1682 due to a lack of recruits. This reduced the number of private militiamen to 200 per company.[9]

---

8   Jürgen Kraus, *Das Militärwesen der Reichsstadt Augsburg 1548–1806* (Augsburg: Stadtarchiv, 1980), p.124.
9   Jürgen Kraus, *Das Militärwesen der Reichsstadt Augsburg 1548–1806* (Augsburg: Stadtarchiv, 1980), p.125.

## Bremen

As with the other Hanseatic towns, Bremen had raised its own *Statdmilitärs* since the end of the sixteenth century. The military organisation was managed by the City Council through the *Kriegskommissar* (war commissioner) and the *Zahlkommissar* (payments commissioner), who directed the work of the respective *Kommissariat*. Both these offices were held by a senator who had their seat in the government's residence. The *Kriegskommissar* also dealt with military justice and for this task he managed the matter with the Court and the City Council. The military force comprised professional troops of foot and the militiaman of the *Bürgerkompanien*.

NCO and Private of a Bremen *Burgerkompagnie* after a watercolour of the *Koster Chronic*, c. 1655. (author's collection)
Both figures wear very dark grey coat and breeches; buttons are of dark grey cloth.

In 1644, the City Council entrusted the command of the professional troops and the militia to *Obrist* Gerhard Ufm Keller from Cleves, replaced in 1672 by the Hessian Johann Albrecht Freyes, who held the office until 1683. In the following years, other foreign senior officers were engaged, with a gap between 1684 and 1689, after the single year of service of the English Colonel William Waller was replaced by *Obristlieutenant* Christian Neubauer who served until 1712.[10] In the years following the Peace of Westphalia, the regular force fluctuated between 500 and 600 professional troops.[11] The state of emergency caused by the Swedish invasion in 1654 and 1666 forced the city to increase the number of troops. About 1,000 professional soldiers were

---

10 Andree Brumshagen, *Das Bremer Stadtmilitär 1618–1810: zur Bedeutung und Funktion des Soldaten in der reichsstädtischen Gesellschaft* (Bremen: Staatsarchiv Bremen, 2010), p.35. Waller had fallen out of favour at the court of Charles II of England and the King had threatened the council with ending friendly relations with Bremen if Waller remained in service

11 Andree Brumshagen, *Das Bremer Stadtmilitär 1618–1810: zur Bedeutung und Funktion des Soldaten in der reichsstädtischen Gesellschaft* (Bremen: Staatsarchiv Bremen, 2010), p.34.

# IMPERIAL FREE CITIES

enlisted in 1654. During the second blockade of the city between February and October 1666, 70 cavalry and 1,500 infantry of professional troops formed the garrison of the city,[12] while a further 6,000 selected militia were gathered as a reserve force.[13] The professional force also included an artillery corps of 80 men under a *Stuckhauptmann* who also dealt with the production of powder and acted as a consultant for the purchase of guns.[14] According to Gualdo Priorato, Bremen had strong walls manned by well-equipped professional troops, who also served at the gates of the city alongside the militiamen.[15] The Italian historian remarks on other fortified towns in the territory of Bremen, such as Stade, Buxtehude, Bremerhaven, Borch and Gestendorf, which were occupied by the Swedes.[16]

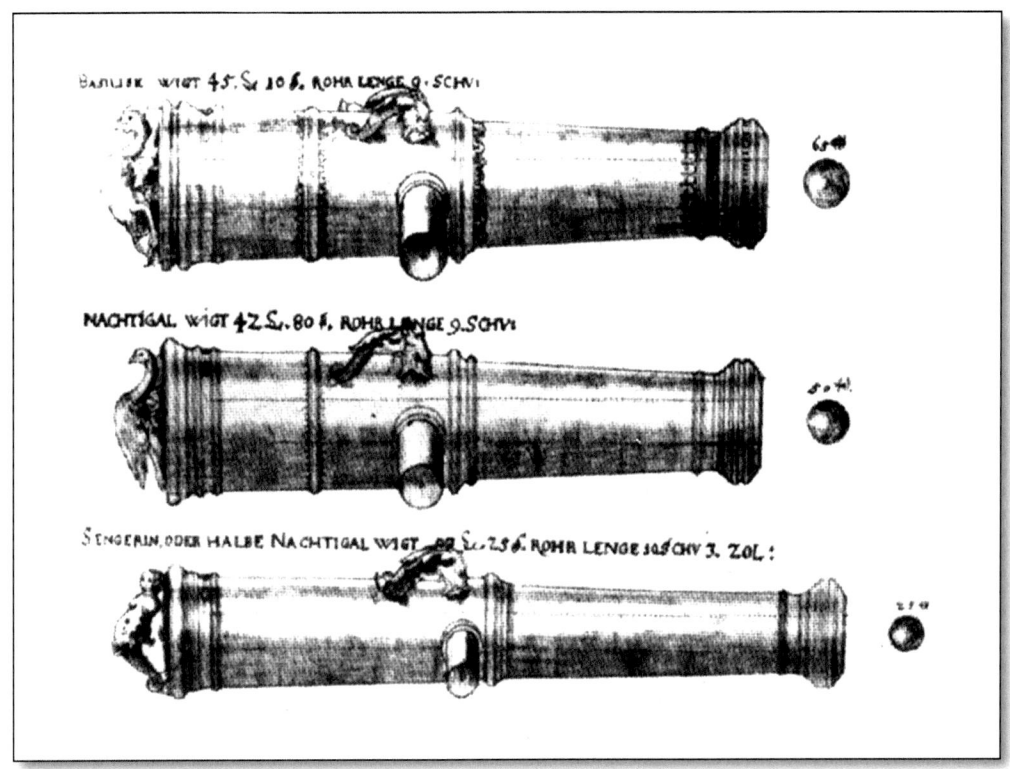

Three of Bremen's heavy artillery pieces which defended the city during the Swedish siege of 1666, named *Der Basilisk*, *Die Nachtgall*, *Die Sängerin*, which defended the city during the Swedish siege of 1666. (author's collection)

---

12 Andree Brumshagen, *Das Bremer Stadtmilitär 1618–1810: zur Bedeutung und Funktion des Soldaten in der reichsstädtischen Gesellschaft* (Bremen: Staatsarchiv Bremen, 2010), p.34
13 Galeazzo Gualdo Priorato, *Relationi delle Città Imperiali & Anseatiche di Colonia, Lubecca, Bremen, & Amburgo, di Norimberg, Augusta, Ulm e Francfort* (Bologna, 1674), p.66. In 1663, the Italian historian fixed the permanent garrison in peacetime to 900 men.
14 Andree Brumshagen, *Das Bremer Stadtmilitär 1618–1810: zur Bedeutung und Funktion des Soldaten in der reichsstädtischen Gesellschaft* (Bremen: Staatsarchiv Bremen, 2010), p.58.
15 Galeazzo Gualdo Priorato, *Relationi delle Città Imperiali & Anseatiche di Colonia, Lubecca, Bremen, & Amburgo, …. delle Corti e Stati de' Serenissimi Elettor di Baviera, e de' Langravi d'Hassia in Kassel e Darmstadt* (Bologna, 1674), pp.68–89
16 Later on Bremen also had to guard against Sweden and not only on a military level. In 1672, Sweden founded Carlsburg at the confluence of the Weser and Geeste rivers to compete with

In 1680, the Senate of Bremen agreed to raise the professional troops to 1,600 infantry, forming a field regiment of three battalions, and the artillery; from 1666 the cavalry no longer existed.[17] In 1681, the infantry received flintlocks, which gradually replaced the older firearms over the next 29 years.[18] As a member of the Lower Saxony Circle, Bremen contributed its quota of troops, of 16 cavalry and 32 infantry in 1663, but the Senate replaced its quota with cash and did the same in 1681.

## Cologne

Cologne was completely surrounded by the territories of the Electorate to which it gave its name but not its possession. Cologne was able to remain unscathed during the Thirty Years' War, due to the city government's decision to keep armies away by paying contributions. However, Cologne benefited greatly from the war through the production of, and trade in, weapons. Cologne became a centre of refuge for high-ranking Catholic leaders who sought to regain their territories lost to Sweden or other Protestant princes. Moreover, wealthy Cologne bankers were involved in the Thirty Years' War as important financiers of the Catholic party.[19] After 1648, concerns came around the Electorate, which demanded the city's acceptance of its state as a vassal. The pressure increased in the 1660s, and in 1671 arrangements were made for Cologne to accept a Dutch garrison should the Elector threaten force.[20]

Cologne differed from the other German Imperial Cities, in having the power shared between the nobility and the bourgeoisie, which made it similar to the United Provinces of The Netherlands, and like these, the government recognised freedom of faith. The political power was held by the

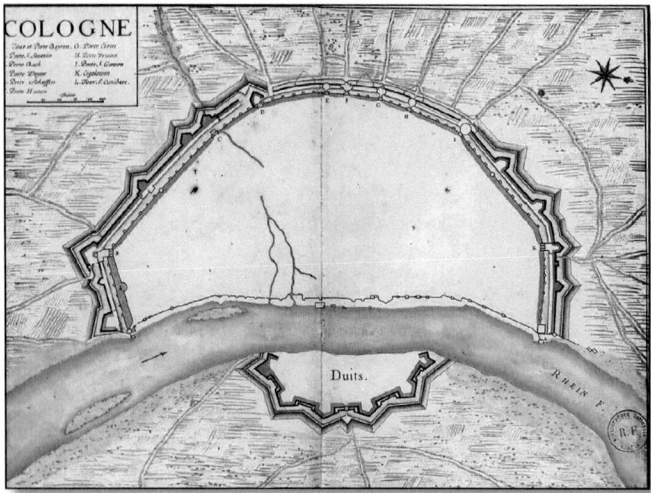

Plan of Cologne, from the *Livre des Plans des Places de l'Alsace et des Batailles qui le Roi a Gagné en ces Quartiers là*, dating to the 1680s. (author's collection) The fortifications were updated after 1668, but these were still incomplete in the early 1680s.

---

Bremen, but the settlement did not prosper.

17   Andree Brumshagen, *Das Bremer Stadtmilitär 1618–1810: zur Bedeutung und Funktion des Soldaten in der reichsstädtischen Gesellschaft* (Bremen: Staatsarchiv Bremen, 2010), p.57.
18   Peter Galperin, *In Wehr und Waffen – Wehrbürger, Söldner und Soldaten in Oldenburg und den Hansestädten* (Stuttgart, Motorbuch Verlag, 1983), p.146.
19   Hans-Wolfgang Bergerhausen: 'Die Stadt Köln im Dreißigjährigen Krieg', in S. Ehrenpreis (editor), *Der Dreißigjährige Krieg im Herzogtum Berg und in seinen Nachbarregionen* (Neustadt an der Aisch: Verlagsdruckerei Schmidt, 2002), p.103.
20   Georg Tessin, *Die Regimenter der Europäischen Staaten im Ancien Régime des XVI bis XVIII Jahrhunderts* (Osnabrück: Biblio Verlag, 1986), Teil 1, p.196. In April 1671, Cologne quartered the Dutch infantry regiment Bampfield and paid it as a regular city force.

major and minor Senate, to which the six *Burgermeisters* and three more majors, who presided over the government's affairs and managed the city's offices, all belonged. One of these dealt with the military matters, which included the maintenance of the fortifications and the arsenal. According to Gualdo Priorato, the walls protecting Cologne were high but not modern.[21]

The *Stadtmilitär* was divided into three organisations: the mercenary troops, the contingent for the Upper Rhine Circle, and the *ausschuss* (militia) with the *Bürgerkavallerie*, the latter with a more representative than military function. In 1663, there were 300 professional infantry who manned the city's gates, the public house, and other posts, but in the event of war Cologne had enough resources to muster 6,000 mercenaries.[22] The *Auschuss* numbered 53 companies, which in turn joined the professionals in their tasks, and at night formed pickets and sentinels to guard the city inside and outside the walls. The city of Cologne belonged to the Westphalian-Rhine Circle. In 1664, the city recruited its own contingent for the regiment *Post zu Pferd* and *Waldbott zu Fuss*, 70 cavalry and 300 infantry respectively.[23]

When the Franco-Dutch War broke out, the Dutch garrison was replaced by a Circle regiment under *Obrist* Waldbott (KoI-1), which formed the main garrison until 1679. In 1688, Cologne had to quarter 1,200 Palatine infantry and 1,200 Brandenburg infantry for protection. The garrison increased to 3,073 men in 1691 with soldiers from Brandenburg, the Palatinate, Münster's, Paderborn and from the city.[24]

## Frankfurt am Main

The ancient seat of the Imperial Diet and the location of the coronation of the Holy Roman Emperors with their private residence in the Braunfeld, Frankfurt managed to maintain its neutrality during the Thirty Years' War. Though the City Council always avoided siding with one opponent or another, the issue became critical between 1631 and 1635, when the Swedish army came to Frankfurt demanding accommodation and provisions. However, the city mastered these adversities more easily than the ones that followed the war, when the plague devastated the city. In 1648, the settlements of Westphalia confirmed for Frankfurt the status of Imperial Free City, and it soon reached new heights of prosperity. The town was a centre of the cloth industry, which formed the basis of the wealth of many families, some of which became owners of trade companies and bankers. The city also had a

---

21  Galeazzo Gualdo Priorato, *Relationi delle Città Imperiali & Anseatiche di Colonia, Lubecca, Bremen, & Amburgo, .... delle Corti e Stati de' Serenissimi Elettor di Baviera, e de' Langravi d'Hassia in Kassel e Darmstadt* (Bologna, 1674), p.7.
22  Galeazzo Gualdo Priorato, *Relationi delle Città Imperiali & Anseatiche di Colonia, Lubecca, Bremen, & Amburgo, .... delle Corti e Stati de' Serenissimi Elettor di Baviera, e de' Langravi d'Hassia in Kassel e Darmstadt* (Bologna, 1674), p.17.
23  Georg Tessin, *Die Regimenter der Europäischen Staaten im Ancien Régime des XVI bis XVIII Jahrhunderts* (Osnabrück: Biblio Verlag, 1986), Teil 1, pp.196–197.
24  Georg Tessin, *Die Regimenter der Europäischen Staaten im Ancien Régime des XVI bis XVIII Jahrhunderts* (Osnabrück: Biblio Verlag, 1986), Teil 1, p.197.

Plan of Frankfurt am Main in the first half of the seventeenth century. (author's collection). The curtain was considerably strengthened with additional works between the 1640s and 1650s with additional works.

large Jewish population, who also included many traders and bankers active in supplying money, uniforms and equipment to the German states.

The territory of the city included not only the town but also the territory around, as well as a number of exclaves in the Rhine-Main area, such as the villages of Soden and Sulzbach which were shared with Mainz, while Niederrad belonged to Frankfurt for three-quarters, and to the Teutonic Order for the remaining quarter. With his customary Italian suavity, Gualdo Priorato provides a positive portrait of Frankfurt, praising the city for its strong curtain with modern bastions, and the arsenal provided with all kind of weapons.[25]

Senate and *Burgermeisters* shared the political power and all the government's colleges were formed by senators and magistrates belonging to the aristocracy, including that dealing with the army. Sources relate the existence of a standing regiment of infantry since at least 1619.[26] According to Gualdo Priorato, in 1663 Frankfurt had 200 professional infantry under

---

25 Galeazzo Gualdo Priorato, *Relationi delle Città Imperiali & Anseatiche di Colonia, Lubecca, Bremen, & Amburgo, .... delle Corti e Stati de' Serenissimi Elettor di Baviera, e de' Langravi d'Hassia in Kassel e Darmstadt* (Bologna, 1674), p.185.

26 Georg Tessin, *Die Regimenter der Europäischen Staaten im Ancien Régime des XVI bis XVIII Jahrhunderts* (Osnabrück: Biblio Verlag, 1986), Teil 1, p.157.

an *oberstleutnant*, and 14 companies of the *Burgerwehr*.[27] Additionally, as a member of the Upper Rhenish Circle, Frankfurt provided troops for the *Reichsarmee*. In 1664, 60 cavalry joined the regiment *Nassau zu Pferd*, while two companies of 170 men, and a third of 80, 420 men at all, marched to Hungary as part of the regiment *Solm zu Fuss*.[28] In the following years, Frankfurt only contributed with two infantry companies in 1674 and 1685 as its quota for the Circle contingent. However, this measure revealed its weakness in October 1688, when the French demanded contributions and that the City accept a garrison. After the refusal by Frankfurt's authorities, the villages of Riedhof, Oberrad, and Niederrad were burnt as retaliation, and only the arrival of troops from Hessen-Kassel, Hessen-Darmstadt and Hannover prevented the French occupation of the city.

Illustration after Michael Mieth's *Artilleriae Recentior Praxis* (Frankfurt am Main: 1684). (Nationaal Militair Museum, Soesterberg) Although the Imperial Free Cities were second-rate military actors, they were very active centres of experimentation in technical matters like artillery and fortifications. Frankfurt am Main also had renowned weapon manufactories.

# Hamburg

The foundations of Hamburg's wealth and influence were thanks to its favourable location in Northern Germany and its natural harbour on the Elbe River, which connected Saxony, Brandenburg and other territories with the North Sea. This enabled it to survive the Thirty Years' War relatively untouched, as both warring factions heavily depended on its markets. Galeazzo Gualdo Priorato describes Hamburg very positively, attributing to it the primacy of the most populated city of Germany with nearly 100,000 inhabitants in the early 1660s. He praises the trade and industry of the city, the

---

27  Galeazzo Gualdo Priorato, *Relationi delle Città Imperiali & Anseatiche di Colonia, Lubecca, Bremen, & Amburgo, .... delle Corti e Stati de' Serenissimi Elettor di Baviera, e de' Langravi d'Hassia in Kassel e Darmstadt* (Bologna, 1674), p.189.
28  Georg Tessin, *Die Regimenter der Europäischen Staaten im Ancien Régime des XVI bis XVIII Jahrhunderts* (Osnabrück: Biblio Verlag, 1986), Teil 1, p.157.

Plan of Hamburg with its defences in a print dating to 1655. (author's collection) According to foreign travellers, Hamburg was 'the most liberal' city of Germany, but they also commented on the citizens' excessive drinking habits. It was reported around 1650 that 'nowadays people first send for spirits before they go to church on a Sunday'. In 1686, the English envoy, Sir George Etherege, wrote about this, and extending his judgement to the whole of Germany:

the Gentlemen of this Country go upon a quite different Scheme of Pleasure, and they take more care to enlarge their cellars than their patrimonial estates. In short, Drinking is the Hereditary Sin of this Country. … Some drinkers are mentioned with as much Applause as the Duke of Lorain (sic) for his noble Exploits against the Turks and may claim a Statue erected at the public Expense in any Town in Germany.[29]

number of foreign diplomatic mission, and remarks on the freedom granted to the Jews, who, unlike in many other European states, were not obliged to wear any distinctive sign or headgear. Gualdo Priorato also discourses about the new fortifications built on the side bordering Danish territory, defining these as 'very high and strong', and reinforced with modern external works. The defence of the city was also secured by the large quantity of weapons and cannon preserved in the arsenal.[30]

The city was governed by a Senate comprising four *Bürgermeisters*, or consuls, and 20 senators. They formed the colleges which dealt with the government's matters, including the military. The Senate appointed the

---

29  *New Cambridge Modern History*, 'The Ascendancy of France, 1648–1688' (Cambridge: Cambridge University Press, 1968), vol. V, p.439.

30  Galeazzo Gualdo Priorato, *Relationi delle Città Imperiali & Anseatiche di Colonia, Lubecca, Bremen, & Amburgo, …. delle Corti e Stati de' Serenissimi Elettor di Baviera, e de' Langravi d'Hassia in Kassel e Darmstadt* (Bologna, 1674), p.82.

Commander-in-Chief of the city garrison, the military commissioners and other administrative personnel. The army consisted of armed citizens, the *Bürgergarde* or *Bürgerwehr*, and professional troops or *Stadtsoldaten*. By 1637, Hamburg had a professional military force of 1,489 infantry divided into four companies.[31] From 1616 they formed a field regiment entrusted to the city military commander, who was also captain of the *Leibcompanie*. The regiment fell to two companies in 1651 and in 1654 there were only 100 soldiers still in service. The effective strength of the *Stadtmilitärs* can be determined with precision only in 1657, when 1,200 foot were registered and an additional 500 foot together with a company of horse were recruited. In 1663, Gualdo Priorato states that the professional infantry numbered 1,200 men under the experienced Saxon, *Obrist* Copey. In the following decades, the overall number of the professional infantry varied from 3,000 to 4,000 men organised in 12 companies.[32] In 1676, the number of companies decreased to 10, with a strength of 4,134 foot.[33] In 1683, 120 musketeers were converted into grenadiers, and the number of companies was re-established at 12.[34] In 1686, a second regiment of 12 companies was hastily raised to face the Danish intervention, and in the same year, a company of dragoons was also recruited.[35] The professional soldiers additionally included a section of artillery, who managed the 311 guns of the celebrated city arsenal.

As for the city militia, in 1648 there were 4 *Bürgerwehr* regiments, each of 10 companies, that carried the name of the city district where they were raised. The regiments were *St Petri, St Nicolai, St Katharinen, St Jacobi* and *St Michaelis*, with approximately 8,000 militiamen in all.[36] In 1658 the strength was increased to 10,000, divided into 57 companies and distributed across the district regiments in unequal numbers. However, from this force, only 1,500 men actually served in support of the professional infantry.[37] The city militia served alongside the professional infantry alternating with them each night, when one or more companies manned the gates and other posts in the city.[38]

---

31 Georg Tessin, *Die Regimenter der Europäischen Staaten im Ancien Régime des XVI bis XVIII Jahrhunderts* (Osnabrück: Biblio Verlag, 1986), Teil 1, p.161.
32 Andree Brumshagen, *Das Bremer Stadtmilitär 1618–1810: zur Bedeutung und Funktion des Soldaten in der reichsstädtischen Gesellschaft* (Bremen: Staatsarchiv Bremen, 2010), p.61.
33 Georg Tessin, *Die Regimenter der Europäischen Staaten im Ancien Régime des XVI bis XVIII Jahrhunderts* (Osnabrück: Biblio Verlag, 1986), Teil 1, p.161.
34 Peter Galperin, *In Wehr und Waffen – Wehrbürger, Söldner und Soldaten in Oldenburg und den Hansestädten* (Stuttgart, Motorbuch Verlag, 1983), p.152. According to Georg Tessin, *Die Regimenter der Europäischen Staaten im Ancien Régime des XVI bis XVIII Jahrhunderts* (Osnabrück: Biblio Verlag, 1986), Teil 1, p.161, both regiments had only 10 companies.
35 Thomas Muhsfeldt, 'Tracht Einiges über Hamburger Stadtsoldaten' in Richard Knötel, *Mittheilungen zur Geschichte der Militärischen Tracht* (Rathenow, 1896), Nr. 8, p.18.
36 Peter Galperin, *In Wehr und Waffen – Wehrbürger, Söldner und Soldaten in Oldenburg und den Hansestädten* (Stuttgart, Motorbuch Verlag, 1983), p.155. Each regiment was identified by a distinctive colour, which presumably was used for ensigns and scarves. These were: red for St Petri, blue for St Nicolai, yellow for St Katharinen, green for St Jacobi, white for St Michaelis.
37 Peter Galperin, *In Wehr und Waffen – Wehrbürger, Söldner und Soldaten in Oldenburg und den Hansestädten* (Stuttgart, Motorbuch Verlag, 1983), p.155.
38 Galeazzo Gualdo Priorato, *Relationi delle Città Imperiali & Anseatiche di Colonia, Lubecca, Bremen, & Amburgo, …. delle Corti e Stati de' Serenissimi Elettor di Baviera, e de' Langravi*

Hamburg adopted very up-to-date administrative and judicial instruments compared to others existing in Germany and even in the rest of Europe. In 1683, the Senate established a special 'Imperial Court', separate from civil jurisdiction, which dealt with professional troops. The office was held by a Military Auditor, or in the second instance, by a Senate member, who was responsible for conducting the trials. Unlike other German territories, in Hamburg there was even a separate superior court-martial for appellate matters. All offences committed on duty by soldiers were tried by this military court. It could sentence offenders to a reduction of salary, 'honour castigations', corporal punishments and, in the case of particularly serious offences, such as desertion or murder, the death penalty. However, the latter was imposed relatively rarely, and corporal punishment and fines were more common.[39] As with the other Hanseatic towns, Hamburg belonged to the Lower Saxony Circle, but did not provide troops for the *Reichsarmee* replacing its quota with a cash payment. In the last quarter of the seventeenth century, Hamburg became an active centre for the recruitment of soldiers by German and foreign states.[40]

## Lübeck

As with the other Hanseatic cities, Lübeck did not provide troops to the *Reichsarmee* although a member of the Lower Saxony Circle, but paid cash for the equivalent. Information on the actual strength of the regular troops serving the city is very fragmentary before 1750, but travellers' accounts and other information indicate that they formed a field battalion of 700 to 800 men between the 1650s and the 1690s.[41] On this matter, Gualdo Priorato refers to four companies of 200 'paid infantry', under an *obrist* and other field officers.[42] The professional troops included an artillery company of 40 men in 1684. In 1663, the Italian historian mentions the 33 companies of armed bourgeoisie, of whom 200–300 were always in active service as support for the regular infantry.[43]

---

d'Hassia in Kassel e Darmstadt (Bologna, 1674), pp.83 and 142, reports that the service of the militia consisted mainly in suppressing the prostitution market inside the city, which was only allowed in the outside suburbs, where other guards were assigned.

39  Andree Brumshagen, *Das Bremer Stadtmilitär 1618–1810: zur Bedeutung und Funktion des Soldaten in der reichsstädtischen Gesellschaft* (Bremen: Staatsarchiv Bremen, 2010), p.120.

40  See Bruno Mugnai, *Wars and Soldiers in the Early Reign of Louis XIV, volume 5: The Portuguese Army, 1659–1690* (Warwick: Helion & Company, 2021), p.61.

41  Thomas Schwark, *Lübecks Stadtmilitär im 17. und 18. Jahrhundert, Untersuchungen zur Sozialgeschichte Einer Reichsstädtischen Berufsgruppe. Veröffentlichungen zur Geschichte der Hansestadt Lübeck*, Reihe B, 18 (Lübeck: Schmidt-Röhmhild, 1990), p.47.

42  Galeazzo Gualdo Priorato, *Relationi delle Città Imperiali & Anseatiche di Colonia, Lubecca, Bremen, & Amburgo, .... delle Corti e Stati de' Serenissimi Elettor di Baviera, e de' Langravi d'Hassia in Kassel e Darmstadt* (Bologna, 1674), p.37.

43  'The writer Johann Peter Hillebrand described Lübeck's city militia as a respectable, well-trained and well-dressed force, present but certainly not numerous due to the external and internal peace of the city.' Thomas Schwark, *Lübecks Stadtmilitär im 17. und 18. Jahrhundert,*

# IMPERIAL FREE CITIES

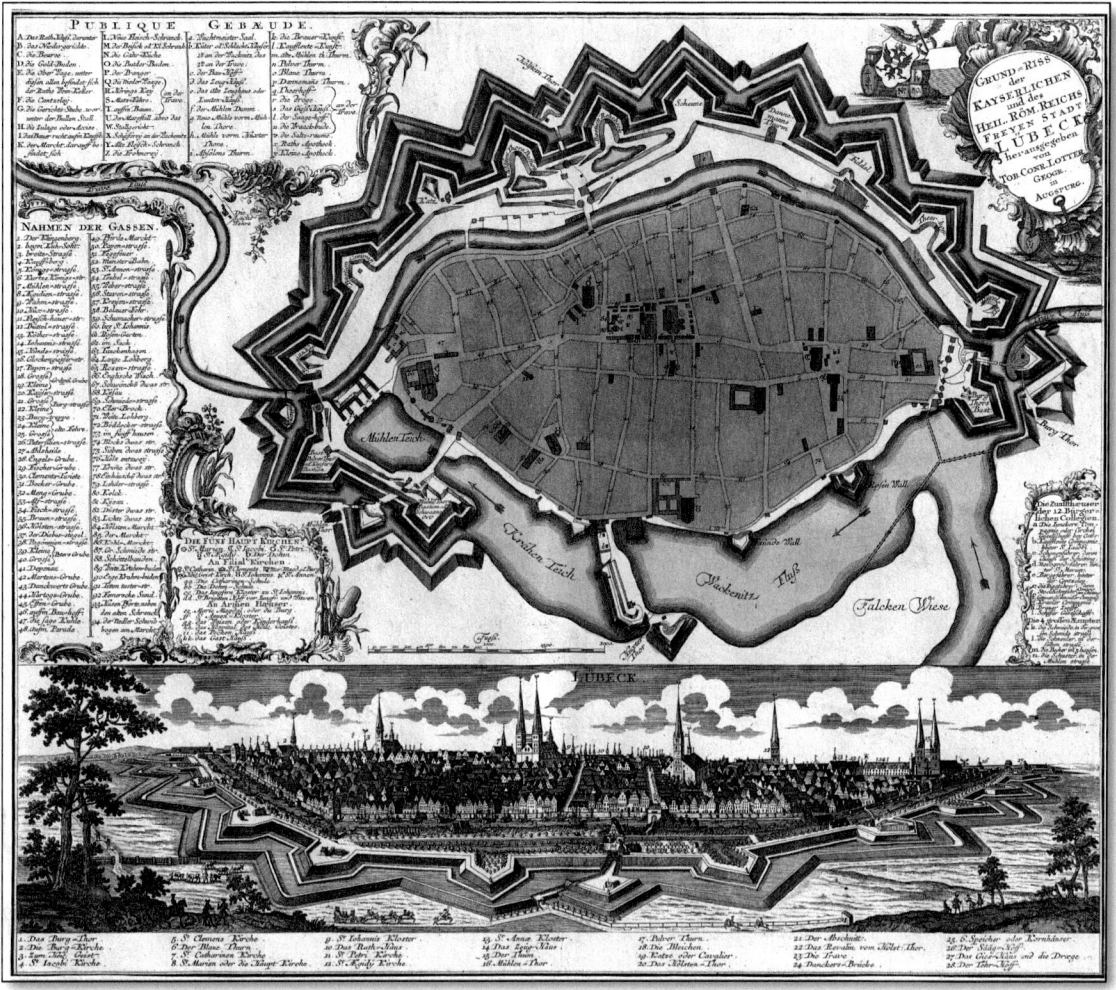

Plan and view of Lübeck in the early eighteenth century, print after the engraving by Matthäus Seutter. (author's archive)

As in Bremen and Hamburg, in Lübeck military justice was managed by a separate court through the war commissioner, but on disciplinary matters, the officers were subject to the City Council. The military authorities already had a Hall by 1665, which branched off from the Löwensaal of the Town Hall and was located next to the Wettstube. In 1665, the seat of the military authorities was moved to another location.

Compared to the other Hanseatic towns, military service in Lübeck was very bad, even by the standards of that time. By the end of the 1680s, the payment of wages was greatly in arrears. In 1691, the accumulated arrears was 28 months, the reason for the professional soldiers declaring that they would no longer serve if the City Council did not pay their wages. The Senate opened talks, but some of the soldiers' spokesmen were taken into custody, and four companies of militia were put on alert as a precaution. The senators in charge of military affairs admonished the remaining soldiers to remember

---

*Untersuchungen zur Sozialgeschichte Einer Reichsstädtischen Berufsgruppe. Veröffentlichungen zur Geschichte der Hansestadt Lübeck*, Reihe B, 18 (Lübeck: Schmidt-Röhmhild, 1990), p.45.

# WARS AND SOLDIERS IN THE EARLY REIGN OF LOUIS XIV – VOLUME 7 PART 3

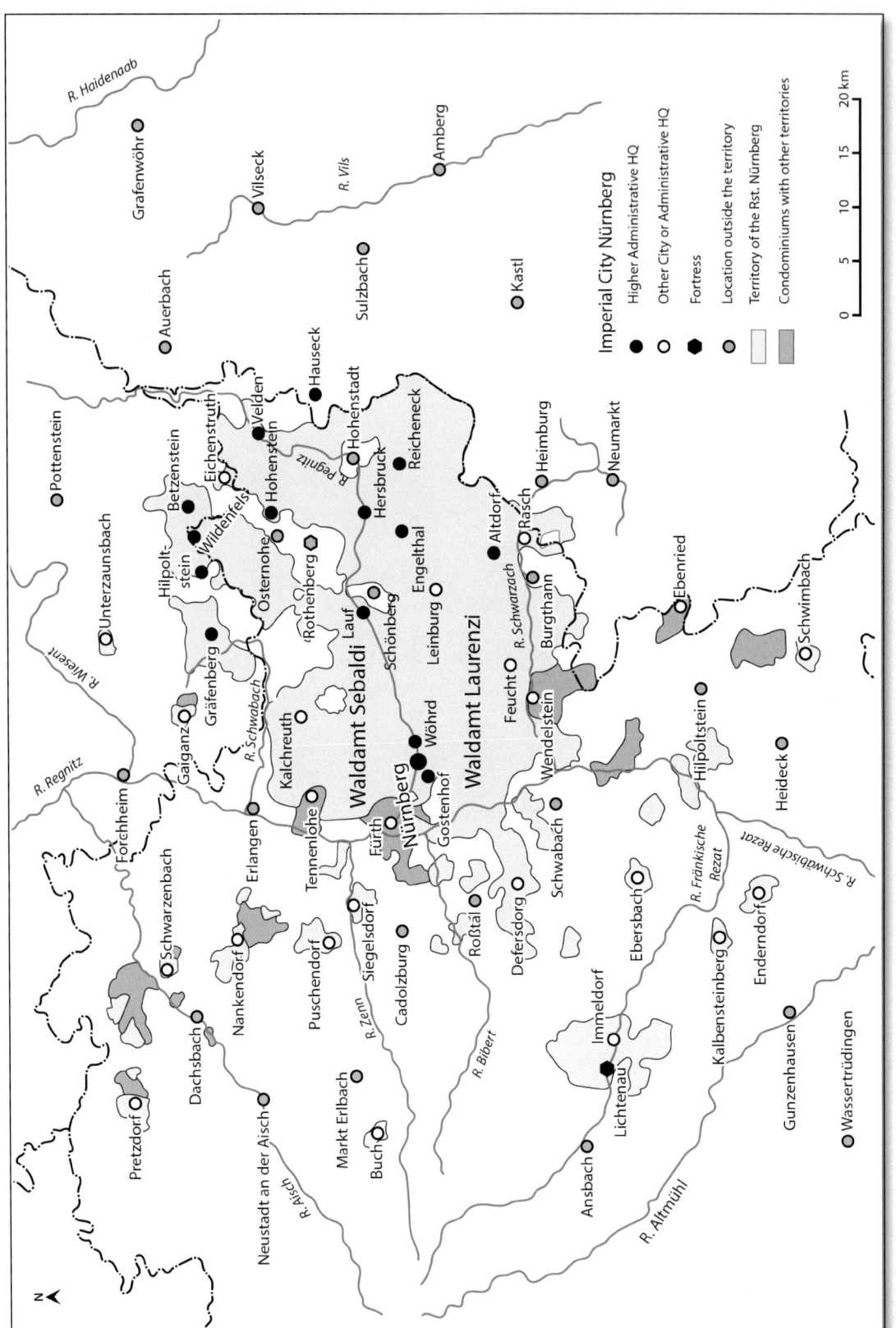

Map of Nuremberg by George Anderson (© Helion & Co. 2024)

their oath of service and to remain silent in the future, but above all to refrain from further seditious acts.[44] A characteristic of the armies of the Imperial Cities, and very common in Lübeck, was the advanced age of the soldiers, and it was easy to meet soldiers over 60, with the majority of the professional force married with children.[45]

## Nuremberg

The largest in terms of territory of all of the Imperial Cities, the Republic of Nuremberg belonged to the Circle of Franconia.

In the Thirty Years' War, the city was involved in the campaign of Gustav II Adolph in Germany. Although it was not taken by the Swedes, it was permanently weakened economically by the devastation in the surrounding area, as well as the contribution extorted by Wallenstein for the billeting of his army in 1632. In admiration that a single city had supported such a large army, the Dutch representatives granted the senators of Nuremberg the title 'Mighty Lords'.[46]

Plan of Nuremberg dating to 1648, print by Matthäus Merian the Elder. (author's collection)
Notwithstanding its remarkable extension, the policy of Nuremberg was no different from that of other German republics. Following Montesquieu's vision, and in contrast to monarchies, the political objective of peace and moderation was inherent in the Free Imperial City.

---

44 Thomas Schwark, *Lübecks Stadtmilitär im 17. und 18. Jahrhundert, Untersuchungen zur Sozialgeschichte Einer Reichsstädtischen Berufsgruppe. Veröffentlichungen zur Geschichte der Hansestadt Lübeck*, Reihe B, 18 (Lübeck: Schmidt-Röhmhild, 1990), p.13. If the soldiers could survive at all was probably due to the fact that they had other jobs as well.
45 Thomas Schwark, *Lübecks Stadtmilitär im 17. und 18. Jahrhundert, Untersuchungen zur Sozialgeschichte Einer Reichsstädtischen Berufsgruppe. Veröffentlichungen zur Geschichte der Hansestadt Lübeck*, Reihe B, 18 (Lübeck: Schmidt-Röhmhild, 1990), p.11.
46 Galeazzo Gualdo Priorato, *Relationi delle Città Imperiali & Anseatiche di Colonia, Lubecca, Bremen, & Amburgo, .... delle Corti e Stati de' Serenissimi Elettor di Baviera, e de' Langravi d'Hassia in Kassel e Darmstadt* (Bologna, 1674), p.166.

Print from *Die Drillkunst. Das ist Kriegsübliche Waffenhandlung der Musqueten ünd Pique Allen Tapfern Soldaten zu nutzlicher beliebüng*, after an engraving of Peter von Isselburg (Nuremberg: 1664). (author's collection)

Portrait of an unknown Nuremberg officer by Johann Heinrich Roos dating to the early 1670s (Bayerischen Staatsgemäldesammlungen, Munich). The painting offers a very detailed image of a *Kollet* and he is wearing a gorget with gold fittings and a scarf in the Nuremberg colours of red and white.

In 1664, the City Council supplied its contingent to the armies of the Empire and for the war against the Ottomans. These were 112 troopers in the *Zobel zu Pferd* and three companies, 533 men, in the Circle regiment *Pleitner zu Fuss*. In 1676, Nuremberg reduced its quota and thereafter there were two companies with 270 foot – instead of the establishment 364 – in the *Avila* Regiment and 2 companies with 145 horse – instead of 182 – in the *Bayreuth Kuirassieren*.[47] In 1681, the *Reichsdefensionalordnung* (the Imperial Defence Ordinance) issued by the Diet obliged Nuremberg to provide nine companies to the three infantry regiments of the Franconian Circle, which would be joined to the Imperial Army guarding the Rhine. The Republic continued to regularly contribute to the contingent of the Franconian Circle until the dissolution of the Empire in 1804. In peace time, 300 infantrymen formed the entire regular force of Nuremberg, along with the artillery corps, which claimed the primacy of the oldest artillery corps in Europe, because, according to tradition, cannon had first been introduced in Nuremberg.[48]

In support of the regular force inside the city and in the other locations, the City Council could rely on the *Burgemilitär*, which numbered 132

---

47 Georg Tessin, *Die Regimenter der Europäischen Staaten im Ancien Régime des XVI bis XVIII Jahrhunderts* (Osnabrück: Biblio Verlag, 1986), Teil 1, p.244.
48 Galeazzo Gualdo Priorato, *Relationi delle Città Imperiali & Anseatiche di Colonia, Lubecca, Bremen, & Amburgo, .... delle Corti e Stati de' Serenissimi Elettor di Baviera, e de' Langravi d'Hassia in Kassel e Darmstadt* (Bologna, 1674), p.125.

companies in 1663, with a strength of approximately 6,000 militia foot.[49] They also served in the other 12 major towns and fortresses of the Republic. Although its military force was relatively large, Nuremberg managed to maintain a high degree of discipline and order, and in the previous century the city's troops already enjoyed a good reputation.

## Strasbourg

After 1648, France began to use the Rhine as a border and, taking advantage of the fragmentation of the Imperial fiefdoms over the Alsatian cities with the Peace of Westphalia, obtained a number of bridgeheads on the right bank. Strasbourg was initially excluded from the French strategy, but was soon targeted by Louis XIV in the course of the Franco-Dutch War. As a member of the Upper Rhine Circle, the Republic of Strasbourg participated in 1664 and 1674 in the formation of the *Reichskontingent*, but declared itself formally neutral. When the conflict extended to the Rhine and Alsace,

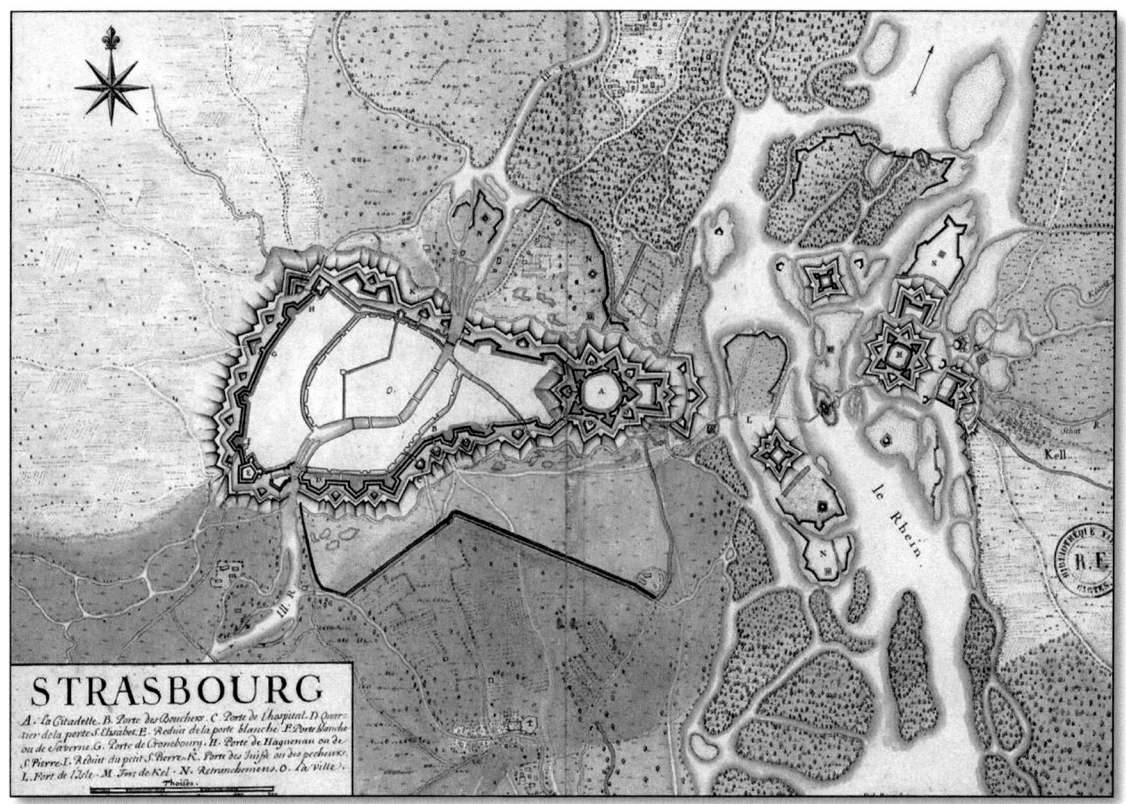

The fortifications of Strasbourg and, right, of Kehl, from the *Livre des plans des places de l'Alsace*. (author's collection) The print shows the improvements built by the French after the annexation of the city in 1681.

---

49   Galeazzo Gualdo Priorato, *Relationi delle Città Imperiali & Anseatiche di Colonia, Lubecca, Bremen, & Amburgo, .... delle Corti e Stati de' Serenissimi Elettor di Baviera, e de' Langravi d'Hassia in Kassel e Darmstadt* (Bologna, 1674), p.148.

Strasbourg became a strategically important location for the allies. By 1675, Montecuccoli and later Charles V of Lorraine used the city as a gateway to Alsace and an Imperial terminal for supplies. Although the city was neutral, the support provided to the Allies had not gone unnoticed by the Louis XIV's generals.[50] On 23 July 1678, the French attempted to take the offensive against Strasbourg, but were prevented by the Imperial cavalry who defeated the French vanguard at Ortenbach; however, Lorraine refused to commit his forces to a general engagement and retreated to Oberkirch. This move was a fatal error, because it cut his army off from the Rhine, leaving *Maréchal* Créquy free to seize Kehl on 27 July after a two-day siege. Before leaving Kehl, he destroyed the strategic bridge and the fortifications, and finally threatened Strasbourg. Then, on 8 August, the French crossed the Rhine at Altenheim on pontoons and turned to Strasbourg to complete the destruction of the bridge on the western side.

Although the Peace of Nijmegen had recognised the independence of Strasbourg under the Imperial protection of Vienna, in September 1681, the city, together with Königshofen and Illkirch, was occupied by the French. The possession of Strasbourg by France was confirmed by the Peace of Rijswijk of 1697.

Apart from the Circle contingent, Strasbourg relied for its safety on the *Bürgerwehr*, which had been formed in the previous century. In 1633, the companies formed a regiment of foot under an *obrist* appointed by the City Council. This was a semi-professional force raised and equipped by the city and officered by citizens appointed after a selection process. In 1665, the regiment numbered 8 companies of foot, and 2 companies of horse were formed before the end of the year.[51] The overall strength was 200 horse and 1,500 foot. In late 1672, the City Council authorised an increase to its *Bürgerwehr* with a further 23 infantry companies.[52] In 1674, mercenaries from the Swiss cantons entered the service of Strasbourg.

Although Strasbourg had proclaimed its neutrality, the Franco-Imperial campaigns in Alsace involved the *Bürgerwehr* in the guarding of the main routes and the borders. In early 1675, the infantry were sent to Willstadt, opposite Strasbourg. The year 1675 marked a turning point of the war in Alsace. The Imperialists were increasingly short of resources, and whereas in previous years Strasbourg had made a good business of trading with the Allies for supplies and transport, from that date onwards the city was forced to accept vague promises of repayment. Other concerns came from billeting and quartering the allied soldiers. On 25 March 1675, *Feldmarschall* Montecuccoli negotiated with the City Council for the quartering of the three companies of the Lower Saxon Circle serving with the allies, together with two Swiss and three Strasbourg companies, the latter later replaced by

---

50   See also Bruno Mugnai, *Wars and Soldiers in the Early Reign of Louis XIV*, volume 2, *The Imperial Army 1657–1687* (Warwick: Helion & Company, 2029), p.170.
51   Joseph Gény, *Die Fahnen der Strassburger Bürgerwehr im 17. Jahrhundert* (Strasbourg: J.E.H. Heitz, 1902), pp.26–27.
52   Joseph Gény, *Die Fahnen der Strassburger Bürgerwehr im 17. Jahrhundert* (Strasbourg: J.E.H. Heitz, 1902), p.36.

a further four Swiss foot companies. In August, the City Council declared that it was unable to pay for the quarters of the troops, so it was decided that Hannover and Lauenburg troops would provide for their own companies, while only the Mecklenburg company would be paid for by Strasbourg. When the Hannover and Saxe-Lauenburg companies were ordered to leave to occupy Mühlberg, Strasbourg refused to keep the Mecklenburg company, forcing it to march home.[53]

---

53 Georg Tessin, 'Mecklenburgisches Militär in Türken und Franzosenkriegen 1648–1718' in *Mitteldeutsche Forschungen*, vol. 42 (Cologne: Böhlau, 1966), p.85.

# 4

# The Duchy of Lorraine

Placed between France and the Holy Roman Empire, the Duchy of Lorraine experienced a turbulent existence during the seventeenth century. Under a geostrategic point of view, Lorraine appeared as an irrational patchwork of different sovereignties and jurisdictions, but formally, Lorraine held the political status of a *Reich*'s state and member of the Upper Rhine Circle through the Margraviate of Nomeny and County of Falkenstein. This allowed Lorraine's rulers to balance their politics in the hard task of exploiting the condition of a buffer state until the situation began to change in the mid-sixteenth century. The following events defined the parameters of Lorraine's geopolitical situation and brought at the final annexation to France in 1766.

Territorial continuity appeared euphemistic, since it was interrupted by enclaves subject to other states, notably France and Spain. The two largest territories were the Duchies of Bar and of Lorraine. Moreover, in the heart of ducal lands lay three former sovereign bishoprics: Metz, Toul, and Verdun which belonged to France. Finally, the town and territory of Merzig was ruled in condominium with the Electorate of Trier. The Duchy's approximately 800,000 inhabitants[1] in the early 1600s occupied an overwhelmingly rural territory of 1,128.63km². The largest urban centre of the area, Metz, boasted a population of around 19,000; in contrast, at the beginning of the seventeenth century, the most important city under ducal control, Nancy, only had about 8,000 residents.[2] French speaking subjects occupied the three *grandes baliages* of Nancy, Vosges, and Luneville, while the Germans were predominant in the fourth of these, Dieuze, located on the Upper Rhine. Straddling the Meuse and Moselle rivers, and stretching from the Vosges Mountains to Luxembourg, Lorraine sat astride two major trading axes, and thus goods, people, and ideas constantly flowed through the Duchy.

---

1   Robert Parisot, *Histoire de Lorraine (Duché de Lorraine, Duché de Bar, Trois-Évêchés)*, (Paris, 1919–1924), tome II (1552–1789), p.139.

2   Agriculture formed the foundation of the duchy's economy, and trade was a positive effect of this activity. Another crucial aspect of Lorraine's economy was its industrial production, especially glass manufacturing and salt mining. These products as well as agricultural surpluses were sold throughout Europe and had favoured the Duchy's prosperity in the sixteenth century. See, Michel Parisse, *Histoire de Lorraine*, (Toulouse: Ouest-France, 1977), p.33.

# THE DUCHY OF LORRAINE

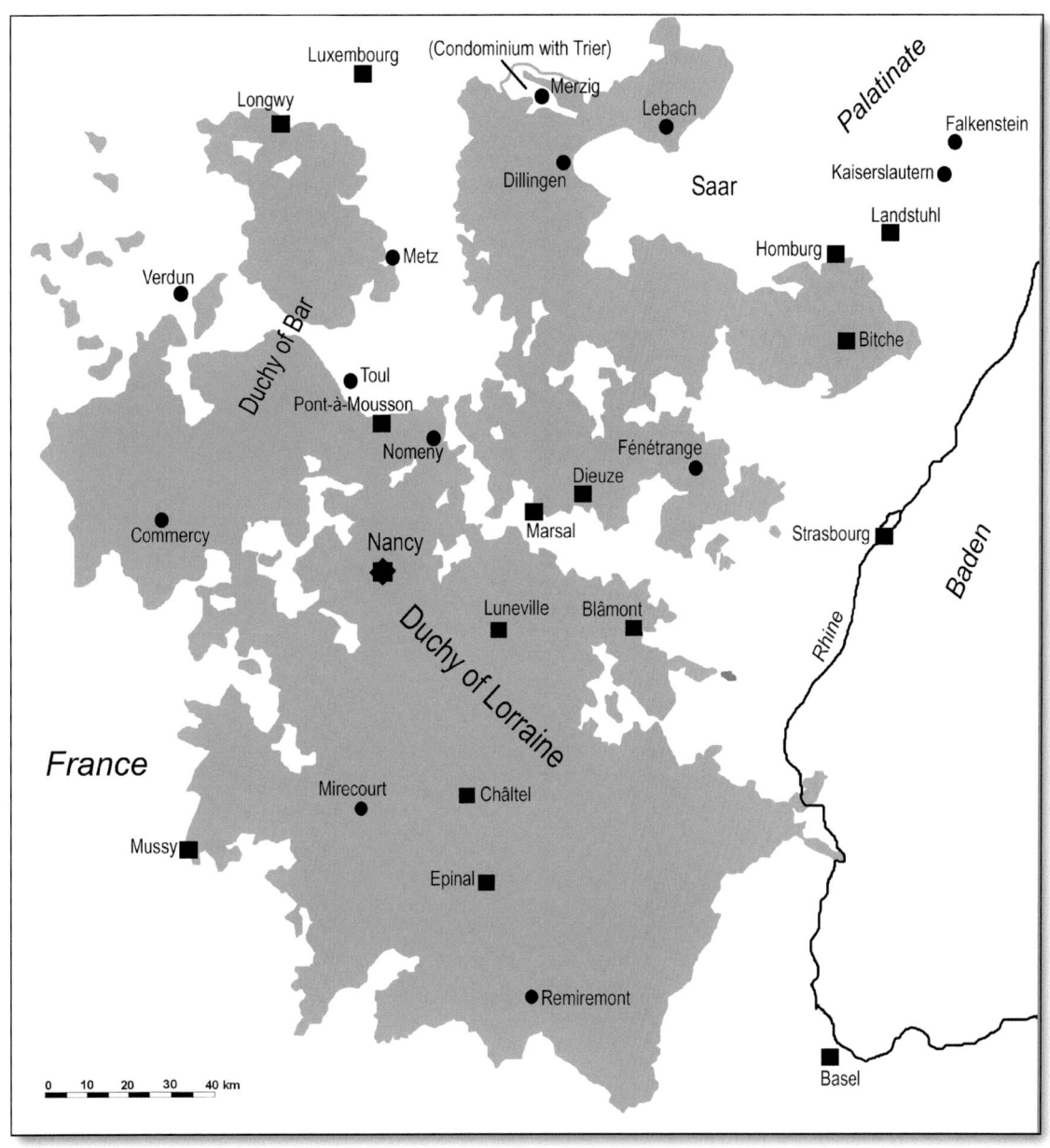

Duchy of Lorraine

In the last quarter of the seventeenth century, Lorraine geopolitical trajectory was similar to that of other German principalities. The European political scenario offered Lorraine the chance to exploit its own 'military' to emerge as a regional power, but notwithstanding this goal failed, the attempt developed along a predictable but at the same time completely original path. Like other buffer states, Lorraine was vulnerable to external invasions and thus could not escape involvement in international affairs. This inherent weakness did not keep larger rivals out of its affairs and territories. Though in the first half of the seventeenth century, Lorraine emerged as a territory capable of fielding 18,000–20,000 professional soldiers, although the average strength was usually closer to 5,000.[3] By the 1630s the economy was affected by several crises, including the French occupation. In addition, there was an epidemic of plague in 1635, and as a consequence, Lorraine lost nearly half of its pre-war population.[4]

## Between France and Empire.

KAREL, Hartogh van Lotharingen.

Although the last quarter of the century witnessed a gradual recovery, by 1654, the Duchy ceased to be a significant military actor. This loss of power resulted in a problematic independence that transformed Lorraine into a satellite of France. However, this goal, carefully aimed at since the age of Richelieu, was achieved with great difficulties, because of the resistance of Duke Charles IV (r. 1624–1675).

Duke Charles IV of Lorraine in a print dating to the 1670s. (author's archive)
Contemporaries left an ambivalent portrait of Charles IV's personality. If some were fascinated by the Duke's reckless temperament, others were scandalised by his behaviour, which increased the perplexity of the contemporaries. If some of his extravagances could be forgiven, others made him disliked. According to his contemporaries, Charles IV's temperament was dominated by a turbulence which was considered excessive even in a boy, and thus absolutely intolerable in a mature man. The Duke's harsh and biting irony did not attract the sympathy of his Spanish allies. In this respect, Fuensaldagne declared that 'the sarcasm, the piquant and venomous words (of Charles IV), pained and wounded the hearts of his interlocutors.'

---

3   Peter H. Wilson, *German Armies. War and German Politics, 1648–1806* (London: UCL Press, 1998), p.29.
4   Guy Cabourdin, *Le Repeuplement en Lorraine apres la Guerre de Trente Ans* (Paris: France Gen Web, 2000), p.2.

A strident Catholic like his countrymen, and more a warrior than a statesman, the Duke actively opposed French policies during the Thirty Years' War. The choice of side as an ally of the Habsburgs did not protect his domains from the French occupations and loss of territories.[5] To the great disappointment of Charles IV, the Congress of Westphalia excluded Lorraine from the peace treaties and forced the Duke, abandoned by the Emperor, to side with Spain, which continued the war against France. Putting his wealth at stake, Charles IV was able to gather a strong army, with approximately 11,000 professional soldiers in 1652.[6] In the next years, he remained an enemy of France and in the 1650s offered his support to the *Fronde* against Mazarin. He also managed to confirm himself as an effective military entrepreneur. In 1652, he signed an agreement with the Duke of Pfalz-Neuburg for the hiring of 5,000 men to face Brandenburg's claims over Jülich.[7]

At the end of the 1653, Charles IV was back in possession of some of the Lorraine territories, but serious problems emerged concerning the allocation of winter quarters. The Spanish Low Countries refused to host the Duke's troops and every other solution seemed impracticable as the alternatives offered few resources. In early 1654, Charles IV went to Liège to negotiate with the Prince-Bishop about the quartering of soldiers in the country, but had to surrender the quarters to Condé's army. Consequently, in February, the Lorraine troops were scattered over a large area to the great complaints of the Duke. The situation became even more unfavourable on 16 February, when the Duke, in Brussels for a war council, was arrested by the Spanish who immediately transferred him to Antwerp, and from there took him to Spain, where he remained as a prisoner until 1655.

---

5  In 1632, Duke Charles IV signed the Treaty of Liverdun, that obliged him to consign Clermont, which was definitely annexed by France in 1641 with the Treaty of Saint-Germain-en-Laye. The agreement opened a period known as 'the Short Peace' between Lorraine and France. The treaty contained political and military clauses obliging the Duke to support France's plans. In particular, Charles IV was 'to remain inviolably bound to the interests of the French crown' and to sever all relations with the House of Austria and other European nations both in time of war and peace. In 1632, the Duke managed to recover his states, but with the reservation of the 'pledge of faith and homage' that left France in possession of all the major towns, fortresses, including Nancy, Marsal and Dun, and other strategically important places for the duration of the war. As far as military aspects were concerned, Charles IV undertook to give free access to French troops in transit through Lorraine, and to cede part of the troops he had in his service. The Duke regained his possessions and fortresses by his own troops, estimated at between 4,000 and 6,000 men. As in every peace treaty of this age, this one also contained secret articles, the most important of which stipulated that at the end of the war between France and Spain, the fortifications of Nancy would be demolished, and that the Duke, whenever he was not on campaign with the French troops, could not reside in the Palace of Luneville, considered too close to Nancy. After a year, the peace was broken and in the summer of 1642 French troops invaded Lorraine again, forcing Charles IV into exile. New agreements for a truce were signed in October 1642 at Viviers and Dieuze, which returned Lorraine to the situation existing before 1641. The Duke and his troops found asylum in the Imperial Army, participating in campaigns until 1648. See also, Robert Parisot, *Histoire de Lorraine (Duché de Lorraine, Duché de Bar, Trois-Évêchés)*, (Paris, 1919–1924), vol. II (1552–1789), tome II, pp.138–139.

6  Jean-Charles Fulaine, *Le Duc Charles IV de Lorraine et sonAarmée* (Metz: Editions Serpenoise, 1997), p.160.

7  Galeazzo Gualdo Priorato, Relatione *degli Stati del Serenissimo Filippo Guglielmo Duca di Juliers, Neuburg ecc.* (Cologne, 1668), p.5.

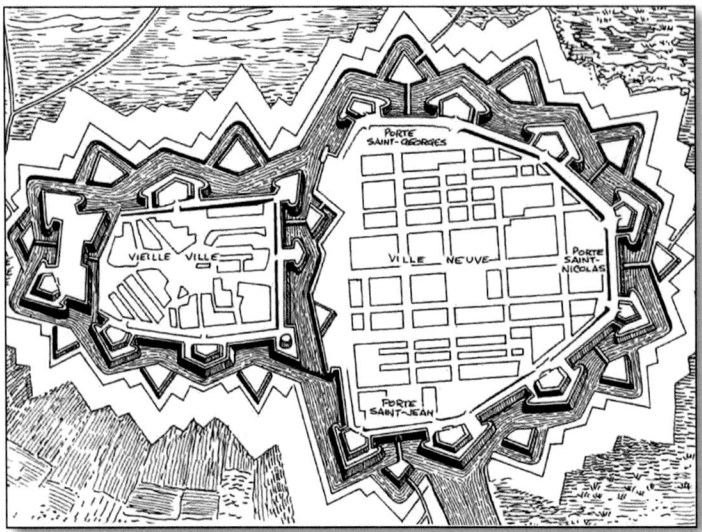

Plan of Nancy showing the fortifications before their destruction in 1670 by the French under Vauban. (author's collection)
Although in 1641 Charles IV realised that Lorraine occupied a secondary position in the plans of the allies and that he himself was a pawn in the hands of the Imperialists and the Spaniards to exclusively support their interests, he was also aware that little good could be expected from supporting France. As expected, this stance resulted in French occupation of Lorraine and ducal exile. Excepting the 1660s, the French invaded Lorraine three times from 1634 to 1697.

The event caused a great sensation across Europe, but to the most attentive observers it seemed a natural consequence of the Duke's actions.[8] Increasingly unwilling to go along with Charles IV's bold plans, and compelled by the need to find an exit strategy from the war against France, the Spanish had decided to rid themselves of an ally considered more of a problem than a resource. For his part, Charles IV lost Madrid's support with his outrageous behaviour too. Resentful of the lack of respect they felt was due to their prestige, the Spanish Governor and ministers held the Duke's excesses in contempt, accusing him of bigamy and other vices. Moreover, his manoeuvres with neighbouring states to bargain for recruits and subsidies, and his stubborn refusal to follow any policy other than his own, alienated any residual support. The issue concerning winter quarters for his troops had been the source of other disagreements. Charles IV declared that his men were forced to eat dead dogs and horses; at the height of this problem, he informed his Spanish allies that the soldiers had boiled the bodies of two elderly nuns in order to feed themselves.[9]

Thinking they had solved the problem by arresting the Duke, the Spanish triggered an even worse crisis. From captivity, the Duke managed to send a message to his officers, in which he expressed his resentment and indicated the action to be taken:

> Let it never be said in the world that I am held back from my service because of traitors and rascals …. You have the most favourable opportunity to make it clear to everyone who I am. Do not fear that I may be killed, and put the whole country (of the Spaniards) to the sword![10]

---

8  Mazarin expressed 'great concern' over the Duke's arrest and remarked that 'the incident that occurred to Monsieur de Lorraine is unprecedented'; Jean-Charles Fulaine, *Le Duc Charles IV de Lorraine et son Armée* (Metz: Editions Serpenoise, 1997), p.162.

9  Jean-Charles Fulaine, *Le Duc Charles IV de Lorraine et son Armée* (Metz: Editions Serpenoise, 1997), p.163.

10  Robert Parisot, *Histoire de Lorraine (Duché de Lorraine, Duché de Bar, Trois-Évêchés)*, (Paris, 1919–1924), tome II (1552–1789), p.79. According to some historians, Ligniville denied having received the letter containing the order, however the tone and words seem to belong to Duke

# THE DUCHY OF LORRAINE

However, the dispersion of the soldiers into winter quarters far from each other and the inaction of the Lorrainer commander, Philippe Emmanuel de Mazz, did not allow the troops to assemble to demand the release of the Duke.

On 25 February 1654, Archduke Leopold of Habsburg, who wanted to keep the services of the Lorraine troops, sent a letter inviting all the senior officers and colonels of the Lorrainer army to join the Spanish service,[11] and asked Nicolas-François de Vaudemont, bastard brother of Charles IV, to take command of the army. Nicolas-François realised that he did not have the same influence over the troops as Charles IV and hesitated to take command.

The uncertainty regarding orders and the lack of resources favoured desertion. Meanwhile, from his captivity, Charles IV granted full powers to his wife Nicole, urging her to order the troops to abandon the Spanish, while his brother finally ended his hesitation and was ordered to remain. The chaos within the army was further increased when it became known that Charles IV was negotiating with the King of Spain for his release in exchange for maintaining the alliance. In May 1654, Nicolas-François left Vienna to join the troops, but soon realised their poor state. Furthermore, he met resistance from the Spanish ministers and could not come to an agreement for the troops' maintenance. The conflict fuelled Archduke Leopold's mistrust for the Lorraine family, to the point that even Nicolas-François was suspected of passing intelligence to France.[12]

In the summer of 1650, the Lorrainer Commander-in-Chief, Philippe Emmanuel de Ligniville, managed to re-take several fortresses, but on 9 October he was defeated by La Ferté at Lignières-sur-Aire. This setback curbed the ambitions of Charles IV, who had remained in Brussels throughout this period waiting for a triumphant return to his Duchy. The subsequent campaigns saw both sides engage in hampering the opponent's progress according to the doctrines of warfare of the seventeenth century.

Against this desolating scenario, the remaining Lorrainer troops continued to serve with the Spaniards in the campaigns of 1654 and 1655. In 1654, the Lorrainer troops numbered 1,500 cavalry and 3,500 infantry 'in good state' not including a further 500 men distributed in the forts still under Lorrainer control.[13] The most important action in which they participated was the siege of Lens, from 3 July to 25 August 1654, which ended in a disastrous retreat. In December 1654, two entire infantry regiments deserted together with

---

Charles IV. Jean-Charles Fulaine, *Le Duc Charles IV de Lorraine et son Armée* (Metz: Editions Serpenoise, 1997), p.162

11  Ferdinand Des Robert, *Charles IV et Mazarin (1643–1668) d'aprés des documents inédits* (Paris: 1890), p.698.

12  Jean-Charles Fulaine, *Le Duc Charles IV de Lorraine et son Armée* (Metz: Editions Serpenoise, 1997), p.165.

13  Ferdinand Des Robert, *Charles IV Et Mazarin (1643–1661): d'Après des Documents Inédits Tirés des Archives du Ministère des Affaires Étrangères des Archives de la Maison de Ligniville* (Nancy, 1899), p.709.

Nicolas-François de Lorraine (1609–1670), also known as Nicolas II, was briefly Duke of Lorraine and duke of Bar for a few months in 1634, spanning the time between the abdication of his older half-brother and his own resignation.

their officers, and entered the service of France.[14] Despite these setbacks, in spring 1655 the Lorrainer Army numbered 5,054 horse and 3,900 foot.[15] The campaign of 1655 was marked by a series of Spanish defeats, which included the loss of some strongholds in Lorraine. Furthermore, the poor treatment received from the Spaniards caused new complaints among the troops, resulting in a high rate of desertion.[16]

In early September 1655, two envoys from Lorraine arrived in Madrid to demand the release of Charles IV. The negotiations were rather confused and met with little success. Only after further secret negotiations, directly conducted by the Duke, was an agreement reached. On 9 October, the treaty was signed, which stipulated that the Lorraine troops were to pass into the service of Spain, with the exception of a small corps that would continue to serve in the Ducal army. This was not the Duke's first sleight of hand with treaties: gaining an immediate advantage in exchange for giving up an asset, which he intended to use again later when the timing was more favourable. However, bringing his army under Spanish control was not to his liking, nor was it for other senior commanders.

Despite the explicit act of swearing an oath to the King of Spain by the Lorraine officers and soldiers, on 12 November 1655, four cavalry regiments, 1,200 men in all, deserted together with their General, the Marquis d'Haracourt – the desertion caused Nicolas-François to resign command of the army. At the same time, Charles IV began to prepare his coup. The abandonment of the alliance with Spain had been carefully prepared and it was just a matter of waiting for the right moment. The opportunity was offered by the Spaniards, who planned the siege of Condé in November 1655. For the operation, the Lorrainers were to form the vanguard. On 19 November, moving from their quarters northeast of Charleroi, Ligniville, who had been in command again for a week, gathered his troops without arousing the slightest suspicion and marched on Condé. In the afternoon, the columns abruptly changed direction and headed for Landrecies, the nearest French

---

14   Robert Parisot, *Histoire de Lorraine (Duché de Lorraine, duché de Bar, Trois-Évêchés)*, (Paris, 1919–1924), tome II (1552–1789), p.79.

15   Jean-Charles Fulaine, *Le Duc Charles IV de Lorraine et son Armée* (Metz: Editions Serpenoise, 1997), p.169.

16   'The colonels tried to get the soldiers to return to their companies, since some regiments consisted almost exclusively of officers and NCOs. The soldiers protested that if they had stayed in places suitable for Christians they would have endured the hardships better, but since they had been treated like animals, they refused to return.' Jean-Charles Fulaine, *Le Duc Charles IV de Lorraine et son Armée* (Metz: Editions Serpenoise, 1997), .168.

place, which they reached after a three-day and three-night march through forests, having crossed the River Sambre on improvised barges.

## L'Armée de Lorraine

Throughout these years, Charles IV had resorted to every expedient to keep his army at a considerable strength level, spending considerable resource in enlisting soldiers in Germany, Flanders and in the Lorraine territories still under his control. The bulk of his army included foreign and native professional regiments under veteran commanders. On 11 December 1655, after their arrival in Paris, the troops were mustered. They comprised the *Maison Militaire* with two companies of the *Gardes du Corps* and the company of the *Chevaux-Lègers*, 224 men in all, who tactically formed one squadron. 12 cavalry regiments and 6 infantry regiments were formed from 72 cavalry companies and by 89 infantry companies. Overall, the number of professional soldiers still in the Duke's service was around 6,000 men.[17]

The cavalry regiments fielded variously 5, 6 or 7 companies, but with many soldiers without horses. By contrast, the infantry fielded regiments of 4, 5 and even 15 companies. Compared to six months before, the army had been reduced to less than half. In detail, there were 18 colonels, 144 captains, 164 lieutenants and ensigns, 255 sergeants, and 2,947 infantrymen and cavalrymen; the muster also included 182 valets. The infantry regiments fielded between 170 and 403 men; the cavalry had a similar incomplete strength, with regiments from 112 to 225 men.[18] Two-thirds of the cavalry companies comprised less than 20 men, while the establishment number would have been 100 rank and file.[19] With regard to nationality, the information is imprecise and can only be accurate with regard to officers. The muster of Paris shows that 35.5 percent came from Lorraine.[20]

The field army was increased with the cavalry that had deserted in November, but two cavalry regiments entered French service. Finally, there were the troops quartered in the fortresses in northern Lorraine, which 'on paper' numbered five cavalry and five infantry regiments. The cavalry was quartered at Nancy and Châtel, while the infantry formed garrisons in Mussy, Dieuze, Landstuhl, Homburg and Bitche. However, the overall number was almost insignificant. Sources record that 37 infantry companies had less than 10 men, and some had only a single soldier; the situation in the cavalry

---

17  Jean-Charles Fulaine, *Le Duc Charles IV de Lorraine et son Armée* (Metz: Editions Serpenoise, 1997), p.172.
18  Jean-Charles Fulaine, *Le Duc Charles IV de Lorraine et son Armée* (Metz: Editions Serpenoise, 1997), p.169.
19  Jean-Charles Fulaine, *Le Duc Charles IV de Lorraine et son Armée* (Metz: Editions Serpenoise, 1997), p.171. Officers and NCOs accounted for 12.5 percent of the total; a fact that prompted the field commanders to urge the colonels to recruit the soldiers missing from their regiments.
20  Jean-Charles Fulaine, *Le Duc Charles IV de Lorraine et son Armée* (Metz: Editions Serpenoise, 1997), p.170.

was no better, fielding from 8 to 54 troopers per company.[21] Numerically, the Lorraine Army represented a modest contribution, but Mazarin and his generals agreed that overall these were excellent troops commanded by veteran officers. In the words of the Cardinal: 'even butts make light like new candles when lit!'[22]

In 1656, the Lorraine troops took part in the campaigns alongside the French under Turenne. They fought at Valenciennes, then in 1657 at Montmédy and finally in 1658, they formed the left wing at the decisive Battle of the Dunes, receiving praise from the French commander. The next year, with the Peace of the Pyrenees, France began to demobilise its army. The treaty also sealed the destiny of the Lorraine troops, who were also dismissed. However, the alliance with France proved no less problematic for Charles IV who, freed from Spanish captivity, tried to negotiate with Mazarin for the restitution of the Lorraine territories still under French control. In 1660, Charles IV still kept 1,500 professional soldiers in his service, and this contingent, despite its modest size, represented one of the main arguments in the diplomacy of the two states, first with Mazarin, and later, after the Cardinal's death, with the young and no less intransigent Louis XIV.[23] On 18 February 1661, Charles IV obtained a modest satisfaction of his demands with the Treaty of Vincennes, by which he regained possession of the Duchy of Bar, in exchange for the restitution of the Rhine territories to the Count of Nassau-Saarbrücken. Despite this success, the treaty contained an article damaging the Duke's aspirations. In return for the concessions granted, Paris demanded the demobilisation of all professional troops. Furthermore, some border corrections were agreed with France, including the free passage through the territory of the three Bishoprics of Metz, Toul and Verdun. This guaranteed to France a considerable strategic achievement, since the concessions and the free military passage through the Bishoprics allowed Louis XIV to keep Lorraine in fear, and to intercept any aid coming from Germany.[24]

After many vicissitudes, battles, years of exile and imprisonment, Charles IV was once again the hostage of the powers with which his state shared increasingly insecure borders. Moreover, the Duke's unstable character had unfortunate consequences for the Duchy. After the signing of the Peace of the Pyrenees and the return of the Lorraine provinces to their rightful ruler, his absolutist tendencies turned the nobility against him. He maintained the power and refused to re-establish the assizes of the nobility; nevertheless,

---

21  Jean-Charles Fulaine, *Le Duc Charles IV de Lorraine et son Armée* (Metz: Editions Serpenoise, 1997), p.171.
22  Ferdinand Des Robert, *Charles IV Et Mazarin (1643–1661): d'Après des Documents Inédits Tirés des Archives du Ministère des Affaires Étrangères des Archives de la Maison de Ligniville* (Nancy, 1899), p.477.
23  Robert Parisot, *Histoire de Lorraine (Duché de Lorraine, Duché de Bar, Trois-Évêchés)*, (Paris, 1919–1924), tome II (1552–1789), p.82.
24  French free passage of the *Chemin des Évêchés* (the route of the Bishoprics) runs into the Lorraine territories trough Maizeray, Marcheville, Harville, Labeauville, Malatour, Gorze to Verdun, and the routes through Solgne, Moncheux, Delme, Gremecey, Chambray, Burthécourt, Moyenvic, Leey, Donnelay, Ormange, Azoudange, Gonfrexange, Heming, Sarrebourg, Niderviller, Garrebourg, Kourtzerode, Phalsbourg to Metz.

it was the question of succession that complicated everything, as Charles IV would willingly have designated as his heir a son born from his affair with Beatrice de Cusance, but who was illegitimate.[25]

Because of this unfavourable scenario, the Duke was forced to undertake a secret military policy for supporting the difficult diplomatic action that awaited him. This could be achieved exploiting the economic resources of his domain, but in 1662, Lorraine did not have an administrative body capable of collecting taxes and managing the fiscal policy of the state. During the period of his imprisonment, the Spanish had seized all the annuities of the Lorraine territories still in the Duke's possession, returning only part of them after the Peace of the Pyrenees.[26] In the immediate future, there would be no other way to maintain an army than to resort to the Duke's personal funds.

Special attention was paid by the Duke to his mounted Horse Guards, which had faithfully followed him through the dramatic years of exile, and they were the only troops whom he could retain in his service. However, the Lorraine Guards were not simple horsemen who performed escort duties, but actually an elite military corps that had participated on the campaigns as a true fighting unit. The Duke held the command of the whole Horse Guards as titular captain. In 1664, the *Maison Militaire* still included the *Gardes du Corps* and the *Chevaux-Légers*. These units were the most ancient corps of the Lorraine Army, being established in 1624 and 1627. The actual strength of the Horse Guards is difficult to establish, as many of the members of the aristocracy held honorary positions in the companies. Also, unfortunately, only a few muster roles are known, and only from the court's registers can the number of members be determined with any accuracy. Between 1660 and

Portrait of Charles V of Lorraine in his youth, after an engraving by Robert Nanteuil (Print Collection of the Metropolitan Museum of Art, Washington, DC). By 1659, the prince had been designated as successor to the title of Duke by his uncle Charles IV. However, throughout this period, Charles IV returned to Lorraine only once, and then only for a few days, preferring to reside in Paris, where he continued his libertine lifestyle. His scandalous conduct did not attract much attention in Lorraine, but at the end of April 1662, bad news arrived about the conclusion of the Treaty of Bar-le-Duc, by which Charles IV ceded the Duchy to France after his death. The Duke's unexpected decision met with strong resistance in Lorraine. Although Charles IV had preserved the rights of 'princes by blood' for his family, his princely relatives opposed the ratification of the treaty, forcing the Duke to reject it and to recognise his nephew, currently serving in the Imperial Army, as his heir and successor and the future Charles V. The immediate effect was the Duke's flight from Paris and his return home in May 1662, after 33 years of exile. Louis XIV took note of his royal cousin's volte-face, but for the young monarch the Lorraine question still remained open.

---

25  Jean Bérenger, 'Un texte inédit de Lisola concernent l'Affaire de Lorraine (1670)' in *Revue Semestrelle de Linguistique et Littératures Romanes*, vol. V, nos 1–2 (2009, Institut d'études romanes de la Faculté des Lettres de l'Université de Bohême du Sud, České Budějovice), p.45. The legitimate heir was his nephew Charles, son of Duke Nicholas Francis. This is why Charles IV at one point wanted to cede Lorraine to France and integrate the House of Lorraine into the Royal Family by signing the Treaty of Montmartre on 6 February 1662. Charles IV was supported by the Guise family, who saw this as a way of consolidating their claim of succession to the French throne.

26  200,000 *pistoles* in gem stones; Jean-Charles Fulaine, *Le Duc Charles IV de Lorraine et son Armée* (Metz: Editions Serpenoise, 1997), p.181.

1664, the number of the 'registered' Guards was 132, but only 10 actually belonged to the *Gardes du Corps* and another 10 to the *Chevaux-Légers*.[27] The next year, the average strength climbed to 66 horsemen for each company of the *Gardes du Corps*. These comprised staff with 1 *capitaine-lieutenant*, 1 *sous-lieutenant*, and 1 *porte étendard*. An undetermined number of lance corporals and *maréchal des logis* completed the ranking personnel of the companies, which maintained the same strength. In 1664, the first company was under the orders of Nicolas de Baillivy, while the Baron de Chauviray commanded the other. In 1666, 1667 and 1669, the total strength varied from 192 to 193 to 180 guards respectively.[28]

The *Chevaux-Légers* also formed two companies. Their organisation was similar to the *Gardes du Corps*, but the overall strength was lower. Between 1664 and 1669, there were 72 men in the first company and 49 in the second, plus another 60 men who were not assigned to either company, and probably were just 'posts of honour'. In 1664, the *capitaine-lieutenant* of the first company was Paul des Armoises d'Alnoy, Governor of Nomeny; the second company was commanded by Jean-Philippe du Plessy, Governor of Dieuze and formerly *obrist* of a cavalry regiment. From only 55 men in 1655, the *Chevaux-Lègers* increased to 212 in 1669.[29] Although the *Gardes du Corps* were the oldest specialist life guard, the *Chevaux-Légers* held the position of honour on the field, and during escort duty.

The third and last mounted unit of the *Maison* were the *Mousquetaires*, whose origin dated back to the 1660s. In 1664, a single company is mentioned for the first time, but little is known about their strength and only the organisation is summarised at least for the officers.[30] The company had its own *capitaine-lieutenant*, *Obrist* Bellerose, who had under him 1 *sous-lieutenant*, 1 *enseigne*, 1 *maréchal des logis* and 1 *brigadier*. In 1665, the *Mousquetaires* were about 60 men in all, but fluctuated between 59 and 61 in the following years. Like the French *Maison du Roi*, the *Maison* of Lorraine formed a field 'brigade', of 400–450 horsemen.

For the Foot Guards, Charles IV had a company of Swiss. Originally, the company was quartered at Épinal, but in 1669 it was transferred to Plombières with the exception of a picket which remained at Épinal. At this date, the company comprised 1 *capitaine*, Emmanuel Zörnlin, 1 *lieutenant*, 1 *enseigne*, 1 *intendant*, 2 *sergeants*, 1 *tambour*, 1 *fifre*, 1 *prévôt*, 3 *caporals* and 97 guards.[31] In the following years, the company is referred as the *cent-suisses*, and like their countrymen in French service, performed as palace guards at the duke's residences. In the early 1660s, these units represented

---

27 Jean-Charles Fulaine, *Le Duc Charles IV de Lorraine et son Armée* (Metz: Editions Serpenoise, 1997), p.191.
28 Jean-Charles Fulaine, *Le Duc Charles IV de Lorraine et son Armée* (Metz: Editions Serpenoise, 1997), p.192.
29 Jean-Charles Fulaine, *Le Duc Charles IV de Lorraine et son Armée* (Metz: Editions Serpenoise, 1997), p.194.
30 Jean-Charles Fulaine, *Le Duc Charles IV de Lorraine et son Armée* (Metz: Editions Serpenoise, 1997), p.195.
31 Jean-Charles Fulaine, *Le Duc Charles IV de Lorraine et son Armée* (Metz: Editions Serpenoise, 1997), p.193.

approximately a third of the whole Lorraine 'military', which still included 15 cavalry regiments and 3 infantry regiements of unequal strength, with approximately 1,300 to 1,500 men in all. This little force had 22 colonels, who served as regiments commanders as well as governors of the fortresses and garrisons.[32]

New military confrontation did not take long to appear. One of the articles of the 1662 treaty between Charles IV and Louis XIV included the ceding of Marsal and Nomeny to France, but in 1663 both places were still in the duke's possession. Realising that this loss further weakened the autonomy of his state, Charles IV tried to procrastinate the handing over by resorting to all sorts of expedients. On the other hand, Louis XIV was perfectly aware that the possession of Marsal and Nomeny represented another piece in the jigsaw he was putting together to keep Lorraine under control.[33] As occurred on other occasions, Charles IV tried to go back on his word, but by 1663,

The surrender of Marsal on 1 September 1663, in a print after a tapestry at Versailles. (author's collection)
The tapestry shows a group of Lorrainer officers wearing red, yellow and buff coats. The second officer from the left bowing to Louis XIV wears a red coat laced and lined with yellow, which could be the one issued to the *Gardes du Corps*. Louis XIV personally directed the siege of Marsal, which opened on 17 August. After this episode, resentment against France increased, and in 1664, some Lorrainer officers quartered in Mainz, fired on the French residence, risking opening a new crisis in relations between Louis XIV and Charles IV.

---

32  Jean-Charles Fulaine, *Le Duc Charles IV de Lorraine et son Armée* (Metz: Editions Serpenoise, 1997), p.199. The officer corps also included 30 captains, 7 lieutenants, 3 ensigns and further 4 with unspecified rank; 57 officers were natives of Lorraine and 9 were foreigners.

33  In this regard, Louis XIV wrote: 'The situation of Lorraine did not allow me to doubt that it would not be very advantageous for me to be its master, and made me wish for it'; cited in Philip McCluskey, 'From Regime Change to Réunion: Louis XIV's Quest for Legitimacy in Lorraine,

the international scenario was becoming unfavourable for him. Spain was engaged against Portugal, while the Emperor was fighting the Ottomans in Hungary, and this allowed Louis XIV to plan a military operation to re-establish his 'grandeur' and 'dignity' against the recalcitrant Duke of Lorraine, and on 17 August 1663, French troops blockaded Marsal. From the headquarters established at Metz, Louis XIV joined his troops on 31 August, just one day before the surrender of the garrison and Charles IV's acceptance of a new agreement. With the Treaty of Nomeny, Lorraine ceded this latter city as well as Marsal to France, but the Duke obtained the cancellation of some clauses of the old 1662 treaty, albeit only by way of verbal assurance from Louis XIV.

After the surrender of Marsal, only a few fortresses worthy of the name remained under the Duke's control. The first in order of size was Bitche, located in the north near the German border and capable of housing a large garrison. In 1663, Bitche was under the command of one of the most experienced Lorrainer veteran commanders, Baron François de Romécourt. The other major forts, from northwest to southeast, were Longwy, Épinal, Châtel, Pont-à-Mousson, Homburg and Landstuhl. Other small places completed the weak defence of Lorraine.[34] These forts housed garrisons but were mostly without modern artillery. With the exception of three culverins, all the Lorraine artillery had been transported to Metz and taken over by the French during the war against Spain.

In 1663, the ranks of *Grand Maitre* and *Capitaine General* of the artillery still existed, although these were entirely honorary charges. The command was held by Jean-Philippe de Savigny-Bey, Baron of Ferrières, who was entrusted with the task of rebuilding the artillery.[35] By 1664, arsenals for the manufacture and maintenance of cannon, and stores for ammunition were established in each fortress. However, Savigny's work was abruptly interrupted in December 1665, when, due to embezzlement, he was exiled from the Duchy and replaced by the Baron de Saffre-d'Haussonville, Antoine de Moisy de Cléron, an opponent of the *Grand Maitre*, who had returned to the Duke's good graces in 1661. The artillery staff also included a lieutenant, a paymaster, and a *concierge*, but only the latter is reported as still existing between 1667 and 1668.[36]

The regulations established in July 1664 for gunners and artillery personnel testify to the growth in activity.[37] In the following years, the arsenals registered an increase of the personnel, with two or three master

---

1670–97' in *The English Historical Review*, vol. 126, no.523 (Oxford: Oxford University Press, December 2011), p.1388.

34 The other forts were Bar-le-Duc, Vaudrevange, and Mussy.

35 Jean-Charles Fulaine, *Le Duc Charles IV de Lorraine et son Armée* (Metz: Editions Serpenoise, 1997), p.189.

36 Jean-Charles Fulaine, *Le Duc Charles IV de Lorraine et son Armée* (Metz: Editions Serpenoise, 1997), p.189; in place of the other two officers there is a judge delegate and a *greffier* (clerk).

37 'the regulation marked a real turning point in the Lorraine military. The part dealing with *maistrez et compagnons, canoniers, faiseurs de canons, arquebusiers, et monterurs d'armes* comprises 50 articles that covered the rules of service, those of the profession and those of the artillery corps.' Jean-Charles Fulaine, *Le Duc Charles IV de Lorraine et son Armée* (Metz: Editions Serpenoise, 1997), p.191.

foundry-men, and one or three powder masters; however, the production of weapons only concentrated on artillery, while no manufactories in Lorraine produced cavalry or infantry firearms, which continued to be purchased in Liège. The number of artillerymen climbed to 14 in 1668.[38] In 1664, the Duke also appointed eight commissioners, including three *commissaires des salpêtres*; the latter increased to eight in 1667, while at the same time the number of commissioners fell to only one.

The reconstitution of the army was accompanied by the creation of new offices dealing with military justice. On his return to Lorraine, Charles IV appointed the *maréchaussée* with the task of managing the matter that had until then been handled by the provosts in the regiments or the captains in the companies. The office was intended to speed up the trials of military personnel, but the most serious cases involving high-ranking officers continued to be handled by the Commander-in-Chief on behalf of the Duke. The patent of 12 May 1661 marked the start of the office's activities, which was initially entrusted to two provost marshals. The *maréchaussée* was organised as a military company with its own commanders and lieutenants, non-commissioned officers and assistant staff.[39]

In great secrecy, and despite diplomatic setbacks, Charles IV embarked on a policy of military reinforcement despite the agreements made with France. In February 1663, using the insubordination of the Count of Aspremont as a pretext, the Duke complained that he needed to maintain his own professional army. Unfortunately, this was an argument, insufficient to change the agreements and therefore, other possibilities had to be exploited, at least to an extent that would not disturb his Royal cousin. Like the other Princes of the Empire, Charles IV could exploit his troops commanded by veteran officers to turn them into useful political and economic instruments and make them available to the highest bidder. The twofold result of this trade produced a third, as the action would keep the troops in a state of efficiency and favoured the selection of the best men. Moreover, the commitment signed with the Princes would allow the Duke to postpone the disbandment of the army until a date yet to be defined.

A first opportunity materialised in the autumn of 1663, when the Duke received an envoy from the Prince-Archbishop Elector of Mainz, Johann Philip von Schönborn, who had come to Nancy to negotiate the hire of troops. Schönborn had decided to intervene *manu militari* against the town of Erfurt, which refused obedience to him and claimed the title of Free Imperial City. The affair reverberated throughout the courts of Germany, and the Elector gained support from both the Emperor and the King of France, an ally in the Rhenish League. Confident that he could take advantage of this event, at the end of November 1664 Charles IV agreed with Schönborn to provide soldiers. The negotiations and the preparations for the setting up of this contingent provide an interesting insight into the economic dynamics

---

38  Jean-Charles Fulaine, *Le Duc Charles IV de Lorraine et son Armée* (Metz: Editions Serpenoise, 1997), p.190.
39  Jean-Charles Fulaine, *Le Duc Charles IV de Lorraine et son Armée* (Metz: Editions Serpenoise, 1997), p.197.

of this type of agreement. The Elector was to pay the amount to the Duke in advance and the latter was to pay half of the wages, while the other half was to be paid by the municipalities. In this way, Charles IV ensured himself a considerable profit. For during the time it took to assemble the troops, accommodation was still paid by the Duke's subjects, who had to provide the barracks for the private soldiers, and their homes for NCOs and officers.

The troops began to gather in Nancy and Luneville. Between December and January, the Duke issued two *Règlements* for the subsistence of his troops on campaign; one concerning the cavalry of the life guard, and the other for professional soldiers. The daily pay for the private soldiers was half in cash and the remainder had to be provided in kind.[40] The horses could be housed in the Duke's stables, if these were present at the mustering locations. On 10 February 1664, the Duke ordered the cavalry destined for Erfurt to move from Luneville to Dieuze, near the border with the Palatinate, and to await new orders. Charles-Henry de Lorraine, Prince of Vaudemont was appointed as Commander-in-Chief.

Charles-Henry de Lorraine-Vaudemont (1649–1723) in a print dating to the 1680. (Public domain). Charles-Henry was the third, but only surviving, son born from the second marriage of Charles IV of Lorraine; there were no children from his first marriage. This second marriage was annulled by the Pope due to the fact that the separation of the Duke from his first wife, Nicoletta of Lorraine, was not accepted by the Holy See. For this reason, Charles-Henry was not entitled to the title of Duke. After serving in the Lorraine Army, in 1670, he entered the service of Spain as colonel proprietor of a cavalry and an infantry regiment. He served in the War of The League of Augsburg in Flanders under William III of England, and in 1698 became Governor of Milan.

The preparation of the contingent must have been meticulous and accurate, and this caused a considerable delay, since by the mid of August the troops were still in Lorraine. Negotiations between the Duke and the Elector also contributed to this delay, but finally both agreed to a contingent of 400 horse and 480 foot. The cavalry formed a regiment of 300 horse with five companies of 60 *maitres*, plus an independent company of 100 horse. Three infantry companies of 50 men, combined with eight others formed with soldiers from the garrisons completed the contingent destined for Erfurt. Finally, these troops left Lorraine in September 1664 and the body consisted of 396 horse and 550 foot.[41] Although sources do not indicate it, it is probable that a detachment from the *Maison Lorraine* joined the contingent on campaign.

The siege of Erfurt ended on 15 October 1664 with the surrender of the city. At the end of the campaign, the Lorrainer troops did not return home, but took winter quarters in the Electorate of Mainz. The reason for this delayed return is unclear, but in the end it was functional for the plans of Charles IV, who was involved in the *Wildfang* War against the Palatinate in the following

---

40 'a *livre* and a half of bread; the same ration of meat, a mug of beer, while horses were required to have 15 *livres* of hay, 3 *picotins* of oats and 4 *livres* of straw for the stable.' Jean-Charles Fulaine, *Le Duc Charles IV de Lorraine et son Armée* (Metz: Editions Serpenoise, 1997), p.201.

41 Jean-Charles Fulaine, *Le Duc Charles IV de Lorraine et son Armée* (Metz: Editions Serpenoise, 1997), p.202.

year.[42] The conflict, also involved the Prince-Bishopric Electorates of Mainz, Trier and Cologne, and although limited to small to medium-sized states, lasted intermittently until 1669, allowing the Duke to strengthen his army. In 1664, the professional troops had increased from about 1,000 to 1,500 a year later, and to 3,000 in 1666.[43] In 1665, the Duke also ordered the mobilisation of the militia, resurrecting the *arriere-ban* obligation for all subjects. He also called the forester and river traffic personnel to form a mounted militia. In particular, on 25 October, the Duke ordered the personnel of the districts of Arches, Blâmont, Darney, Dompaire, Luneville, Saint-Dié, La Croix and l'Avant Garde to assemble in Luneville.[44] The next year the military strength increased to almost double the 1,500 men of two years earlier.[45] In early 1666, the Lorrainer troops were deployed between Falkenstein, Landstuhl, Homburg and Schaumburg under Vaudemont's orders, and between Bitche and Speyer under Lillebonne and Bassompierre. After the Peace of Heilbronn, signed on 7 February 1667 with the mediation of France, instead of disbanding the army, Charles IV retained all the soldiers still in service, which together with the guards of the *Maison Lorraine* brought the total to more than 4,000 men.

Although this was a relatively large number of soldiers, it was an army that was not supposed to exist according to the treaty with Louis XIV, which required its demobilisation. Despite this, Charles IV continued to pursue his personal career as a military entrepreneur, convinced that he could reap further benefits from the trade. In February 1667, the Duke, as was his custom, tried an *autout* by offering Louis XIV Lorrainer soldiers for the war he was preparing against Spain. The French King regarded the help offered by Charles IV with suspicion, but did not refuse it, although he replied that he would not take on any expenses for the Lorrainer soldiers on campaign except for the ration of bread. On 9 March 1667, the French agent in Lorraine informed Paris that Charles IV could provide 1,800–1,900 horse and 1,600–1,700 foot, and thus confirmed that this was a very modest contribution. However, Charles IV was convinced that he could bargain his soldiers for new concessions from the King of France.

The mobilisation of the troops, planned for the end of March, was delayed by new negotiations. Louis XIV again demanded the disbandment of the Lorrainer army at the end of the war against Spain, because the conflict with the Elector of the Palatinate had ended. Charles IV pretended to accept and immediately afterwards began to devise new plans. On 2 June 1667, the Lorraine troops destined for the campaign in the Spanish Low Countries had gathered at Pont-à-Mousson, under Lillebonne and Vaudemont, and from there, they headed for Arras where they stopped at the end of a two-day march. The review carried out by the French commissioners recorded

---

42  See Chapter 10: Wars and Factions in Germany (1653–1689).
43  Jean-Charles Fulaine, *Le Duc Charles IV de Lorraine et son Armée* (Metz: Editions Serpenoise, 1997), p.221.
44  Jean-Charles Fulaine, *Le Duc Charles IV de Lorraine et son Armée* (Metz: Editions Serpenoise, 1997), The overall figure of this mounted militia is uncertain.
45  Jean-Charles Fulaine, *Le Duc Charles IV de Lorraine et son Armée* (Metz: Editions Serpenoise, 1997), p.212.

a strength of 1,500 horse and 1,200 foot; a number therefore lower than the total force initially estimated.[46] Days later, the Lorrainets joined the corps under Turenne for the first campaign in Flanders.

As an ally of Louis XIV, the Duke well understood that his space for manouevre was increasingly reducing, since the presence of a French corps of 4,000 men under Créqui on the Luxembourg border appeared more like a pending threat than support in case of danger. Deprived of his troops, but forced to maintain them at his own expense, Charles IV waited for an event that could turn the situation around, but since this did not come, he provoked it himself. The Duke caused a state of emergency in Nancy, declaring that the town was in danger of being plundered by the Spanish and therefore ordered the transfer of the Court with all its furniture and tapestries to Épinal. He also issued an edict to collect 40,000 *écus* of voluntary contributions to pay the Spaniards as compensation to secure Lorraine from invasion. A letter of 22 November to the Governor of Luxembourg written by a very irritated Viceroy of the Spanish Low Countries, ordered a contribution of 100,000 *écus* to be imposed on Lorraine.[47] Charles IV had finally succeeded in provoking Spain by appearing as a victim, but the charade did not allow him to recover his soldiers or obtain favourable conditions to strengthen his army.

The War of Devolution continued the following year, but the Lorrainer troops remained idle in Flanders, where they had spent the winter quarters. The peace preliminaries, which began on 15 April 1668, ended on 2 May with the Peace of Aix-le-Chapelle allowing Charles IV to recover his soldiers. On 18 May, he sent the Prince of Vaudemont to Flanders with the aim of bringing the troops back, but his plan ran up against the unresolved problem of disbanding all professional troops as requested by France. There was no option other than the inescapable one of bowing to the will of the strongest, but once again, Charles IV managed to postpone the execution of the agreement by taking advantage of Pope Clement IX's appeal to come to the aid of the Venetians in Candia who were besieged by the Ottomans. The pretext appeared to be excellent, especially as Louis XIV himself had acceded to the Papal request. Charles IV received a *bevvy* of congratulations from Clement IX, after promising to send 4,000 men to Crete, that is the whole army, and thus avoiding the disbandment. The Venetian Senate examined the proposal in turn, but when the extent of Charles IV's economic demands became clear, the number of soldiers had fallen dramatically. The Duke complained a great deal to the Republic, claiming that the Senate had not agreed to support him in his plan in refusing to provide vessels to transfer the soldiers to Crete. At the same time, the news of his troops' rebellion at the idea of going to fight in such a remote location further reduced the amount of aid from Lorraine.[48]

---

46    Jean-Charles Fulaine, *Le Duc Charles IV de Lorraine et son Armée* (Metz: Editions Serpenoise, 1997), p.214.

47    Robert Parisot, *Histoire de Lorraine (Duché de Lorraine, Duché de Bar, Trois-Évêchés)*, (Paris, 1919–1924), tome II (1552–1789), p.149.

48    'As soon as the news spread, the soldiers mutinied against the officers. In the infantry regiment de Maulon, the colonel was received with stones, while a lieutenant was hit in the head with a pistol butt. Three companies of German cavalry deserted en masse.' Jean-Charles Fulaine, *Le Duc Charles IV de Lorraine et son Armée* (Metz: Editions Serpenoise, 1997), p.214.

Facing these events, Charles IV renounced the Cretan project, but managed to enlist recruits in Provence, with the permission of Louis XIV, and to raise an infantry regiment which, in 1668, joined the French expeditionary corps sailing from Marseille.[49]

Never short on imagination, Charles IV resorted to other expedients to achieve his goals. After disbanding six cavalry regiments in June, on August 1668, the French agent in Lorraine informed Paris that 'the Duke was selling his troops to Spain.'[50] According to the French spies, cavalry companies were actually on the march to Franche-Comté, then, the agreement between Charles IV and the Spanish became public a few days later. Predictably, Louis XIV's furious reaction was not long in coming. Faced with the King's repeated requests to dismiss the troops, Charles IV could no longer refuse, but once again, exploited the political scenario to postpone the order. In his letter of reply, the Duke informed his French cousin that Elector Carl Ludwig of the Palatinate was increasing his troops in order to support his right in the *Wildfang* quarrel, and therefore Charles IV could not dismiss the army as long as there was an external threat. The Elector, for his part, argued the same against the Duke, who was secretly recruiting soldiers. After a further exchange of letters, on 12 August, Charles IV promised to disband all foreign troops within a week, but on 19 August, no soldiers had been released. The Duke confirmed the disbanding, but actually had issued only temporary permissions to officers and soldiers, who retained horse and salaries. On the same day, troops from the Palatinate were seen assembling close to the Lorraine border; six days later, Lillebonne confirmed that these were heading for the Duchy. Now Charles IV could justify his resistance to dismissing the army. However, signals of the Elector's offensive had been noticed since July, and demands to cede some posts on the border were issued to Charles IV before the end of the month. During the summer, Charles IV reinforced the army with new enlistments at home and abroad. Two infantry regiments were recruited in Germany, while additional cavalry companies reinforced the existing regiments. The total strength never fell below 4,000 men. French mediation again put an end to hostilities in November 1668. At this date, 16 colonels were still in service, with 86 captains, 25 lieutenants and 16 ensigns, distributed among 12 cavalry and three infantry regiments.[51]

Unfortunately for Charles IV, the Palatine threat was not sufficient to postpone the disbandment of the army indefinitely. On 5 January 1669, the French request admitted no reply. A memorandum, with the tones of an ultimatum, requested Charles IV's immediate dismissal of the troops with the exception only of the companies of the *Maison Militaire*, 300 horsemen in all.[52] To make it even clearer to the Duke that this time it would not be

---

49   See in *The Cretan War, the Ottoman-Venetian struggle for the Mediterranean, 1645–1671* (Warwick: Helion & Company, 2018), p.112.
50   Jean-Charles Fulaine, *Le Duc Charles IV de Lorraine et son Armée* (Metz: Editions Serpenoise, 1997), p.216. The six cavalry 'regiments' numbered 400–500 men in all.
51   Jean-Charles Fulaine, *Le Duc Charles IV de Lorraine et son Armée* (Metz: Editions Serpenoise, 1997), p.221.
52   Jean-Charles Fulaine, *Le Duc Charles IV de Lorraine et son Armée* (Metz: Editions Serpenoise, 1997), p.221.The memorandum, delivered to Nancy on 16 January 1669, specified that the

possible to avoid the order, a corps of infantry and cavalry under Créqui was assembling not far from Metz. The ultimatum demanded that the foreign mercenaries should leave the country immediately, while the Lorrainer troops would be dismissed between 18 and 22 January. On 17 January, the Duke convened his council and then demanded of Louis XIV the postponement the disbandment of the army, in the hope of reaching an accommodation that would be advantageous to him. However, the answer was clear: no postponement and the disbandment within the terms expressed in the memorandum of 5 January. The dismissal began a few days late and was completed in early February 1669. On day 17 of the same month, Créqui's report arrived in Paris with the confirmation that the Duke had finally dismissed his army. The *maréchal* described in detail the size of the garrisons and regiments, and also revealed that the Duke was secretly negotiating to recruit new troops in Germany with the intent of assembling a professional force estimated at least 11,000 men.[53]

The disbanding of the army calmed tensions between Charles IV and Louis XIV, but new problems were about to arise. Louis XIV did not hide his irritation at the fact that some members of the ducal family and many Lorrainer aristocrats were serving in the Imperial and Spanish armies. The picture was made bleak again by French agents, who informed the King that the name and address of officers and soldiers of the disbanding units had been recorded, that troops were quartered at the Duke's expense, and that weapons and equipment were still in the fortresses.[54] Moreover, Charles IV continued to maintain diplomatic relations with all foreign powers and his emissaries regularly visited Den Haag, London, the Spanish Low Countries, Vienna, Madrid and the princes of Germany. Information that reached Paris also reported on the constant changes and reforms ordered by the Duke regarding his Life Guards. Many officers from the disbanded units had been attached to the *Maison Militaire* and these moves seemed to conceal new manoeuvres to cheat the agreement. French agents soon realised that despite the reforms, some companies of the Life Guard had a larger strength. In April 1669, the Duke had formed a new company of *Gardes du Corps* for the Duchess with 50 horsemen, while a new cavalry company under Vaudemont was formed shortly afterwards. Other evidence confirms that Charles IV kept six cavalry regiments in Franche-Comté, 'camouflaged' in the Spanish garrisons. Although there is no certain information on the size of these troops, their number was estimated at around 3,000 men: notwithstanding the disbanding of February, the Lorrainer army still existed.

---

dismissal of the troops was to be 'real and effective' and that the duke was not to quarter his troops outside the borders 'while continuing to pay them salaries and food as he had done before'. *Maréchal* Créqui had been ordered to enter Lorraine with his troops if he did not receive a positive answer from the duke by 18 January, so that he himself could proceed with the dismissal of the Lorraine troops.

53   Jean-Charles Fulaine, *Le Duc Charles IV de Lorraine et son Armée* (Metz: Editions Serpenoise, 1997), p.224.

54   Jean-Charles Fulaine, *Le Duc Charles IV de Lorraine et son Armée* (Metz: Editions Serpenoise, 1997), p.217.

This was a modest force, but sufficient to disturb Louis XIV, especially since it was an outrageous failure to comply with his ultimatum. When asked for an explanation, Charles IV replied that these were troops sold to the Spanish and therefore no longer concerned him. As for the mercenaries he had recruited in Germany, these were troops intended to support the election of his nephew to the Polish throne, or to accompany his son who was about to marry the niece of the Elector of Trier, Katharina von der Leyen.[55] In Paris, these explanations convinced no one and persuaded Louis XIV to resolve the Lorraine issue once and for all – and by force. Louis XIV waited a year before proceeding, and this decision was confirmed after the news coming from international diplomacy. On 2 November 1669 Louis XIV rejected the Treaty of Montmartre of 1662 by formally renouncing the Lorraine succession, but this appeasing attitude did not improve relations between Paris and Nancy, because Charles IV had resumed contact with the Austrian representatives at Den Haag, with a view to joining the Triple Alliance which had just stopped the French Army in the War of Devolution.[56] Meanwhile, accustomed to negotiating on several tables, Charles IV took advantage of the proposal of the Elector of Mainz to include the Lorraine Army in the new *Deutsche Allianz*.[57] An increasingly irritated French King reproached Charles IV for maintaining more troops than he had agreed to and, above all, for promoting an alliance of the German princes of Rhineland against France.[58]

On 20 July 1670, having avoided falling victim to an assassination attempt orchestrated by France, Charles IV left the country pursued by Créqui's troops, who completed the occupation of the Duchy the following October. The attack on the Duke's person and the invasion of his territories without a formal declaration of war, and in a time of peace, aroused the indignation of courts all over Europe.[59] The Emperor sent his representatives to negotiate with Louis XIV for the return of the Duchy to Charles IV, but the negotiations

---

55  Nicolas Buat, *La France et Les 'différends palatins'. L'intervention de Louis XIV dans la querelle du droit de Wildfang en Allemagne, 1660–1674*. (Chartes: Ecole Nationale – HAL, 1995), p.150
56  The main architect of the negotiations was the talented François de Risaucourt, who managed the complex net of relations and links in Austria and in the Empire since the 1660s. Nicolas Buat, *La France et Les 'Différends Palatins'. L'Intervention de Louis XIV dans la Querelle du Droit de Wildfang en Allemagne, 1660–1674*. (Chartes: Ecole Nationale – HAL, 1995), p.8.
57  Peter H. Wilson, *German Armies. War and German Politics, 1648–1806* (London: UCL Press, 1998), p.174.
58  Jean Bérenger, 'Un texte inédit de Lisola concernent l'Affaire de Lorraine (1670)' in *Revue Ssemestrielle de Linguistique et Littératures Romanes*, tome V, nos 1–2 (2009, Institut d'etudes romanes de la Faculté des Lettres de l'Université de Bohême du Sud, České Budějovice), p.49. The Elector of Mainz also implied that he would support Charles IV if Louis XIV took any military action against Lorraine, while he continued his diplomatic negotiations with a view to a rapprochement with the Triple Alliance in Den Haag. The Elector of Mainz sent his minister Boineburg in June to the Elector of Trier to join him and give his guarantee to the Duke of Lorraine.
59  In 1671, Franz Paul von Lisola, a diplomat of the Imperial court, published a 255-page document with a bilingual French-German text entitled *Eclaircissements sur Les affaires de Lorraine pour tous Les Princes Chrestiens*, complaining about the French outrageous act against Charles IV and his domains.

fell on deaf ears.⁶⁰ The French occupation of Lorraine continued until 1697, when the Treaty of Ryswick finally returned it to its rightful sovereign.

## The Never-Disbanded Army (1670–1675)

The French occupation of Lorraine did not interrupt the history of its army. As happened in the past, the Duke went through a new exile, a situation to which he seemed to have become accustomed. The army had lost about 2,300 infantry as prisoners of war after the surrender of the major fortresses between September and October 1670, but the Duke did not lose time raising new troops. From his exile in the Vosges, he gathered the few soldiers still available in the garrisons quartered on the eastern border and then marched to Coblenz, Mainz, Cologne and finally camped near Frankfurt am Mein in early November, accompanied by a small group of officers. Despite the absence of a regular train and with very few resources, Charles IV divided the troops into three regiments of horse and two regiments of foot, about 1,200 men in all, which were increased in the following days by the officers and men who had escaped French captivity. Not being able to sustain the expenses required to maintain the troops for long, in late May, the Duke ceded half of his soldiers to Spain, but achieved a significant political success thanks to the Elector of Mainz, who in August sent his own troops to Bitche to avoid retaliation by the French after the passage of the troops heading for the Spanish Low Countries.⁶¹ With Imperial protection through Schönborn, in the following weeks the Duke also obtained the help of the Elector of Trier, which sent its own soldiers to Hamburg, while the Spaniards put the territories on the border with Luxembourg under their protection. However, the last horse and foot still in service were sold in 1672 to the Elector of Cologne, an ally of Louis XIV.⁶²

With only a small detachment of his *Maison*, Charles IV took residence in the Electorate of Mainz; for him this was the first time without an army, but this condition was not to last for long. Reports dating to the spring of 1673 indicate that Charles IV still had the cavalry quartered in Franche-Comté

---

60 'Un texte inédit de Lisola concernent l'Affaire de Lorraine (1670)', p.49. Charles IV had also turned to the Diet of the Empire to request the help of the German princes, while between September 1670 and March 1671 there was an exchange of emissaries between France and the duke. The Diet was not very favourable because the German princes had never appreciated the equivocal attitude of the duke. This is why the Diet sent Charles IV's request for an intervention to the Emperor. The Diet suggested that Leopold I should take Charles IV under his protection to ask France for the return of Lorraine. Jean Bérenger, 'Un texte inédit de Lisola concernent l'Affaire de Lorraine (1670)' in *Revue Ssemestrielle de Linguistique et Littératures Romanes*, tome V, nos 1–2 (2009, Institut d'études romanes de la Faculté des Lettres de l'Université de Bohême du Sud, České Budějovice) p.50.

61 Robert Parisot, *Histoire de Lorraine (Duché de Lorraine, duché de Bar, Trois-Évêchés)*, (Paris, 1919–1924), tome II (1552–1789), p.201. To meet the expenses, on 25 February 1671, Charles IV sold the lordship of Marmontier to the Bishop of Strasbourg, Franz Egon von Fürstenberg.

62 Jean-Charles Fulaine, *Le Duc Charles IV de Lorraine et son Armée* (Metz: Editions Serpenoise, 1997), p.238. These were *Bellerose zu Fuss* (KkI-7), *Lippe zu Pferd* (KkC-6) and *Salins zu Pferd* (KkC-7). See also the Appendix.

## THE DUCHY OF LORRAINE

'concealed' in the Spanish garrisons. News of recruitment of mercenaries in Mainz are recorded on 5 September under the command of the *Obrist Monsieur* de Creange; then weeks later, three German captains received the patents to each raise a company of 50 horse.[63]

The Spanish involvement in the Franco-Dutch War gave the Duke scope for new enterprises. In early 1674, the army had been reconstituted. It is difficult to establish with certainty whether the decision to form an army of cavalry alone was the idea of Charles IV, who surely possessed a visionary attitude and was well-disposed to unconventional choices. The French invasion of Franche-Comté in 1673 caused concerns for transferring the Lorraine cavalry to the north. On 25 March, Charles IV gathered his force waiting for the arrival of the Imperialists for a campaign in Franche-Comté. The agreement stated that the Duke would serve under the orders of the Emperor's commanders. The overall strength of the Allies was calculated at less than 4,000 men, including one cavalry regiment and two Imperial infantry regiments. Possibly this meant that Charles IV could field 1,000 horsemen in all, but in all likelihood, the strength increased in the following weeks, if, according to reports, 2,000 'Lorraine horse' participated in the Battle of Sinsheim on 16 June 1674, signalling itself very positively despite the final defeat.[64] Charles IV and his cavalry joined the Imperial Army for the campaign in Alsace in October.

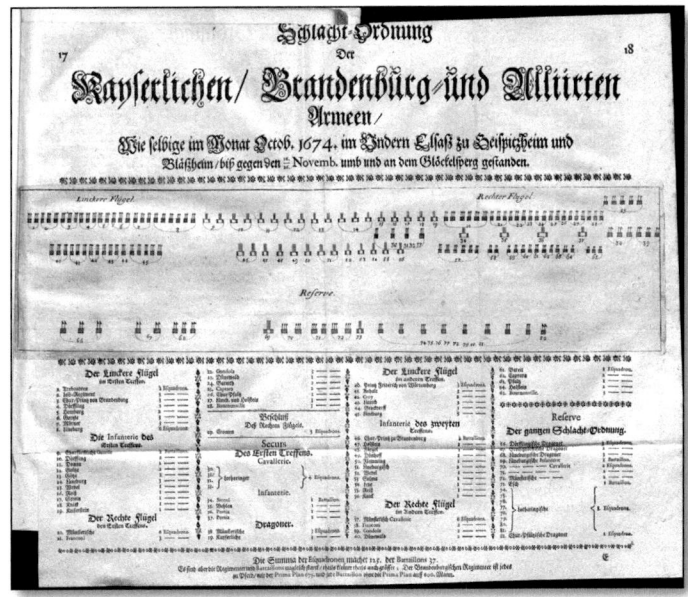

Order of battle of the Imperial-Allied Army in Alsace in November 1674. (Author's collection) The Lorraine cavalry deployed four squadrons on the right wing, and further eight squadrons in the reserve.

---

63   Jean-Charles Fulaine, *Le Duc Charles IV de Lorraine et son Armée* (Metz: Editions Serpenoise, 1997), p.241.
64   Jean-Charles Fulaine, *Le Duc Charles IV de Lorraine et son Armée* (Metz: Editions Serpenoise, 1997), p.242. It is likely, therefore, that the cavalry that was in Franche-Comté rejoined those already under the orders of the Duke in Alsace.

Pierre Ernest de Mercy (1641–1686), father of the talented Claude-Florimond, who became *Feldmarschall* of the Imperial Army serving under Prince Eugene of Savoy. Pierre entered a military career in the Lorraine Army as a volunteer and later became an officer of cavalry.

After taking winter quarters around Strasbourg, Charles IV asked to move against the French rearguard, exploiting the numerical superiority of the allied cavalry. He intended to enter Lorraine by outflanking the enemy who were camped between Hagenau and Saverne in order to cut off the supplies and take the winter quarter in his Duchy. The plan was discussed in the council of war, but the Imperial commander, Bournonville, expressed his negative opnion. Determined to return one way or another to his own state, Charles IV waited for a new propitious opportunity. At the end of October, Charles IV learned that the French had gathered 500 'gentilhommes' of the Anjou *arriere-ban* (mounted militia) on their way through Lorraine escorting the supplies to Turenne's army. This time Bournonville agreed. The departure was set for 2 November with a cavalry corps under *Obrist* Du Puy comprising four regiments of horse and 100 dragoons. Other officers from illustrious families also took part in the expedition, such as Count Pierre Ernest de Mercy, who had just been released from captivity in Sinsheim, the *Rheingraf*, and Compte de la Roche.

After three days of marching through the rough terrain and exploiting the dense fog of the region, undiscovered the Lorrainers advanced cautiously and finally intercepted the enemy convoy and escort near the village of Bénéménil. The action succeeded perfectly and took the French by surprise as they abandoned both supplies and baggage and fled almost without a fight.[65] The Lorrainers took 700 prisoners including drivers, valets, cavalrymen and 17 *gentilhommes*, along with 400 horses, 13 mules and 40,000 French *livres*. The victors claimed that they lost 14 officers and 40 men dead or wounded.[66]

Upon receiving the news of the success, Charles IV, escorted by his life guards, left Strasbourg to meet Du Puy and establish a new plan of action. After joining the cavalry corps on 12 November, the duke and his horse moved to distrupt the enemy communications. On 20 November, Charles IV sent to Obrist Allamont, who commanded the rest of the cavalry in Alsace, an order to join him and seize Épinal and Remiremont. Allamont and his troops arrived seven days later. Both towns were without defences since the French had demolished the curtains in 1670, and the Lorrainers succeeded in taking both places. Encouraged by the poor French resistance, Charles IV intensified the operation. On 4 December, Du Puy moved against the French depots at Saint-Dié with 700–800 horse. Days later, he received the order to

---

65 Bénéménil's action was the last one supported by the French *arriere-ban* during the reign of Louis XIV.

66 Jean-Charles Fulaine, *Le Duc Charles IV de Lorraine et son Armée* (Metz: Editions Serpenoise, 1997), p.243.

**Plate A – the Hansa and *Reichstädte*, 1686–90**

1 – Hamburg, Uffeln zu Fuss, Musketeer. 1686; 2 – Bremen, Infantry, Musketeer, 1689–90; 3 – Augsburg, Infantry NCO, 1690s

(Illustration by Bruno Mugnai © Helion & Company)

*See Colour Plate Commentaries for further information.*

**Plate B – Feldabzeichen**
1) Celle and Hanover; 2) Wolfenbüttel; 3) 3 Hessen-Kassel; 4) Hessen-Darmstadt (late version); 5) Electoral Cologne (1672-74); 6) the Palatinate; 7) Württemberg; 8) Mecklenburg; 9) Holstein-Gottorf; 10) Brandenburg-Bayreuth and Ansbach-Bayreuth; 11) Salzburg; 12) Lorraine.
(Graphic by Bruno Mugnai © Helion & Company)
*See Colour Plate Commentaries for further information.*

**Plate C – Infantry Colours**
1-3) Hannover, 1660-80; 4) Celle, 1690s; 5) Wolfenbüttel, 1690s
(Graphic by Bruno Mugna © Helion & Company)
*See Colour Plate Commentaries for further information.*

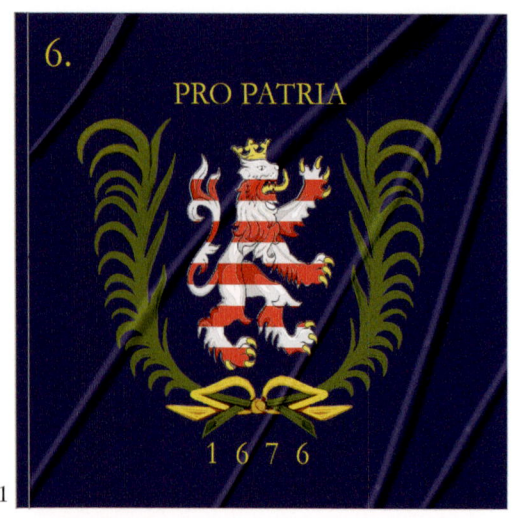

**Plate D – Infantry Colours**
1) Hessen-Kassel, 1676-78; 2) Hessen-Darmstadt, 1663; 3) Lorraine, 1650-60; 4) Brandenburg-Bayreuth, 1687: 5-6) Osnabrück, 1670s
(Graphic by Bruno Mugnai © Helion & Company)
*See Colour Plate Commentaries for further information.*

**Plate E – Infantry Colours**

1) Holstein-Gottorf, 1664; 2) Mecklenburg, 1664; 3) Pfalz-Neuburg, 1650-60; 4) Hamburg, 1684; 5-6) Würzburg, 1680s
(Graphic by Bruno Mugnai © Helion & Company)
*See Colour Plate Commentaries for further information.*

**Plate F - Cavalry Standards and Dragoon Guidons**
1-2) Hannover, 1673-1689; 3-5) Celle, 1690s; 6) Hessen-Darmstadt, 1677-78; 7) Electoral Cologne, 1672; 8-9) Osnabrück 1670s; 10-11) Lorraine, 1660-70s; 12) Frankfurt am Main, 1660s.
(Graphic by Bruno Mugnai © Helion & Company)
*See Colour Plate Commentaries for further information.*

**Plate G – Cavalry Standards**
Hessen-Kassel, standards of the cavalry regiment Hornhumb, 1677-78.
(Army Museum of Stockholm)
*See Colour Plate Commentaries for further information.*

**Plate H - Strasbourg. Infantry and cavalry ensigns of the Burgewehr, (1665-69)**
From Joseph Gény, *Die Fahnen der Strassburger Bürgerwehr im 17. Jahrhundert* (Strasbourg, 1902).
See Colour Plate Commentaries for further information.

**Plate I – Infantry Ensigns: late 17th–early 18th century**
1) Hannover, Bremer zu Fuss (BhI-13), company colour.
2) The Palatinate, Kurprinz zu Fuss (KpI-6) life colour; 3) Sachsen-Meiningen zu Fuss (KpI-9), company colour.
4) Frankfurt am Main, company colour.
Copies after *Les Triomphes du Louis XIV*
See Colour Plate Commentaries for further information.

**Plate J - Cavalry Standards: late 17th–early 18th century**
1) Hannover, attributed to Öffener zu Pferd (BhC-10), company standard; 2) Raugraf zu Pferd (BhC-9), company standard.
3) The Palatinate: Leibregiment zu Pferd (KpC-2) life standard; 4) Franckenberg zu Pferd (KpC-3) company standard.
5) Wolfenbüttel, Öst-Friesland zu Pferd (BwC-10), life standard.
Copies after *Les Triomphes du Louis XIV*
*See Colour Plate Commentaries for further information.*

move against the villages of Badonviller and Rambervillers, but the shortage of fodder and the cold season arrested his brilliant campaign in Lorraine.

If Charles IV's plan had also been supported by the Allies, the famous winter manoeuvre that Turenne performed a few weeks later with the victories of Mulhouse and Türckheim would perhaps have had a less unfavourable outcome for them. In fact, far from being weakened, Turenne surprisingly reopened the campaign by defeating the allies at Mulhouse on 29 December 1674. The Lorainer cavalry, commanded by Allamont, are mentioned positively in the battle reports, where it is said that they charged seven times against the French. The fighting was certainly fierce, as Allamont had his horse wounded, and a number of other officers were killed or wounded in the battle. The overall losses were however modest, as only 35 to 40 men remained on the field. The Lorrainers captured the French *Maréchal de Camp* Montauban along with 12 officers and 103 private soldiers.[67] The Lorrainers also participated at the Battle of Türckheim on 5 January 1675, but there is little information concerning their actual involvement in the fighting, except for the bitter commentaries by Charles IV and Allamont on Bournonville's performance.[68]

Charles IV and his troops took part in the 1675 campaign under Montecuccoli, which culminated in the death of Turenne at Salzbach, and the subsequent operations in Alsace and on the Rhine until the siege of Trier. In August 1675, Charles IV was among the commanders who in the council of war strongly advocated an assault on Créqui's corps, which was marching to relieve the besieged city. On 11 August, four cavalry regiments and one dragoon regiment under Grondeur formed the right wing at the Battle of Conzer Brücke, where they performed a decisive action.[69]

The last information concerning the strength of the Lorraine Army provides conflicting data. On the eve of the Battle of Sinsheim, there were 3,500 men divided into 9 cavalry regiments, one dragoon regiment, and an unknown number of autonomous companies of 40 to 50 men each at most. However, not all of these soldiers took part in the battle of 16 June. A year later the matter became even more intricate, as the total strength fell to 2,500 men, who nevertheless formed a larger number of regiments: 14 of cavalry and two of dragoons. As for the officers, 22 colonels, 22 captains,

---

67 Jean-Charles Fulaine, *Le Duc Charles IV de Lorraine et son Armée* (Metz: Editions Serpenoise, 1997), p.244.
68 Jean-Charles Fulaine, *Le Duc Charles IV de Lorraine et son Armée* (Metz: Editions Serpenoise, 1997), p.245. Obrist Allamont died several days after the Battle of Türckheim.
69 Marchese Ottone Enrico del Carrettto, Imperial commander at Conzer Brücke, left an eloquent report concerning the positive behaviour of the Lorrainer cavalrymen. He wrote, 'to do justice to the brave Lorraine, who went into battle with great order and discipline, to wait for the infantry that was deploying, and showed considerable cold blood, it is sufficient to prize the impetus with which they attacked the enemy, and despite the losses of so many good people did not stop them from pursuing the enemy, …. and it was a not inconsiderable effort to hold back the second line that wanted to launch itself against the fleeing enemy.' The sources do not agree about the strength of the Lorraine cavalry at the battle. Fulaine estimates the Lorrainers at about 2,000 men, whereas Anton Marr, 'Der Feldzüg im Jahre 1675 in Deutschland', in *Österreichische Militärische Zeitschrift* (Vienna: Kaiserl. Koenigli und Hof und Staatsdruckerei 1839), vol. III, p.121, gives a strength of 3,500 horsemen and dragoons.

1 lieutenant, 2 ensigns were still still serving in 1674; 32 Lorrainers and 15 were foreigners.[70]

Shortly after the Battle of Conzer Brücke, Charles IV fell ill and after two days spent in bed, he died on 18 September 1675. The Duke's death marked the actual end of the Lorraine Army, and the disappearance of a commander with the unshakeable energy of the late duke was a vacuum not easily filled: the Prince de Vaudemont was in Spanish service; his nephew Charles, designated in the Will as the new duke, was serving in the Imperial Army and in 1676 replaced Montecuccoli as Commander-in-Chief; other skilled officers, such as Haracourt and Beauvau, ranked as colonel in Bavaria. From this date, the diasporas of the Lorrainer captains in the armies of Europe began.

Charles V of Lorraine portrayed as Imperial cavalry officer in the 1670s (Author's collection). He was appointed as colonel of an Imperial cuirassier regiment in1664, serving in Hungary and on the Rhine under Montecuccoli, who appreciated the qualities of the Duke and recommended him as commander on the Rhine. In 1675, Charles V succeeded to his uncle, and he was appointed Commander-in-Chief of the Imperial Army, becoming the natural leader of the exiled Lorraine aristocrats, who served in great number in the Spanish and Imperial armies.

---

70  Jean-Charles Fulaine, *Le Duc Charles IV de Lorraine et son Armée* (Metz: Editions Serpenoise, 1997), p.247.

5

# Wars and Factions in Germany (1653–1689)

The Treaty of Westphalia had ended the war between the states of Germany, but new tensions returned to threaten the peace, albeit at a less devastating level. However, these disagreements were not amplified by religious issues, but arose from purely dynastic matters or territorial claims. Just three years after the Treaty of Westphalia, Brandenburg and Pfalz-Neuburg were involved in the contest centred on the disputed Jülich-Cleves inheritance in Westphalia. Brandenburg had acquired Cleves, Mark and Ravensberg by 1614, but Pfalz-Neuburg still held Jülich and Berg along with the Circle executive post. In June 1651, Elector Friedrich Wilhelm of Brandenburg mobilised 16,000 men, but he was only able to deploy 3,800 in the immediate vicinity, while Wolfgang Wilhelm of Pflaz-Neuburg mustered 12,000. The conflict threatened to escalate as the Duke of Lorraine backed Pfalz-Neuburg, while the Orangist faction agitated for Dutch intervention in support of Brandenburg.[1] However, actual operations were relatively bloodless, while the still-united Jülich-Cleves estates refused financial assistance to both princes, leading to the contemporary label of the 'Düsseldorf Cow War.'[2] In December, Brandenburg was forced to back down and the conflict was defused by Imperial mediation.[3] Further bilateral negotiations led to a split of the inheritance along the territorial *status quo* of 1666, leading to the emergence of a de facto third Westphalian executive post for Brandenburg as well as joint cooperation to break estates' opposition to military taxation.[4]

---

1 This connection did not survive beyond the war, but the latter was cemented by dynastic ties between the Hohenzollerns and the House of Orange-Nassau, who had considerable influence within the Republic as well as German possessions in Westphalia and the Upper Rhine.
2 Peter H. Wilson, *German Armies. War and German Politics, 1648–1806* (London: UCL Press, 1998), p.33.
3 Essentially, the Great Elector was forced to back down because Pfalz-Neuburg mustered enough troops and was supported by Lorraine, while the Dutch failed to make good their promise of support for Brandenburg. See Joachim Whaley, *Germany and the Holy Roman Empire. Vol. 2: from the Peace of Westphalia to the Dissolution of the Reich. 1648–1806* (Oxford-New York, NY: Oxford University Press, 2012), pp.16–17.
4 Hanschmidt Alwin, 'Kurbrandenburg als Kreisstand im Niederheinisch- Westfälischen Kreis vom Westfälischen Frieden bis zum Spanischen Erbfolgekrieg' in O. Hauser (ed.), *Preußen,*

Nonetheless, an extremely tense and potentially dangerous crisis was finally defused by an Imperial arbitration which set the combatants on the path towards the lasting settlement of the full range of territorial and religious issues relating to Jülich-Cleves in 1672.

Further concerns came from other German territories. In 1653, Imperial intervention forced the Swedes to relinquish Western Pomerania to Brandenburg. In the same year, the Duke of Lorraine, together with the Prince de Condé, invaded the Archbishopric of Liège, and another time the Imperial Diet averted military intervention by the Electors of Brandenburg, Mainz, and Trier on behalf of the Archbishopric's ruler, the Elector of Cologne.[5] If the *Reich* managed to limit the spread of violence within its frontiers, it found it impossible to prevent it originating beyond them. The growth of extraterritorial violence stemmed from a coincidence of international and German factors. The attitude of the German principalities was equally complex. In myriad combinations, each was dependent on a mix of constantly fluctuating regional security issues and dynastic interests, they concluded alliances they believed would guarantee their security, promote dynastic interests, or simply secure them financial gain in the form of subsidies. It is often difficult to define clear groupings, for most continually adapted their policies, changing course as events unfolded, often hedging their bets by simultaneously pursuing, with varying degrees of openness, mutually contradictory options.

By the 1660s, German involvement in international conflict continued to increase, and some German principalities like Brandenburg, Bavaria, Münster, Cologne, Württemberg, and Mainz were signatories to the string of treaties negotiated by French diplomats to isolate the Spanish Low Countries as the intended target of Louis XIV's first major war.

## First Swedish War on Bremen, 1653–1654

The Treaty of Westphalia had allocated the former Prince-Bishoprics of Bremen and Verden to Sweden. Years before, Bremen and other Hanseatic ports requested that they become Imperial Cities; Bremen being successful with the *Linz Privilege*. The act had been signed in 1646 with the aim of preventing Sweden from gaining the city.[6] This had a strong repercussion in Stockholm, since King Carl X Gustav interpreted the city of Bremen as being included in the Duchy allocated to Sweden, and his Governor, Hans Christoph von Königsmarck, renewed this claim whenever he could. Bremen City Council thought otherwise, insisting on the long practised immediate status of Free City. Additionally, among other concessions, Bremen paid to Sweden about 100,000 thalers in subsidy.[7] Owing to Swedish diplomatic

---

*Europa und das Reich* (Cologne: Böhlau, 1978), pp.47–64.
5 Joachim Whaley, *Germany and the Holy Roman Empire. From the Peace of Westphalia to the Dissolution of the Reich, 1648–1806* (Oxford: Oxford University Press, 2012), p.17.
6 Konrad Elmshäuser, *Geschichte Bremens* (Munich: Beck, 2007), p.58.
7 Konrad Elmshäuser, *Geschichte Bremens* (Munich: Beck, 2007), p.59

# WARS AND FACTIONS IN GERMANY (1653–1689)

efforts however, the text of the 1648 treaty did not determine whether or not Bremen was to be excluded from the Swedish Duchy. Making the scenario less secure for Bremen, a dispute about custom duties between the City and the Emperor led to the latter imposing an Imperial ban in 1652. Sweden, which had never accepted Bremen's Imperial immediacy, immediately moved on to the action. In the summer of 1653, Swedish troops occupied all the villages on Bremen territory. Bremen's authorities strengthened the City's defences and prepared to face an assault, but the Swedes did not besiege the city, because of their lack of artillery. In September 1654, a truce was agreed upon, and on 28 November the Treaty of Stade sealed a peace. The city of Bremen made territorial concessions ceding the territories of Bederkese and Lehe, and promised to pledge allegiance to the Swedish King, Carl X Gustav, to follow Stockholm's foreign policy, and to promote Swedish trade in the Hansa.

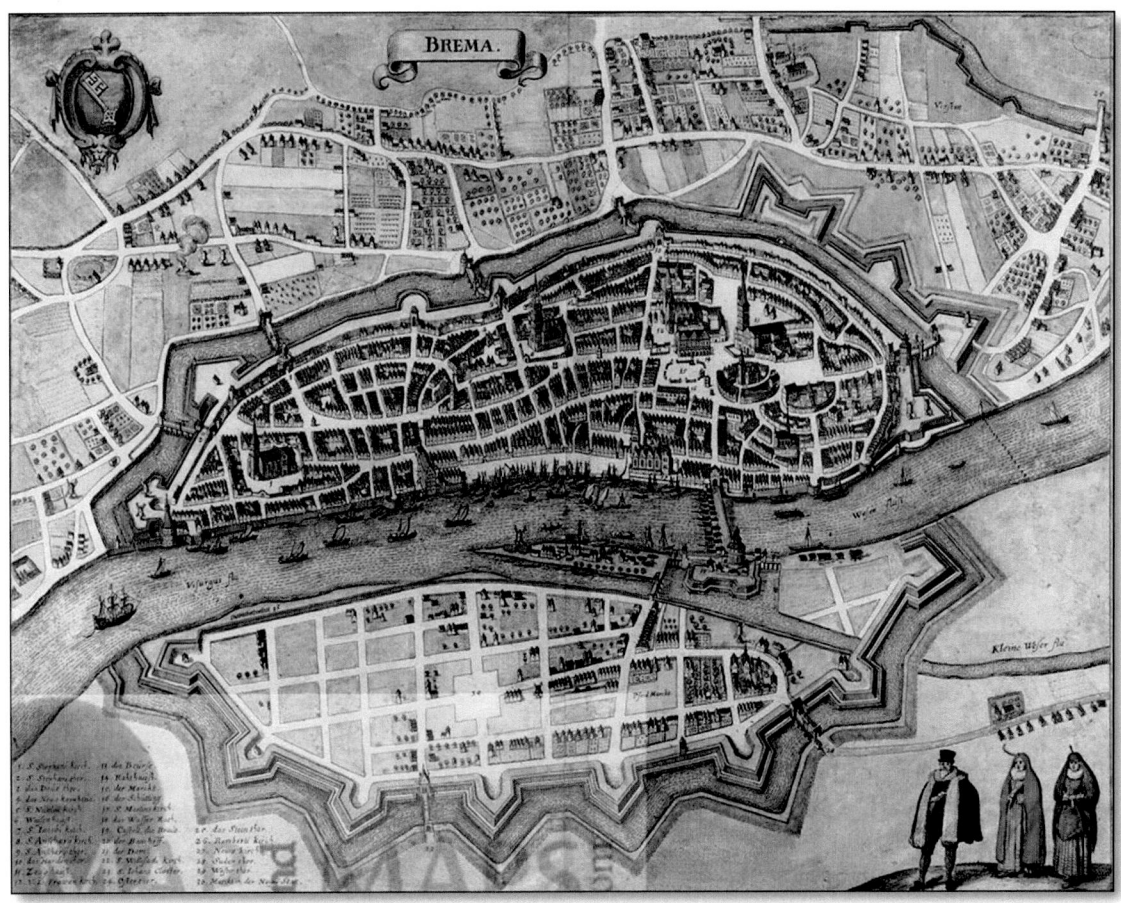

The fortifications of Bremen in the 1640s, shown in a print by Matthäus Mrian the Elder. (Author's collection)
Since the 1620s the City Council had updated the defences with modern bastions and external works; a decision that saved the city from the Swedish attempt to seize it with a regular siege.

## The *Wildfang* War, 1665–1668

Also known as the *Wildfang* Dispute, the dispute had its origins in a prolonged struggle for influence on the middle Rhine that initially involved Mainz and the Palatinate in 1651 and rendered the Electoral Rhenish circle inoperative for many years. The term *Wildfang* originated from a medieval right which allowed the ruling prince to grant people who were homeless or engaged in seasonal activities the status of subjects.[8] The Elector of the Palatinate, Carl Ludwig von Wittelsbach, resumed this right to increase the number of inhabitants of his state, which was hardly improved by the Thirty Years' War that had halved the population. Soon, this right turned into an actual immigration, since the Elector favoured the settlement of people by favourable concessions. As a consequence, the extension of this right affected neighbouring states, which lost significant population share.[9] In the 1650s, this prolonged struggle menaced the influence of the Elector Prince-Archbishop of Mainz, Johann Philip von Schönborn, who by 1663 also held the Bishopric of Worms, close to the Palatinate. The matter involved other states such as Electoral Cologne, Trier, and Lorraine, all concerned to stop the application of the *Wildfang* on their subjects. In 1663, the dispute reverberated in the Diet of Regensburg, which imposed on the Palatinate an order for the interruption of the *Wildfang*, but this could not be enforced and the year after the tension resumed. In the county of Falkenstein the situation became more intense. As the enclaves of such states were encompassed by Palatine territories, the Elector intended to extend his rights on these, as in the case of Falkenstein. Though the County was under Lorraine administration, Carl Ludwig had held the feudal lordship of Falkenstein since 1648. In order to better protect the territory, Charles IV of Lorraine had quartered a cavalry regiment, with orders to fight any attempt to establish the *Wildfang*. In February 1664, Carl Ludwig sent 3,000 regular soldiers and militia into Falkenstein, who disarmed the Lorraine troops in a surprise action. This event caused the protest of the Lorraine deputy to the Diet, and from Mainz, Schönborn suggested that if the Duke retaliated, the Empire would not disapprove. However, an initiative by Schönborn pre-empted the reprisals planned by the Duke of Lorraine.[10]

---

8    In the Middle Ages, the lawless strangers who placed themselves under the protection of the sovereign and thus became his serfs were called *Wildfänge* (animals' catchers). Even if there were no longer any serfs in the original sense by the seventeenth century, the Electoral Palatinate continued to exercise this privilege, even beyond the borders of the state. In 1667, the village of Mundenheim, which today is included in the municipality of Ludwigshafen am Rhein, housed 115 *Wildfänge* out of 122 residents. This suggests that this right was widely exercised by the Elector. Cf Johann Samuel Esch, and Johann Gottfried Gruber, (eds), *Allgemeine Encyklopädie der Wissenschaften und Künste in Alphabetischer Folge. Erste Section: A-G* (Leipzig: Brockhaus, 1840), Teil 33, p.121.

9    Karl Brunner, *Der Pfälzische Wildfangstreit unter Kurfürft Karl Ludwig (1664–1667)* (Innsbruck: Wagner'schen Universität-Buchhandlung, 1896), p.44. According to the author, in 1661, out of the 16,630 residents in 119 villages of the Bishoprics of Speyer and Worms, 12,759 were claimed by the Palatine Elector as his subjects by the right of the *Wildfang*.

10   Nicolas Buat, *La France et Les 'Différends Palatins'. L'Intervention de Louis XIV dans la Querelle du Droit de Wildfang en Allemagne, 1660–1674.* (Chartes: Ecole Nationale – HAL, 1995), p.147:

## WARS AND FACTIONS IN GERMANY (1653–1689)

It took Schönborn no more than a month to put in place a wider alliance, the aims of which were explicitly anti-Palatine. Also siding with Mainz, were the Bishops of Speyer and Strasbourg, the Wild- and Rhingraves and the immediate lesser nobility of the Empire on the Rhine, Swabia and Franconia. The allies, or *die Gravierten*, as they called themselves, were determined to obtain satisfaction from the Palatinate, and came together in an alliance that was both defensive and offensive, which was concluded at Regensburg on 31 March 1664.[11]

However, diplomacy did not stop in attempts to settle the dispute. On 11 February 1665, the complaints were forwarded to Vienna, but the mediation had little effect.[12] The Palatinate's stubbornness in enforcing the *Wildfang* was further aggravated by the toll and conduct fees imposed on the neighbouring states, which were considered to be outright vexations.[13] In May, Schönborn assembled a military force that was intended to secure his hold on the Bishopric of Worms. He gathered about 600 foot with a further 900 Lorraine cavalry and infantry still quartered in Mainz after the campaign against Erfurt in 1664. Cologne and Trier increased the allied side with 300 to 400 infantrymen each.

Elector Carl Ludwig considered this assembly of troops as an openly hostile act and prepared to face the threat. A resolute reply had to be given and therefore Carl Ludwig turned his attention to the fortified town of Ladenburg. Situated on the Neckar, Ladenburg occupied an important strategic position half a day from Heidelberg, and was surrounded by territories that mostly belonged to the Palatinate. In late April, regular soldiers and pioneers from the Palatinate entered the territory of Ladenburg and demolished the medieval curtain, leaving intact only a tower guarded by a small garrison. Schönborn and all the *Gravierten* interpreted this act as a declaration of war, and after asking for an explication from Carl Ludwig, ordered their forces to prepare to move.

---

'The Duke of Lorraine first asked Carl Ludwig for the return of weapons and horses from the Palatine soldiers, but the reply he received gave him no hope. In return, the Elector demanded that the Duke of Lorraine no longer hinder the exercise of *Wildfang*'s right in the county of Falkenstein until the dispute had been settled peacefully, either by treaty or by an Imperial sentence. He also proposed resuming the talks that had already been established to achieve this goal.'

11   Nicolas Buat, *La France et Les 'Différends Palatins'. L'Intervention de Louis XIV dans la Querelle du Droit de Wildfang en Allemagne, 1660–1674.* (Chartes: Ecole Nationale – HAL, 1995), pp.146–147: 'This alliance exceeded all expectations in terms of size, showing that the *Gravierten* were determined to defend themselves as a block.'

12   The issue was very complex and negotiations also involved the diplomacies of Sweden and Spain. The latter, the great protector of Catholicism in Europe, refused to support a Protestant prince who opposed a predominantly Catholic alliance; but the Palatinate, which had been the great victim of the Habsburgs in 1619, were turning to them to assert its rights. See also Karl Brunner, *Der Pfälzische Wildfangstreit unter Kurfürft Karl Ludwig (1664-1667)* (Innsbruck: Wagner'schen Universität-Buchhandlung, 1896), pp.23–24.

13   Nicolas Buat, *La France et Les 'Différends Palatins'. L'Intervention de Louis XIV dans la Querelle du Droit de Wildfang en Allemagne, 1660–1674.* (Chartes: Ecole Nationale – HAL, 1995), p.94.

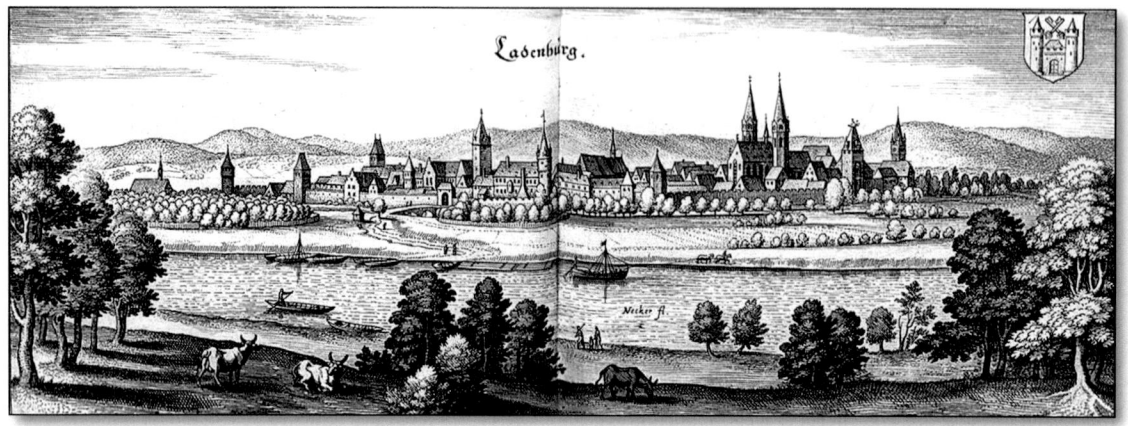

Ladenburg in a print of the mid-seventeenth century. (Author's collection)
The status of Ladenburg was the worst source of conflict imaginable. Since the fourteenth century, the Palatinate had owned half of the territory of Ladenburg, with the exception of the bishop's palace, since the Bishop of Worms had pledged the town to the Palatinate with the right to buy it back. However, the Electors of the Palatinate considered the city as their territory and when Schönborn, Prince-Bishop of Worms since 1663, expressed his wish to re-take the city entirely, the claim was unacceptable to Carl Ludwig. The cession of a fortified place in the middle of the Palatinate to the Elector of Mainz would have posed a threat to him and his subjects now that a war seemed increasingly likely.

Initially, the conflict remained of low intensity and only a few skirmishes took place between the Palatine outposts facing the troops of the three Archbishops, but this soon escalated when the Duke of Lorraine ordered Charles-Henry de Vaudemont to cross the border. On 22 May, Lorrainer troops looted some villages in the Palatinate and in June, alongside those of Mainz, besieged the small garrison of Ladenburg, which surrendered on terms. Carl Ludwig raised further troops and tried to cut the communication of his enemies but without success. In July, Vaudemont seized Odenheim and other minor posts, forcing Carl Ludwig to call for a truce. Meanwhile, he turned to Sweden, Brandenburg and other Protestant princes for help. Peace talks began with the mediation of Duke Philipp Wilhelm of Pfalz-Neuburg, cousin of Carl Ludwig, and soon involved the Emperor as well, who was concerned for the possible interference of France and Sweden in the Rhine affairs. However, the negotiations were interrupted in late August when an unfortuitous incident occurred between some Lorrainer horse and a Palatine officer and his men, causing a fight which resulted in the death of seven of the Elector's soldiers.[14]

During the summer, Carl Ludwig had exploited the truce to gather more professional troops and more militia to assault the Lorrainer troops quartered near Mainz in the night of 2/3 September. The action proceeded in a confused manner and allowed Vaudemont to face the approaching enemy with the infantry, which covered the retreat of the rest of the troops. The Lorraine cavalry took advantage of a favourable position and halted the

---

14  Reports refer to the Lorraine horse killing a barking dog belonging to a Palatine officer. This latter arrested the horsemen and confiscated their horses. The Lorraine reaction was directed against the quarters of the Palatinate soldiers who refused to release the prisoners. Jean-Charles Fulaine, *Le Duc Charles IV de Lorraine et son Armée* (Metz: Editions Serpenoise, 1997), p.208.

Palatines' assault with actions against the flanks of the unprotected enemy infantry. At dawn, Carl Ludwig became aware of the strong enemy position and tried to dislodge them with artillery, but with little success. News of the arrival of reinforcements from Mainz persuaded the Elector to order the withdrawal of his troops. The retreat ended on the night of 3/4 September, but the chaos generated by trumpet and drum signals dispersed the soldiers over too wide an area, and many of them were taken prisoner or deserted. The Allies did not take advantage of the situation and days later Carl Ludwig sent a request for a new truce of four months.[15]

Without waiting for the negotiations to progress, Charles IV of Lorraine sent Prince François-Marie de Lillebonne with a mixed corps to again invade the Palatinate. On 21 September, Lillebonne with 600 horse, 2,000 foot and three field guns routed the Electoral militia that had tried to bar his way at Frankenthal.[16] In the meantime, mediation from Vienna and other German princes led to a common agreement and a truce was finally signed on 31 October 1665, allowing all contenders to take up their winter quarters. Both Lorraine and the Palatinate took advantage of the truce to reinforce their respective armies and, by the beginning of the new year, the war had become an affair between Duke Charles IV and Elector Carl Ludwig.

Exploiting a pretext of the application of the *Wildfang* on some Lorraine subjects, in late February 1666, Charles IV ordered a punitive expedition into Palatine territory, to which a response followed days later Carl Ludwig opened the siege of Kislau, in the Bishopric of Speyer, with 1,700 horse and foot. The garrison, comprising two companies of Lorrainer cavalry under Falquemont, performed valiantly and allowed Vaudemont to relieve the fortress, forcing the Palatines to abandon the siege. On 20 March, after the arrival of more troops, the Lorrainers crossed the border and laid siege to Billigheim, which immediately surrendered. Again, Vaudemont with 1,500 horse, advanced into the Palatinate, looted seven or eight villages, and carried away 400 horses and cattle. Then he waited for new orders from Nancy. Schönborn and the other ecclesiastical princes did not join the Lorrainer plan and deplored the looting of the Electorate, because, according to them, this action would be followed by a more violent response by Carl Ludwig. As expected, on 24 August, the Elector Palatine assembled a party of cavalry and infantry supported by field guns and entered the enemy territory. The Palatine troops looted many villages in the Bishoprics of Worms and Speyer, and the properties of the minor nobility were not spared, such the town of Hernsheim, belonging to the Dalberg Counts. Here, the Electoral soldiers pillaged the castle and drank all of the wine and beer in the cellars. The

---

15  Nicolas Buat, *La France et Les 'Différends Palatins'. L'Intervention de Louis XIV dans la Querelle du Droit de Wildfang en Allemagne, 1660–1674.* (Chartes: Ecole Nationale – HAL, 1995), p.172. The negotiations had some effect and between Mainz and the Palatinate it was decided to leave the decision concerning Ladenburg to an Imperial arbitration. However, Carl Ludwig was trying to gain time, because he was alarmed by the news coming from Lorraine referring the formation of a strong party of intruders.

16  Nicolas Buat, *La France et Les 'Différends Palatins'. L'Intervention de Louis XIV dans la Querelle du Droit de Wildfang en Allemagne, 1660–1674.* (Chartes: Ecole Nationale – HAL, 1995), p.172.

Bishop of Speyer took advantage of the situation to ask for the protection of the King of France.[17]

After a series of skirmishes, the war resumed in intensity in the last days of August, when the Palatines again laid siege to Kislau. Days later, Lillebonne received orders to relieve the fortress with 400 horse and 500 foot.[18] The Lorrainer commander conducted the operation skilfully, crossing the Rhine with improvised boats, and recovered the lost time by forced marches on Kislau. For the second time, the Palatines abandoned the siege, avoiding a field engagement.

While the war continued, diplomacy tried to find a solution and this time Schönborn himself asked for new negotiations. He realised that the conflict was leading to an undesired aftermath. Although the Hertzog von Lorraine was an indispensable partner, being 'the spearhead of the coalition', he was prone to abuse his position to pursue a personal policy in which the general interest of the Allies took second place. He could be an adversary equal to Carl Ludwig; since both princes had the reputation of being equally reckless and the Duke was as good a captain as the Elector and was gifted with skill at cheating, they were destined for perpetual dissension. Therefore, after a short discussion with the Electors of Trier and Cologne, Schönborn called for the mediation of France.[19]

In the meantime, the conflict showed no signs of decreasing in intensity. Knowing that most of the Lorrainer troops were outside of the Duchy, on 2 September 1666, Carl Ludwig's *Generalleutnant* Chauvet, a Frenchman, crossed the Rhine at Gemersheim and entered Lorraine to extort contributions. The few Lorrainer troops under Haraucourt were quartered on the west bank of the great river, and found themselves threatened by the advancing enemy. On 4 September, a series of cavalry skirmishes began with alternating successes, but ended by the arrival of the vanguard of Lillebonne's corps, which had been hastily recalled. The fighting continued in the following days, involving the cavalry of both sides.

At the end of September, France and Sweden intervened as mediators to put an end to the conflict, as guarantors of the Treaty of Westphalia. The envoys of the two Kings asked the contenders to cease hostilities and enter peace negotiations, and to make the request more effective, on 29 September, the Duke of Lorraine received a letter from Louis XIV warning him to suspend operations immediately. On 18 October, the Lorrainer troops left the Palatinate and headed for home. At the beginning of November, a new letter stated Louis XIV's satisfaction at the end of the military operations. Days later, Swedish and French representatives assured Charles IV and the Archbishops of Mainz, Cologne and Trier about the Palatinate's forthcoming

---

17 Nicolas Buat, *La France et Les 'Différends Palatins'. L'Intervention de Louis XIV dans la Querelle du Droit de Wildfang en Allemagne, 1660-1674*. (Chartes: Ecole Nationale – HAL, 1995), p.204.
18 Jean-Charles Fulaine, *Le Duc Charles IV de Lorraine et son Armée* (Metz: Editions Serpenoise, 1997), p.210.
19 'Unfortunately, the initiative of Schönborn was very badly received by the Duke of Lorraine, and even the bishop of Speyer, whom the devastation of his bishopric had made warlike.' Nicolas Buat, *La France et Les 'Différends Palatins'. L'Intervention de Louis XIV dans la Querelle du Droit de Wildfang en Allemagne, 1660-1674*. (Chartes: Ecole Nationale – HAL, 1995), pp.203–204.

adherence to the peace negotiations.[20] Nevertheless, Carl Ludwig did not lay down his arms and after receiving reinforcements from Pfalz-Neuburg, sent 3,500 soldiers and militia into enemy territory. During the march, the Palatines besieged Kirrweiler, which surrendered after the brief resistance of the small garrison.

Lillebonne's troops, around 2,800 men, were deployed between Speyer, Mainz and the Lorraine border, and were widely separated, but after managing to gather 1,800 horse and foot, he marched southwards to face the Palatines. Cleverly exploiting the terrain and concealing the numerical inferiority of his troops, Lillebonne surprised the enemies not far from Kirrweiler on 7 November and, after routing them, seized a castle manned by a company of dragoons. To protect the retreat, the Palatines had left four squadrons on a height which dominated the marshy plains. With two squadrons including 40 dragoons, Lillebonne succeeded in also routing these. The Palatine cavalry suffered the loss of 80 men; *General* Chauvet had his arm broken, and several of his officers were killed. The Electoral Army could have suffered heavier casualties if it had not ensured control of the paths which passed through the swamps with artillery.[21]

The failure of the expedition persuaded Carl Ludwig to open peace negotiations, which began on 11 November thanks to Franco-Swedish mediation, and a peace was signed on 7 January at Heilbronn. A 'compromise' was pronounced on 17 February 1667 which aimed to restore the *status quo* limiting the right of *Wildfang*, but only after an agreement among the princes. The signing of the resolution had been received 'with good faith on one side as well as the other', but despite the ostensible good intentions, tensions between the Duke of Lorraine and the Elector of the Palatinate remained high, and a mutual hatred fuelled mistrust.[22] Not only had the troops not been dismissed, and were in winter quarters ready to reopen hostilities, but both sides had enlisted further men.

The last campaign had shown that the limited number of troops had affected the effectiveness of operations and consequently it had not been possible to prevail against the enemy. Therefore, both sovereigns assessed the economic effort required to achieve victory, but resources remained insufficient and additional revenue was difficult to obtain. In early 1667, Lorraine had about 3,600 professional soldiers, while the Prince-Elector could deploy 3,500–4,000 men in all,[23] figures still too low for victory over the enemy. As concerning the Palatinate was the debt it was accumulating,

---

20 Jean-Charles Fulaine, *Le Duc Charles IV de Lorraine et son Armée* (Metz: Editions Serpenoise, 1997), p p.212.
21 Nicolas Buat, *La France et Les 'Différends Palatins'. L'Intervention de Louis XIV dans la Querelle du Droit de Wildfang en Allemagne, 1660–1674.* (Chartes: Ecole Nationale – HAL, 1995), p.244.
22 Robert Parisot, *Histoire de Lorraine (Duché de Lorraine, Duché de Bar, Trois-Évêchés)*, (Paris, 1919–1924), tome II (1552–1789), p.88.
23 Jean-Charles Fulaine, *Le Duc Charles IV de Lorraine et son Armée* (Metz: Editions Serpenoise, 1997), p.215. The French author states 4,000 regular soldiers, while Oskar Bezzel, *Geschichte des Kurpfälzischen Heeres von Seinen Anfängen bis zur Vereinigung von Kurpfalz und Kurbayern* (Munich: Lindauer LTR-Verl, 1925), vol. I, p.99, calculates the Palatine Army as 3,416 men.

which was certainly beyond the state's means.²⁴ In June, the departure of the Lorrainer contingent for the War of Devolution shifted the balance in favour of the Prince-Elector, since this allowed Carl Ludwig time to increase the strength of his army. In spring 1668, the Palatine Army was estimated at 2,000 cavalry and dragoons and 6,000 infantry,²⁵ and soon the alarm sounded in Lorraine, since, pressed by the French ultimatum, Charles IV was disbanding his army. In summer, the resumption of the war seemed very probable. Charles IV was able to take the initiative, and on 12 May his troops seized Hoheneck, but on 4 July, news of the Palatine troops heading to Lorraine spread across the Duchy. Despite the concern of many, the event was welcomed by Charles IV, who could exploit the Palatine move to stop the disbandment of his army.²⁶

On 18 July 1668, the Palatine Army quartered before Kaiserslautern, where it could control the enemy approaches.²⁷ Carl Ludwig offered peace if Charles IV ceded Homburg, Landstuhl and Hoheneck. Having received no reply, the campaign resumed on 21 August, the previous day the Elector himself had joined the troops. Convinced that the truce was not broken, two Lorrainer officers, one of whom was a relative of the Duchess, were captured on their way from Landstuhl to Nancy. On 23 August, after a 24-hour siege, of which 12 hours was of cannon bombardment, the garrison laid down arms and was transferred to Homburg under escort.²⁸ Charles IV of Lorraine learned the news while in a brothel near Nancy, but wasted no time and immediately moved to his residence to call a war council. Dispatches were sent to gather all available troops and for the return of the contingent quartered in Flanders.²⁹

Meanwhile, on 29 August the castle of Hoheneck, 10km from Landstuhl, surrendered to Elector Carl Ludwig after a three-day siege; the garrison, numbering about 100 men, were given leave to evacuate the castle with their weapons. Thinking he had sufficiently intimidated his enemy, Carl

---

24  Karl Brunner, *Der Pfälzische Wildfangstreit unter Kurfürft Karl Ludwig (1664–1667)* (Innsbruck: Wagner'schen Universität-Buchhandlung, 1896), p.29.
25  Jean-Charles Fulaine, *Le Duc Charles IV de Lorraine et son Armée* (Metz: Editions Serpenoise, 1997), p.216. Again the sources notably differed on the Palatine strength. According to Oskar Bezzel, *Geschichte des Kurpfälzischen Heeres von Seinen Anfängen bis zur Vereinigung von Kurpfalz und Kurbayern* (Munich: Lindauer LTR-Verl, 1925), Band I, p.100, Elector Carl Ludwig had gathered just 6,500 men in all.
26  Robert Parisot, *Histoire de Lorraine (Duché de Lorraine, Duché de Bar, Trois-Évêchés)*, (Paris, 1919–1924), vol. II (1552–1789), tome II, p.89.
27  Nicolas Buat, *La France et Les 'Différends Palatins'. L'Intervention de Louis XIV dans la Querelle du Droit de Wildfang en Allemagne, 1660–1674.* (Chartes: Ecole Nationale – HAL, 1995), p.341: 'The Palatine expedition much irritated Louis XIV and his ministers, who were determined that the Duke of Lorraine should disarm his army. The latter had continued to repeat over the past weeks that he was threatened on his borders, and now Carl Ludwig's intentions seemed to prove him right.'
28  Jean-Charles Fulaine, *Le Duc Charles IV de Lorraine et son Armée* (Metz: Editions Serpenoise, 1997), p.218. They were 60 infantry privates and officers. Before the siege Lorraine could deploy 50 horse and 200 foot, but their fate is unclear. However, it is certain that there were casualties, since the brother of the Count d'Aspremont, who was in command of the cavalry is recorded as a casualty.
29  Jean-Charles Fulaine, *Le Duc Charles IV de Lorraine et son Armée* (Metz: Editions Serpenoise, 1997), p.218.

## WARS AND FACTIONS IN GERMANY (1653–1689)

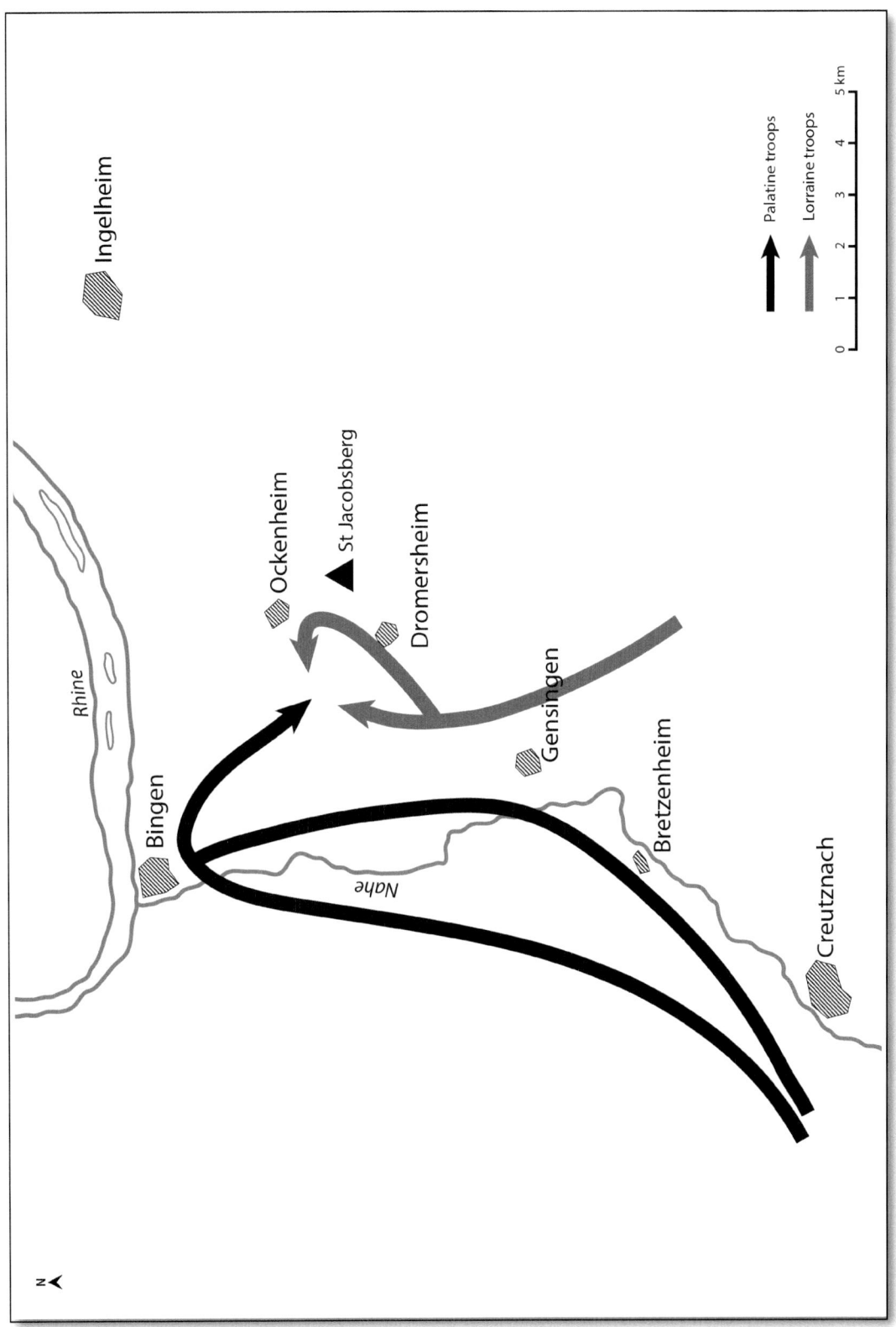

The manoeuvres of the Lorraine and Palatine Army before the Battle of Bingen (George Anderson, © Helion & Co.)

Ludwig interrupted the campaign, and on next day, after leaving a garrison in Hoheneck, the Palatine troops retruned to Lambsheim.

At the same time, Charles IV had completed the assembly of troops for a counter-offensive. These comprised 3,000 cavalry and 1,600 infantry, including 200 bourgeoisies of Nancy who formed two companies of foot, and two light guns.[30] By 30 August, under Lillebonne, the Lorrainer troops had reached Homburg, but it was not until 9 September that their approach became known to the Palatines. Marching in two columns, the Lorrainer infantry crossed the River Nahe at Bingen, in the territory of Mainz, while the cavalry led the way to the ford at Bretzenheim, after having extorted contributions in enemy territory. In mid-September, Lillebonne halted the advance and moved to a few kilometres south-east of Bingen, with the River Rhine to the north and the River Nahe to the west, deploying the troops with a front facing south towards Lambsheim, where reconnaissance had spotted the Palatine troops. Carl Ludwig could still deploy 1,500 horse and dragoons, but he had little knowledge about the enemy strength, since his cavalry performed very poorly in reconnaissance. Meanwhile, a last attempt to avoid the fighting was made by Schönborn. On 17 September, three deputies came to visit the two camps. The hope of agreement on a truce soon vanished. Carl Ludwig was sure to achieve the victory, and Lillebonne, who knew the inferiority of his forces, dispatched an officer to Mainz to ask for reinforcements and ammunition.[31] On 22 September, realising their mission had failed, the deputies returned to Mainz.

After two days of waiting, on 25 September the fighting began. The engagement, later known as the Battle of Bingen, lasted until the evening of 26 September, and was the major field encounter of the entire war. Lillebonne realising his shortage of food moved the army to the east in order to deploy the troops on the hills of Inghelsheim, where he could better sustain horses and men. Soon after the Palatine Army left its position and marched to close the passage to the enemy, occupying the routes and placing artillery on the hills of Ockenheim. During the march, cavalry parties engaged small bodies, and the Palatines avoided the full engagement and withdrew after a brief cannonade. Then, they decided to move onto the hills in order to dominate the right wing of the Lorrainers. All of this was the only action of the first day. During the night, the Lorrainers strengthened their position with embankments.

The following day, 26 September at 7 am, the Palatine artillery targeted the enemy infantry and cavalry deployed in the first line on the left. The fire caused few casualties, but succeeded in destroying two defences. At 2 pm, Lillebonne and his officers met in a council of war, and then ordered the reinforcement of the right wing with the infantry from the centre, replacing these latter with part of the cavalry of the reserve. The orders had been just issued, when the Palatine cavalry was sighted coming from the south-

---

30  Jean-Charles Fulaine, *Le Duc Charles IV de Lorraine et son Armée* (Metz: Editions Serpenoise, 1997), p.219.
31  Nicolas Buat, *La France et Les 'Différends Palatins'. L'Intervention de Louis XIV dans la Querelle du Droit de Wildfang en Allemagne, 1660–1674.* (Chartes: Ecole Nationale – HAL, 1995), p.344.

west. Immediately, Lillebonne called the reserve of cavalry and assaulted the Palatine's flank, while Vaudemont moved to face the enemy frontally. The action was performed by the elite of the Lorraine cavalry, including the *Gardes du Corps, Chevaux Legers*, and *Mousquetaires*. The manoeuvre succeeded in routing the Palatine cavalry, but their officers were able to rally them and soon launched another assault. The encounter turned into chaotic fighting: the Palatines fired at a short distance according to the cavalry tactics of the time, while the Lorrainers, who were short of ammunition, charged with cold steel. This tactic, and the higher quality of the Lorraine horsemen, made the difference and, for the second time, the Palatine cavalry fled from the battlefield.

Seeing the rout of his cavalry, Carl Ludwig moved infantry and dragoons forward, supported by artillery fire, against the enemies behind the embankments in the centre where Bellerose was in command. Under the incessant enemy artillery fire, he withdrew the troops back to take cover, but abandoned the cannon that had lost their train. The five Palatine infantry battalions of the first line were already crossing the unguarded embankments when Lillebonne, realising the emergency, charged the enemy flank with the cavalry still under his command, forcing the Palatine troops to withdraw.[32] Sources conflict regarding the final events of the battle: some state that the Palatines fled in disorder,[33] while other reports say that they retired in good order 'with a fanfare of drums and trumpets'. The Elector sent a messenger to ask the Lorrainers for permission to collect his dead.[34] Wth regards to the casualties the sources also disagree. The Lorraine reports do not refer their losses, but claimed 2,000 dead and missing 1,000 wounded and 400 prisoners for the Electoral Army.[35] In comparison, the German sources state 500 dead and wounded for the Lorrainers and 400 for the Palatines.[36]

Though the defeat frustrated the Elector's ambitions, it did not put an end to the war. In early October, Charles IV sent into the Palatinate 1,500 infantry and cavalry and four heavy cannon (two 24-pounders and two 18-pounders) under Armoises.[37] On 21 October, the Duke asked his nobility to serve as volunteers in the army. On 11 November, the Lorraine troops took up winter quarters on the border with the Palatinate, preparing for a new campaign. Charles IV was convinced that the Elector was unwilling to agree the truce, and was meditating a new assault; subsequent events proved him right. On 28 November, Carl Ludwig took the Castle of Winnweiler and nine

---

32 Jean-Charles Fulaine, *Le Duc Charles IV de Lorraine et son Armée* (Metz: Editions Serpenoise, 1997), p.220. The French reports of the battle testify to the valour of the Lorraine troops, whose commanders performed like 'true heroes'.
33 Jean-Charles Fulaine, *Le Duc Charles IV de Lorraine et son Armée* (Metz: Editions Serpenoise, 1997), p.220.
34 Nicolas Buat, *La France et Les 'Différends Palatins'. L'Intervention de Louis XIV dans la Querelle du Droit de Wildfang en Allemagne, 1660–1674*. (Chartes: Ecole Nationale – HAL, 1995), p.347.
35 Jean-Charles Fulaine, *Le Duc Charles IV de Lorraine et son Armée* (Metz: Editions Serpenoise, 1997), p.220.
36 Oskar Bezzel, *Geschichte des Kurpfälzischen Heeres von Seinen Anfängen bis zur Vereinigung von Kurpfalz und Kurbayern* (Munich: Lindauer LTR-Verl, 1925), Band I, p.101.
37 Jean-Charles Fulaine, *Le Duc Charles IV de Lorraine et son Armée* (Metz: Editions Serpenoise, 1997), p.222.

days later besieged Falkenstein. The Lorrainer's reaction was halted by the intervention of Louis XIV, who ordered the contenders to cease operations and join the mediation offered by France. On 30 December 1668, the war finally ended with the imposition of the Heilbronn's compromise by the French representatives.

## Second Swedish War on Bremen, 1666

By 1663, Gustav Horn was the Swedish Governor of the Duchies of Bremen and Verden. On every occasion he declared the Swedish aim to conquer Bremen, and the city had therefore improved its fortifications and was protected by a garrison of professional bourgeois soldiers, who formed a select militia. In the following year, relations between the City's Council and Sweden further worsened, and in 1665 Bremen refused to pledge allegiance to Carl X Gustav's successor, King Carl XI. Meanwhile, Denmark, Austria and other German princes sympathised with Bremen, and the Swedish King feared that they might declare war. In March, Carl XI decided on war, and 12,000 Swedish troops were transferred to the Duchy of Bremen by the end of the year. In early January 1666, Carl Gustaf Wrangel left from Swedish Pomerania to command the Swedish troops, which by early 1666 numbered 14,000 men. The second Swedish War on Bremen began on 27 January 1666, when the Swedish troops entered the Republic's territory. By summer, all of the area around the city was occupied without resistance, but Wrangel had miscalculated his siege artillery which proved inadequate for seizing the city. Meanwhile, Brandenburg, the Brunswick duchies, Electoral Cologne, and Osnabrück were gathering troops to relieve Bremen. In the face of the reaction from the Bremen allies, Carl XI issued instructions to his envoy in Paris, Esaias von Pufendorf, to ask for the support of Louis XIV, since France was a guarantor of the Westphalia Treaty, in order to definitively bring Bremen under Sweden's control. However, the French King did not agree to this request, because Imperial protection could provoke a larger war, and in 1666 Louis XIV was focused on dividing his enemies and not uniting them.[38]

Meanwhile, Bremen was receiving actual aid from the Brunswick duchies and also from Brandenburg, Denmark, Osnabrück, and the Dutch Republic supporting the city and forging an anti-Swedish alliance. In October, around 25,000–29,000 soldiers under Prince Georg Friedrich of Waldeck headed for Bremen.[39] The two sides did not engage inbattle, and Wrangel failed to lay siege to the city. Negotiations were opened at the Swedish headquarters in

---

38 Hugues de Lionne, the French secretary of foreign affairs, advised the Swedes that they would be better off waiting for a situation when the Dutch Republic, the Emperor and the neighbouring German principalities were involved in other disputes, and then take Bremen by surprise. Further reading: Beate-Christine Fiedler, 'Esaias v. Putendorf (1628–1689). Diplomat in Europa und Kanzler in den Schwedischen Herzogtümern Bremen und Verden – eine biographische Skizze' in Asmus, Droste, Olesen, (editors), *Gemeinsame Bekannte: Schweden und Deutschland in der Frühen Neuzeit* (Berlin-Hamburg-Münster: LIT Verlag, 2003), pp.170–179.

39 Robert Wilhelm Georg von Sichart, *Geschichte der Königlich-Hannoverschen Armee* (Hannover, Hahn'sche Hofbuchhandlung, 1866), band I, pp.351–354.

Habenhausen and, on 14 November, a truce was signed. The Swedes were obliged to destroy the fortresses they had built close to Bremen territory; but the City was forbidden to send representatives to the Diet of the Lower Saxony Circle. Bremen further had to cede its territories north of the city and on the lower Weser River, but the city itself with a number of villages around, maintained its independence.[40] Finally, Bremen had to give up its status as an Imperial City during the current sessions of the Diet. What could not be foreseen at the time of the Peace was that the Imperial Diet was to become the 'Perpetual Diet of Regensburg', lasting until the dissolution of the *Reich* in 1804.

## Hamburg's War, 1685–1686

Having failed to seize Hamburg in 1679, following the actions of Brandenburg, Celle, Hannover and Münster which had forced Christian V to lift his blockade of the city, Denmark waited for a new opportunity. At the beginning of 1685, a dispute began between the citizens and the Hamburg magistrate. At the head of the citizens was the popular merchant Schnittger, who had favoured Mayor Maurer for election to office. As the dispute seemed to be endless, and the magistrates were forced to leave the city, the Diet and the Emperor entrusted Duke Georg Wilhelm of Celle with the task of settling the dispute. Unfortunately, the citizens did not recognise this decision, rejecting it as a violation of their rights. In the meantime, the Duke had the ringleaders tracked down in the surroundings of Hamburg and on 29 March 1685, Schnittger was captured while travelling with an escort of armed men. However, from Hamburg, Schnittger's followers intercepted the Celle soldiers, disarmed them and beheaded nine officers and non-commissioned officers.

On the advice of the Elector of Brandenburg, the citizens of Hamburg sent two deputies to Vienna to denounce the outrage. Anxious to avenge the murder of his men, in January 1686, Georg Wilhelm had 2,000 soldiers from Franke Dragoons and Linstrow Infantry Regiment cross the Elbe at Artlenburg, and from there head to Bergedorf advancing into Hamburg's *Vierlande*. Celle's troops succeeded in taking the Heckaten redoubt, albeit with some losses, and subsequently repulsed an attempt by Hamburg's *Oberstleutnant* Manecke, who attempted to drive them off with 700 infantry. Due to the failure of the action, Manecke was arrested and shot because, according to the Hamburg military court, he had not done his duty. Denmark, Sweden and Brandenburg, however, mediated the problem so that Celle's troops left the Hamburg territory at the beginning of April. In return, they maintained some garrisons on the border and extracted contributions from Moorburg and Moorwerder.

Before the dispute was settled, a new danger materialised against Hamburg. King Christian V of Denmark tried to use the occasion of the

---

40    Konrad Elmshäuser, *Geschichte Bremens* (Munich: Beck, 2007), p.60.

internal unrest and the dispute with Celle to force Hamburg to accept submission and 'hereditary homage'. In early summer 1686, he ordered an advance on the city with an army of 16,000 men. However, the Senate and the rebel citizens not only quickly resolved internal disputes, but also made peace with Celle. Brandenburg, Sweden and Hannover also sided with the city against the Danes. Brandenburg and Celle even supported Hamburg with their own troops. On 21 August 1686, Celle's *Obrist* Linstrow arrived in Hamburg with 1,200 musketeers and dragoons; while soldiers dismissed by Celle, entered the service of Hamburg after an oath to the city. A further 800 horsemen arrived from Celle a few days later. Hamburg united in their efforts and withstood a siege that lasted 21 days. During the hostility initiated by the Danes, Celle's troops performed an excellent service by defending the Sternschanze, a trench that had been erected in front of the Damm Gate, and during the raids against Hamburg, the cavalry engaged the enemies in violent skirmishes.

In Hamburg, however, a conspiracy arose, headed by Schnittger and his follower Gastram, who wanted to hand the city over to the Danes. With the mediation of Brandenburg, Sweden and Celle, a truce with the Danes was agreed upon. In the treaty of 28 October 1686, the Pinneberg Agreement of 1679 was reconfirmed, and the Danes withdrew from Hamburg territory in mid-September. The city magistrates returned to the city in October. After the execution of the two traitors, Gaftram and Schnittger, Mayor Maurer also returned to Hamburg and was reinstated in office.[41]

## Danish Occupation of Holstein-Gottorf, 1684–1689

In the Treaty of Oliva of 1660, Sweden had forced Denmark to recognise the independence of Holstein-Gottorf. The Duchy of Schleswig had previously been a Danish fief. The Kings of Denmark regretted having having made this concession, and repeatedly invaded Schleswig-Holstein-Gottorf during 1675–1679. On 30 May 1684, a Danish force under *General* Fuchs invaded and occupied Holstein-Gottorf again and expelled Duke Christian Albrecht who fled to Hamburg. Holstein-Gottorf, being a patchwork of territories without natural defences, was easy prey; the Danes encountered hardly any resistance. Additionally, Holstein-Gottorf's traditional ally, Sweden, did not act. In 1689, diplomatic mediation and pressure resulted in the Treaty of Altona, which restored Duke Christian Albrecht to his territories and England and the Dutch Republic guaranteed the sovereignty of Holstein-Gottorf.[42]

---

41 Robert Wilhelm Georg von Sichart, *Geschichte der Königlich-Hannoverschen Armee* (Hannover, Hahn'sche Hofbuchhandlung, 1866), band I, pp.405–407.
42 Friedrich Carl Rode, *Kriegsgeschichte Schleswig-Holsteins* (Neumünster: K. Wachholz 1935), pp.34–35.

# Lauenburg's Succession, 1689–1693

The Duchy of Saxe-Lauenburg became an object contested by its neighbours when, in 1689, Duke Julius Franz died without leaving a male heir. Saxe-Lauenburg was an immediate principality of the Empire and a member of the Lower Saxon Circle. Duke Georg Wilhelm of Celle was one of the closest and senior of the male-line claimants to the succession. The other claimants included the five Ascanian-ruled territories of Anhalt, Saxony, Saxe-Wittenberg, Sweden and Brandenburg, and also the neighbouring Mecklenburg-Schwerin and the Danish Duchy of Holstein, whose ruler was King Christian V of Denmark (whose mother was Georg Wilhelm's sister).

Duke Georg Wilhelm of Celle occupied the Duchy creating a 'fait accompli'. King Christian V of Denmark had an old account to settle with Celle over 1686 when approaching troops of Georg Wilhelm had caused him to break off the siege of Hamburg and in 1693 sent an army into the Duchy of Lauenburg, demanding Celle's troops to leave the country. However, only Georg Wilhelm and Christian V of Denmark engaged militarily on the question. When this demand was denied, the Danish troops seized and destroyed the fortress city of Ratzeburg, a part of the Duchy of Lauenburg, except for the Cathedral district (which belonged to Mecklenburg). The fortifications of Ratzeburg had only been strengthened in 1690. The Emperor Leopold I did not interfere directly as he was involved in the War of the Grand Alliance against France, although he condoned the occupation of Lauenburg by Duke Georg Wilhelm. Christian V of Denmark avoided committing to an all-out war and, after the destruction of Ratzeburg, withdrew his troops; the fate of Sachsen-Lauenburg remained tied to Celle.[43] An accord was reached between Celle and Denmark by which on 9 October 1693, in the *Hamburger Vergleich* (the Hamburg Comparison), Georg Wilhelm – who now de facto held most of Saxe-Lauenburg – would retain the duchy in a personal union. Meanwhile, the Emperor Leopold I, who had no direct claim to the duchy, occupied the Land of Hadeln, a Saxe-Lauenburg enclave, and held it in Imperial custody. Apart from that, Leopold did not attempt to use force in Saxe-Lauenburg.

---

43 Robert Sichart, *Geschichte der Königlich-Hannoverschen Armee* (Hannover, Hahn'sche Hofbuchhandlung, 1866), band 1, pp.572–573.

# Colour Plate Commentaries

## Plate A – the Hansa and *Reichstâdte*, 1686–1690

### 1 – Hamburg, *Uffeln zu Fuss* (Hai-1), Musketeer, 1686

On 25 November 1679, the City Council ordered that the *Stadtsoldaten* be dressed in 'certain livery' (uniform) of the Hanseatic colour, namely red. Cavalry and artillery probably followed the same pattern. In the same year, 500 German *Flintmusketen* or *Schnapphahnen* were issued to the infantry but these seemed unreliable, and were replaced a year later with a new order for 300 Dutch flintlocks. In 1683 a grenadier company was also raised, probably wearing a cloth cap with a frontal plate showing the Coat of Arms of the city. For 1688, the records show that in August the rank and file and officers of the *Leibregiment* (the regiment *Uffeln*) were dressed with the new red uniforms lined of blue. The second regiment, in red lined green, followed a few days later.

### 2 – Bremen, Infantry, Musketeer, 1689–1690

In the eighteenth century, Bremen infantry wore uniforms manufactured in the colours of the Hanseatic towns, red and white, which were also common in Lübeck. Although there is no definate evidence, it is likely that the regular infantry was already wearing these colours in the last quarter of the seventeenth century.

### 3 – Augsburg, Infantry NCO, 1690s

The earliest information on a regular uniform issued to the Augsburg infantry dates to 1702, however, the instruction suggests that it is a confirmation of existing regular clothing for rank and file. The uniform consisted of a light grey *Rock* faced and lined in blue for private soldiers, while NCOs could tailor their own coat of blue, laced with gold as a distinction of rank.

German grenadiers in an illustration by Anton Faulhaber from *Die Artilleriekunst* (Ulm, between 1680 and 1702). The author took as an example the grenadier depicted in the *Travaux de Mars* by Mallet (Paris: 1684), however this type of clothing, comprising a broad-brimmed hat, was common in South Germany's armies before the introduction of the *Pelzmütze*.

## Plate B – *Feldabzeichen*

Scarves had identified the nationality of armies since at least the sixteenth century, becoming in the next century the common field distinction for officers in the Western European armies. 1) Celle and Hanover; 2) Wolfenbüttel; 3) Hessen-Kassel; 4) Hessen-Darmstadt (late version); 5) Electoral Cologne (1672–74); 6) the Palatinate; 7) Württemberg; 8) Mecklenburg; 9) Holstein-Gottorf; 10) Brandenburg-Bayreuth and Ansbach-Bayreuth; 11) Salzburg; 12) Lorraine.

## Plate C – Infantry Colours

### 1 – Hannover, regiment *Lippe zu Fuss* (BhI-2), company Colour, 1674

The infantry Colours of Hannover during the reign of Johann Friedrich are very varied in their design and symbols, but tend to have the distinctive colour of the regiment as predominant. However, there is no shortage of exceptions. In the cartoon of the Camp of Jensen in 1674, this regiment has 11

## COLOUR PLATE COMMENTARIES

ensigns consisting of four horizontal stripes of blue, yellow, red and black in various patterns for each company. The regiment was originally identified as *Das Blaue Regiment*, but in this case the distinctive colour appears alongside with a further three unrelated to the regiment. The monogram 'JF' (Johann Friedrich) appears on other ensigns, but not on the ones of this regiment. This could have been an omission because these are very small drawings. The same design, but with stripes of white and gold, is attributed to the *Neue Blau* regiment (BhI-7). A twelfth ensign, the *Leibfahne*, is white with golden designs. At Neerwinden in 1693, the regiment, now under *Obrist* Du Mont, lost a blue ensign with the monogram 'EA' (Ernst August) in yellow-gold.

### 2 – Hannover, regiment *Mücheln zu Fuss* (BhI-7), company Colour, 1674

A blue company Colour represented on the Jensen Cartoon in 1674 is attributed this regiment, originally known as *das Neue-blaue*, alongside with other striped flags as described above.

### 3 – Hannover, regiment *Wiedemann zu Fuss* (BhI-5), company Colour, 1680

Ensigns chequered of green and white are already attributed to this regiment in 1674. Six years later, there is a detailed description of each ensign provided by Schirmer, who mentions seven ensigns of green and white, one with 12 squares and six with 9. Five ensigns with 9 squares carry a design in the centre inside a golden laurel. A company Colour is of yellow, and another has stripes of white, yellow, red and black, with the monogram 'JF'. These latter belonged to companies coming from the 'old yellow' and 'old blue' regiments. The colonel's Colour is white with a right arm holding a green palm emerging from a white cloud, and a sword on the left. The green and white ensign is confirmed for this regiment again in 1693 by a series of flags illustrated in the *Triomphes* of Louis XIV.

Hanover, regiment *Ohr zu Fuss* (BhI-8), Colour lost at Neerwinden in 1693.
Red with yellow monogram 'EA'. After the great variety in infantry ensigns before 1679, there was a considerable simplification with the arrival of Duke Ernst August. The backgrounds are mostly red, or of the distinctive colour of the regiment, more rarely the field is in four colours two of which white. Sometimes, the only decoration besides the monogram is the ducal crown. The same pattern was used in cavalry and dragoon ensigns, but only with the distinctive colour.

### 4 – Celle, regiment *Nettelhorst zu Fuss*, 1690s

In Celle, infantry Colours often had the white horse on a red or white background for the colonel's Colour, however, in certain cases there are flags with different designs and symbols. This company Colour was lost at Neerwinden in 1693, and it has no heraldic symbols or motto. For the same regiment in 1691, Sichart describes a company Colour of carmine red, with a golden lion lying on a green ground at the centre, green laurels tied by a red ribbon, and the motto VIGILANTIA VINCIT of black on a white scroll.

### 5 – Wolfenbüttel, *Leibregiment Anton Ulrich* (BwI-2), colonel's Colour, 1680–1690

White Colours carrying the horse of Brunswick are described in the 1680s for the Wolfenbüttel infantry. Company Colours could be of different hues, but blue was the most common.

The Wolfenbüttel regiment *Bernstorf zu Fuss* (BwI-6) lost one white and nine blue ensigns with crown, golden laurels and monogram at the Battle of Fleurus on 1 July 1690. This pattern differs considerably from the one used in most infantry Colours of this period, which usually carry the white Guelph horse.

## Plate D – Infantry Colours

### 1 – Hessen-Kassel, Company Colour, *Regiment Ufm Keller zu Fuss* (HkI-3), 1676–78.

Most of the knowledge about Hessen-Kassel Colours in the last quarter of the seventeenth century comes from the originals preserved in the Armémuseum in Stockholm, which were copied by Olof Hofmann in the eighteenth century in a series preserved in the Armémuseum's library. The Hessian infantry lost one white and seven blue ensigns at Warskow, in January 1678. The blue ensigns had a golden number on the left corner identifying the company. Devices and mottos were the same for all Colours.

# COLOUR PLATE COMMENTARIES

## 2 – Hessen-Darmstadt, Company Colour, 1663

As in Hessen-Kassel, the infantry of Darmstadt carried blue Colours displaying the heraldic lion and palm leaves of silver or gold. The monogram of the Landgrave is repeated in the corners, as described in a contemporary account.

## 3 – Lorraine, Company Colours, 1650–1660

Most of the Lorraine infantry Colours known today have red and yellow as their main colouring with the double cross, known as the 'cross of Lorraine' disposed in various designs. White ensigns with red or golden cross and the image of Mary with Infant Jesus are mentioned in the 1650s, probably as colonels' Colours.

## 4 – Brandenburg-Bayreuth, *Erbprinz zu Fuss* (BbI-2), Company Colour, 1687

As described in the note written by Obrist Carl Sparre, both regiments hired to Venice carried white ensigns with the Brandenburg eagle and the devise QUO PROPIOR, EO ACRIOR (The Closer To The Enemy, The Braver). The flames in the corners in the regiments' distinctive/facing colour are conjectural.

## 5 – Osnabrück, Regiment *Borch zu Fuss* (OsI-3), Colonel's Colour (?), 1670s

## 6 – Osnabrück, Regiment *Ohr zu Fuss* (OsI-1), Company Colour, 1679

Both Colours belonged to infantry regiments which arrived in Hannover with Herrzog Ernst August in 1679 after he succeeded as the new ruler of the duchy. Two ensigns like the one reproduced are attributed to regiment *Ohr zu Fuss*, while regiment *Borch* also had further white ensigns but without the red wheel of Osnabrück, one with the golden motto CAVE FERIO; one with the motto HONESTUM PRO PATRIA in gold, one white with the motto ITA ET VIRTUS in gold. A third regiment, *Hülsen zu Fuss*, had a yellow-red-yellow-red vertical striped ensign.

## Plate E – Infantry Colours

**1 – Holstein-Gottorf, *Leibgarde zu Fuss* (hgi-1), 1664**

**2 – Mecklenburg, *Reichskontingent*, Company Colour, 1664**

**3 – Pfalz-Neuburg, Company Colour, 1650–60**

The *Gazette de France* in 1655 described the colour 'ensigns' of the Pfalz-Neuburg infantry as black and yellow with a red cross of St Andrew. This type of cross may have been the main symbol for the Pfalz-Neuburg infantry colours. The same cross, in gold, appears on the colonel Colour of the regiment commanded by the Prince of Pfalz-Neuburg serving in the Dutch Army in the 1690s.

**4 – Hamburg, regiment *Uffeln zu Fuss*, Grenadier Company Colour, 1684**

Regiment *Uffeln zu Fuss* formed its grenadier company in 1684, as shown on the Colours. The Colour carries the grenadier's arms and equipment, including the flintlock muskets, with the Arms of Hamburg (the white castle) in the centre, as was typical on the Colours of the Free Imperial City.

In the *Mittheilungen zur Geschichte der militärischen Tracht*, Richard Knötel, and Thomas Muhsfeldt, described the symbols carried on the company colours of the Hamburg infantry regiment Scheiter in 1686, when the *Statsoldaten* paraded though the city:

> *Obrist Kompagnie*: the word Jehovah in Hebrew letters and the motto DER HERR IST MEIN BANNIER UND MEIN SCHILD (The Lord is my banner and my shield).
> 
> *Obristlieutenant Kompagnie*: a rock surrounded by water with the devise ICH STEHE FEST (I stand fast).
> 
> *Obristwachtmeister Kompagnie*: a light on a beacon with the motto ICH ZÜNDE ANDEREN AN (I set others on fire).
> 
> *Hauptmann* Schaffshausen: a lion with the motto ICH FÜRCHTE MICH FÜR NICHTS (I am afraid of nothing).
> 
> *Hauptmann* Brakel: a sun shining on the sea with the motto GESCHWIND UND UNERMÜDET (Fast and untiring).
> 
> *Hauptmann* Westius: a crane with the motto ICH HALTE GUT WACHE (I keep watch well).
> 
> *Hauptmann* Rebenstock: Fortuna with the motto DAS GLÜCK ZU ERGREIFEN, MUSS MAN KEINE GELEGENHEIT VERSÄUMEN (To take hold of fortune you must not miss any opportunity).

# COLOUR PLATE COMMENTARIES

*Hauptmann* Schwarz: a Karl (a man in a coat of mail) with arrows which he is breaking over his knee, with the motto JE MEHR, JE STÄRKER (The more, the stronger).

*Hauptmann* Böhme (grenadier company): the Arms of the City with the grenadier weaponry and the motto NEMO ME IMPUNE TANGET (No one touches me with impunity).

*Hauptmann* Kregel: three leaves with a grenade and the motto GREIFTS DU NACH MIR, SO STECH ICH NACH DIR (If you grab at me I shall prick you).

Unfortunately, there is no information about the colouring, but the field was red with the Coat of Arms of the City of Hamburg.

The city militia companies also carried Colours of a distinctive hue: St Petri red, St Nicolai blue, St Katharinen yellow; St Jacobi and St Georg white, St Michaelis green.

## 5 – 6 Würzburg Company Colours

Contemporary sources report that the Würzburg infantry had white and blue Colours and others of different colours with the Imperial eagle bearing the Coat of Arms of the ruling bishop. The Colour on the left comes from the age of Johann Gottfried II von Gutenberg (1684–1698). Both Colours are reconstructions by the author.

# Plate F – Cavalry Standards and Dragoon Guidons

## 1 – Hannover, Regiment *Massenbach zu Pferd* (BhC-4), Company Standard, 1673–1679

The regiment was formed in 1673, but in 1679 was disbanded and only the colonel's company remained in service. Which is the primary reason for the survival of the standard, today it is preserved in the Marienburg Castle in Germany; approximate size: 60cm x 60cm.

## 2 – Hanover, Regiment *Vitry Dragoner* (BhD-2), Company Guidon, 1680–1691

Wolfenbüttel cavalry standards. Left: *Anton Ulrich Garde zu Pferde* (bwc-i), 1666: white background with golden monogram AU, palm leaves, crown and fringes. Right; cavalry *Leibregiment Rudolph August* (BwC-10), 1689: white background with golden monogram RA, palm leaves, crown and fringes

**3 – Celle, Company Standard, Regiment *Lippe zu Pferd* (BcC-8), 1680–90.**

After *Les Triomphes du Louis XIV*; this standard was lost at Fleurus in 1690. In the collection, the standard is reproduced two times, but with some differences in details and decorations.

**4 – Celle, Company Standard, Regiment *Chauvet zu Pferd* (BCC-1), 1690s.**

The standard was captured by the French at Neerwinden in 1693; the regiment was under the same colonel since 1670.

**5 – Celle, Company Standard, Regiment *Brennecke zu Pferd*, 1690.**

**6 – Hessen-Darmstadt, Company Standard, *Riedesel zu Pferd* (BdC-1) 1677–78.**

Wilhelm Beck attributes four green standards to this regiment, which existed from 1677 to 1678. Obverse and reverse were the same, but the reverse had different mottos applied in a circle: PRO DEO ET PATRIA; OPPORTUNE LUCEBIT; CORONABO; HAUD DORMIO. The pole bears a golden finial with the monogram 'L'.

**7 – Electoral Cologne, Company Standard, 1674.**

This is the only known Electoral Cologne standard, albeit the reverse had probably a different design. It was preserved in the Dutch National Army Museum before the destruction in the World War Two.

**8 – 9 Osnabrück, Company and Colonel Standards, unknown regiments, 1679**

Four standards with the white horse of Brunswick, and another four standards with a lion, belonged to two unknown cavalry regiments arrived from Osnabrück in 1679.

**10 – 11 Lorraine, Companies' Standards, 1660–70s**

**12 – Frankfurt am Main, Company Standard of the City Mounted Militia 1660s**

# COLOUR PLATE COMMENTARIES

The *Grand Étendard* of Lorraine (Author's reconstruction). It is also known as the Charles IV standard, because it was created by the Duke during the Thirty Years' War. The standard has a yellow field and golden fringe, and includes the Coat of Arms of Lorraine surmounted by the ducal crown. It also displays the crosses of Lorraine and the red cross of St John. This standard accompanied the duke in all of his military engagements until 1675.

## Plate G – Cavalry Standards

### Hessen-Kassel, Standards, Regiment *Hornhumb Zu Pferd* (HkC-1), 1677–78

The complete stand of the Standards lost by the Hessen-Kassel cavalry at Warskow, on the island of Rügen, in January 1678. These are today preserved in the Armémuseum in Stockholm. Size: 63cm x 65cm.

Life Colour of the Hessen-Kassel *Leibregiment* in 1689, reconstructed from a written description. White background, green laurels, red scroll with golden letters; goose natural on a green field.

## Plate H – Strasbourg

### Infantry and cavalry ensigns of the Burgewehr, (1665-69)

From Joseph Gény, Die Fahnen der Strassburger Bürgerwehr im 17. Jahrhundert (Strasbourg: J.H.E. Heitz, 1902).

Only two of the eight companies forming the regiments are known, both belonging to the first company. The flag changed every time a new ensign was appointed.

**1 – Martin Andreas König (1653–1669)**

**2 – Matthäus Kniebs (1669–1681)**

The regiment existed from 1633, and continued to serve until 1681, when it was disbanded after the French occupation. The colonels commanding, from 1660 were Johann Jakob Erhardt; Johann Philipp Müth (1664); Franciscus Reisseissen (1676); Johann Leonhard Fröreissen (1677).

**3 – 4 Standards of the cavalry companies**

*Rittmeister* Johann Wencker and *Rittmeister* Johann Reisshoffer.

### Plate I - Infantry Colours (copies after *Les Triomphes du Louis XIV*), late 17th-early 18th century.

1) Hannover, *Bremer zu Fuss* (BhI-13), company colour.
2) The Palatinate, *Kurprinz zu Fuss* (KpI-6) life colour.
3) *Sachsen-Meiningen zu Fuss* (KpI-9), company colour.
4) Frankfurt am Main, company colour.

### Plate J - Cavalry Standards (copies after *Les Triomphes du Louis XIV*), late 17th-early 18th century.

1) Hannover, attributed to *Öffener zu Pferd* (BhC-10), company standard.
2) *Raugraf zu Pferd* (BhC-9), company standard.
3) The Palatinate: *Leibregiment zu Pferd* (KpC-2) life standard.
4) *Franckenberg zu Pferd* (KpC-3) company standard.
5) Wolfenbüttel, *Öst-Friesland zu Pferd* (BwC-10), life standard.

COLOUR PLATE COMMENTARIES

## Plate K – Bremen, Colour of the Bürgerkompanie (late 17th-early 18th century) (on rear cover)

from the *Wappenbuch der Bürgerkompanie der Obern und Langestrasse* (Staats und Universitätsbibliotek Bremen).

The only known Colour of the Bremen city militia is reproduced in the Wappenbuch der Bürgerkompanie dating to 1731. The style and decoration of the ensign suggest that it was already in use in the previous century. The Latin motto SED PACEM BELLUM VOLES AD UTRUNQUE PARATUS (If you want peace and war, be prepared for both) expresses the city's attitude toward a peaceful but not submissive foreign policy (Approximate size cm. 200x200).

Throughout the three parts of this book, the author has used a reference code whilst referring to the units under discussion. The code can be referenced in the appendix chapter containing the history, engagements, and uniforms of the various corps.

# Appendix I

# Orders of Battle and Tabular Data

## German Soldiers' Trade (Auxiliary troops in Foreign Service), 1658–1669

| State: | Agreement: | Partner: | 1658 | 1659 | 1660 | 1661 | 1662 | 1663 | 1664 | 1665 | 1666 | 1667 | 1668 | 1669 |
|---|---|---|---|---|---|---|---|---|---|---|---|---|---|---|
| Holstein-Gottorf | 1658 | Sweden | 1,500 | Passed into Swedish service in 1658 | | | | | | | | | | |
| Bavaria | 1658 | Venice | | 1,000 | 1,000 | ? | ? | ? | ? | 300 | | | | |
| Pfalz-Neuburg | March 1660 | Münster | | | 500 | Passed into Münster service in 1661 | | | | | | | | |
| Cologne | March 1660 | Münster | | | 500 | 500 | | | | | | | | |
| Trier | March 1660 | Münster | | | 500 | 500 | | | | | | | | |
| Münster | January 1661 | Emperor | | | | 3,000 | 3,000 | | | | | | | |
| Ansbach | March 1661 | Venice | | | | 800 | 800 | 800 | 800 | 800 | 800 | 800 | ? | |
| Trier | April 1661 | Emperor | | | | 500 | Passed into Imperial service in 1661 | | | | | | | |
| Mainz | May 1661 | Emperor | | | | 1,200 | Passed into Imperial service in 1661 | | | | | | | |
| Würzburg | May 1661 | Emperor | | | | 1,000 | Passed into Imperial service in 1661 | | | | | | | |
| Brandenburg | October 1663 | Emperor | | | | | | | | 2,000 | | | | |
| Saxony | October 1663 | Emperor | | | | | | | | 1,174 | | | | |
| Lorraine | August 1664 | Mainz | | | | | | | | 880 | | | | |
| Münster | April 1665 | Spain | | | | | | | | | 3,800 | Passed into Spanish service in 1666 | | |
| Hanover & Osnabrück | May 1665 | The Palatinate | | | | | | | | | 500 | | | |
| Osnabrück | May 1667 | The Palatinate | | | | | | | | | | | 1,840 | |
| Lorraine | June 1667 | France | | | | | | | | | | | 2,700 | 2,700 |
| Hanover & Osnabrück | December 1667 | Dutch Rep. | | | | | | | | | | | 4,614 | |

| Celle | March 1668 | Venice | | | 3,300 | 3,300 |
| Celle | June 1668 | Dutch Rep. | | 400 | 400 | |
| Hanover | August 1668 | Venice | | | 400 | 400 |
| Osnabrück | August 1668 | Venice | | | 300 | 300 |
| Bavaria | March 1669 | Venice | | | | 1,000 |
| Austria | April 1669 | Venice | | | | 800 |

# German Soldiers' Trade (Auxiliary troops in Foreign Service), 1672–1679

| State: | Agreement: | Partner: | 1672 | 1673 | 1674 | 1675 | 1676 | 1677 | 1678 | 1679 |
|---|---|---|---|---|---|---|---|---|---|---|
| Brandenburg | August 1671 | Poland | 1,500 | 1,500 | For Ducal Prussia as contingent of the *Bomberger Beitrage* | | | | | |
| Brandenburg | October 1671 | Dutch Republic | 7,000 | 7,000 | Further 7,000 in Brandenburg's pay | | | | | |
| Bavaria | April 1672 | Electoral Cologne | 1,600 | 1,200 | | | | | | |
| Münster | April 1672 | Electoral Cologne | 400 | Passed into Electoral Cologne service in 1672 | | | | | | |
| Reuss-Pleuen | May 1672 | Münster | 1500 | | | | | | | |
| Bayereuth | June 1672 | Brandenburg | 150 | Passed into Brandenburg service in 1673 | | | | | | |
| Waldeck-Pyrmont | June 1672 | Brandenburg | 390 | 390 | | | | | | |
| Bavaria | September 1672 | Savoy-Piedmont | 1,700 | | | | | | | |
| Mecklenburg-Schwerin | February 1672 | France | 250 | Passed into French service in 1673 | | | | | | |
| Mecklenburg-Schwerin | September 1672 | Denmark | 253 | Passed into Danish service in 1673 | | | | | | |
| Mecklenburg-Schwerin | January 1673 | Electoral Cologne | 850 | Passed into Electoral Cologne service in 1673 | | | | | | |
| Saxony | August 1673 | Emperor | | 3,000 | 2,841 | | | | | |
| Reuss-Plauen | June 1673 | Emperor | | 1,000 | Passed into Imperial service in 1673 | | | | | |
| Brandenburg | July 1673 | Poland | | 1,200 | | | | | | |
| Würzburg | February 1674 | Emperor | | | 2,140 | 2,140 | | | | |
| The Palatinate | August 1674 | Emperor, Dutch Republic, Spain | | | 2,500 | | | | | |
| Münster | May 1674 | Emperor | | | 10,000 | | | | | |
| Electoral Cologne | June 1674 | Emperor | | | 700 | Passed into Imperial service in 1674 | | | | |
| Saxe-Eisenach | June 1674 | Emperor | | | 1,000 | 1,000 | 1,000 | Merged with Saxe-Gotha in November 1676 | | |
| Celle | June 1674 | Emperor, Dutch Republic, Spain | | | 7,220 | 6,500 | 4,000 | | | |

| State | Agreement | Partner | | | | | |
|---|---|---|---|---|---|---|---|
| Wolfenbüttel | June 1674 | Emperor, Dutch Republic, Spain | 5,780 | 4,000 | | | |
| Brandenburg | July 1674 | Emperor, Dutch Republic, Spain | 16,000 | 15,400 | Transferred to Pomerania in June 1674 | | |
| Münster | September 1674 | Emperor, Dutch Republic, Spain | | 9,000 | ? | | |
| Osnabrück | December 1674 | Emperor, Dutch Republic, Spain | 5,100 | ? | | | |
| Pfalz-Neuburg | March 1675 | Brandenburg | 500 | 500 | | | |
| Saxony | June 1675 | Emperor | 2,500 | 1,200 | 1,200 | 1,200 | |
| Osnabrück | October 1675 | Dutch Republic, Spain | | 6,000 | 6,000 | 6,000 | |
| Würzburg-Bamberg | November 1675 | Emperor | | 6,000 | 5,000 | | |
| Pfalz-Neuburg | January 1676 | Dutch Republic, Spain | | 6,500 | 7,500 | 5,500 | |
| Brandenburg | February 1676 | Denmark | | 1,800 | Passed into Danish service in 1676 | | |
| Saxony | March 1676 | Emperor | | 650 | Passed into Imperial service in 1676 | | |
| Paderborn | April 1676 | Münster | | 1,500 | | | |
| Paderborn | October 1676 | Dutch Republic, Spain | | 1,500 | 1,500 | | |
| Saxe-Gotha | November 1676 | Emperor | | 3,000 | 3,000 | | |
| Münster | April 1677 | Denmark | | 4.000 | | | |
| Hessen-Darmstadt | April 1677 | Emperor | | 1,100 | 1,100 | | |
| Hessen-Kassel | April 1677 | Denmark | | 2,000 | 2,000 | | |
| Münster | August 1677 | Spain | | 8,500 | 4,286 | | |
| Münster | April 1678 | Denmark | | 6,000 | 6,000 | | |
| Hessen-Kassel | April 1678 | Denmark | | 1,300 | 1,300 | | |

# German Soldiers' Trade (Auxiliary troops in Foreign Service), 1683–1690

| State: | Agreement: | Partner: | 1683 | 1684 | 1685 | 1686 | 1687 | 1688 | 1689 | 1690 |
|---|---|---|---|---|---|---|---|---|---|---|
| Würzburg-Bamberg | May 1683 | Emperor | 3,400 | 3,400 | Passed into Imperial service in 1685 | | | | | |
| Saxony | June 1683 | Emperor | 10,231 | | | | | | | |
| Bavaria | August 1683 | Emperor | 8,200 | | | | | | | |
| Brandenburg | July 1683 | Poland | 1,200 | 2,000 | 2,000 | | | | | |
| Münster | July 1683 | Emperor | 1,940 | 1,940 | 1,940 | 1,940 | 1,940 | 1,940 | | |
| Hildesheim | July 1683 | Emperor | | 1,271 | 1,271 | | | | | |
| Paderborn | October 1683 | Emperor | | 300 | 300 | 300 | 300 | 300 | | |
| Bavaria | February 1684 | Emperor | | 10,000 | 8,000 | 8,000 | 9,133 | 9,900 | | |

| State | Date | Recipient | | | | | |
|---|---|---|---|---|---|---|---|
| Hanover | May 1684 | Venice | | 2,700 | 3.600 | 4,000 | 1,300 |
| Celle, Hanover and Wolfenbüttel | September 1684 | Emperor | | | 12,000 | 6,000 | 6,000 |
| Electoral Cologne | August 1684 | Emperor | 6,500 | About 1,000 infantrymen passed into Imperial service in 1684 | | | |
| Electoral Cologne | January 1685 | Emperor | | 2.400 | 2,400 | 2,400 | 2,400 |
| Brandenburg | January 1686 | Emperor | | | 8,300 | | |
| Saxony | January 1686 | Emperor | | | 4,700 | | |
| Mecklenburg-Güstrow | January 1686 | Emperor | | | 1,150 | 600 | 400 |
| Saxony | March 1686 | Venice | | | 3,000 | | |
| Bayreuth | January 1687 | Venice | | | | 2,000 | 2,000 |
| Liège | January 1687 | Venice | | | | 1,000 | 1,000 |
| Württemberg | February 1687 | Venice | | | | 1,000 | 4,000 | 2,142 |
| Hessen-Kassel | March 1687 | Venice | | | | 1,000 | 1,000 | 1,000 |
| Wolfenbüttel | June 1687 | Venice | | | | 1,210 | 1,210 | 1.210 |
| Bayreuth | August 1687 | Emperor | | | | 950 | Passed into Imperial service in 1688 | |
| Hessen-Darmstadt and Saxe-Meiningen | December 1687 | Württemberg (for Venice) | | | | 1,000 | | |
| Saxony | January 1688 | Emperor | | | | 2,000 | | |
| Waldeck-Pyrmont | January 1688 | Venice | | | | 1,000 | | |
| Liège | March 1688 | Venice | | | | 1,000 | 1,000 | |
| Hessen-Kassel | July 1688 | Dutch Republic | | | | 2,442 | 2,442 | 2,442 |
| Württemberg | July 1688 | Dutch Republic | | | | 1,296 | Passed into Dutch service in 1689 | |
| Brandenburg | August 1688 | Dutch Republic | | | | 6,000 | 6,000 | 6,000 |
| Wolfenbüttel | August 1688 | Dutch Republic | | | | 1,388 | 1,388 | 1,404 |
| Celle | August 1688 | Dutch Republic | | | | 2,720 | 2,720 | |
| Saxe-Coburg | October 1688 | Emperor | | | | 1,200 | Passed into Imperial service in 1690 | |
| Saxe-Gotha | May 1689 | Dutch Republic | | | | | 425 | 425 |
| Celle | June 1689 | Spain | | | | | 500 | |
| Wolfenbüttel | January 1690 | England | | | | | | 1,604 |

# German Leagues

## The *Rheinbund*, 1658–1668

| State: | Year of Membership: | Military Contingent: | |
|---|---|---|---|
| | | Infantry: | Cavalry: |
| Mainz | 1658 | 600 | 300 |
| Cologne (Electorate) | 1658 | 800 | 420 |

| | | | |
|---|---|---|---|
| Pfalz-Neuburg | 1658 | 800 | 400 |
| Sweden (for Bremen-Verden) | 1658 | 1,000 | 420 |
| Brunswick-Wolfenbüttel | 1658 | 900 | 420 |
| Brunswick-Lüneburg Celle | | | |
| Brunswick-Lüneburg Hanover | | | |
| Hessen-Kassel | 1658 | 400 | 180 |
| France | 1658 | 1,600 | 800 |
| Hessen-Darmstadt | 1659 | - | - |
| Münster | 1660 | 800 | 400 |
| Württemberg | 1660 | 200 | 100 |
| Trier | 1661 | 400 | 180 |
| Pfalz-Zweibrücken | 1663 | - | - |
| Brandenburg | 1665 | - | - |
| Strasbourg (bishopric) | 1665 | - | - |
| Basel (bishopric) | 1665 | - | - |
| Ansbach-Bayreuth | 1665 | - | - |
| Brandenburg-Bayreuth | 1665 | - | - |

Source: Peter H. Wilson, *German Armies. War and German Politics, 1648–1806* (London: UCL Press, 1998), p.172.

## Contingents of the *Deutsche Allianz* for Hungary (1664)

| State: | official strength: | actual strength: |
|---|---|---|
| Brunswick-Wolfenbüttel | 1,320 | 1,320 |
| Brunswick-Lüneburg Celle | | |
| Brunswick-Lüneburg Calenberg | | |
| Mainz | 900 | 1,200 |
| Cologne | 1,200 | 1,200 |
| Trier | 380 | 380 |
| Münster | 1,200 | 1,200 |
| Pfalz-Neuburg | 1,100 | 1,110 |
| Hessen-Kassel | 300 | 460 |
| Württemberg | 300 | 370 |
| Hessen-Darmstadt | 230 | 350 |
| Pfalz-Zweibrücken | 150 | 90 |
| Sweden | 650 | 180 |

Source: Wilson, *German Armies. War*, p.42; Oskar Bezzel, *Geschichte des kurpfälzischen Heeres von seinen Anfängen bis zur Vereinigung vonKurpfalz und Kurbayern*, vol. I (Munich, 1925), p.151.

## The Marienburg Alliance, 1671–1672

| State: | Infantry: | Cavalry; | Dragoons: | Total: |
|---|---|---|---|---|
| Austria | 400 | 1,000 | 400 | 5,400 |
| Mainz | 1,000 | 150 | - | 1,150 |
| Trier | 500 | 75 | - | 575 |
| Saxony | 500 | 800 | 200 | 1,500 |
| Münster | 500 | 800 | 200 | 1,500 |
| Brandenburg-Bayreuth | 50 | 30 | - | 80 |
| Paderborn | - | - | - | - |
| TOTAL: | 6,550 | 2,855 | 800 | 10,205 |

Source: Wilson, *German Armies*, p.177.

## The Brunswick Union, 1672

| State: | Infantry: | Cavalry: | Total: |
|---|---|---|---|
| Austria | 6,000 | 3,000 | 9,000 |
| Brandenburg | 6,000 | 3,000 | 9,000 |
| Lüneburg Celle | 1,200 | 600 | 1,800 |
| Brunswick-Wolfenbüttel | 1,000 | 500 | 1,500 |
| Hessen-Kassel | 800 | 400 | 1,200 |
| TOTAL: | 21,000 | 10,500 | 31,500 |

\* not including 6,000 foot and 3,000 horse from Denmark.

Source: Wilson, *German Armies*, p.177.

## 'The Magdeburg Concert', October 1688

| State: | Troops: |
|---|---|
| Saxony | 10,000* |
| Saxon Duchies | 1,000* |
| Hessen-Kassel | 6,000* |
| Hanover | 8,000* |
| Münster | 6,000* |
| Brandenburg | 1,500* |
| Brandenburg | 18,400** |
| TOTAL: | 50,900 |

\* on the Middle Rhine.
\*\* on the Lower Rhine under Dutch subsidy.

Source: Wilson, *German Armies*, p.183.

# Brunswick-Lüneburg Celle

## Professional Troops in 1665

### Infantry:

| # | Unit: | Strength: | | Quarter: |
|---|---|---|---|---|
| | | Coys: | Men: | |
| bci-i | Garde zu Fuss | 1 | ? | Celle |
| BcI-1 | Leibregiment | 10 | 600 | |
| BcI-2 | Flüte | 10 | 600 | |
| BcI-3 | Rasfeldt | 10 | 600 | |
| - | Schloss-Compagnie Bremer | 1 | ? | |
| - | Schloss-Compagnie Kuppel | 1 | ? | Lüneburg |
| - | Schloss-Compagnie Red | 1 | ? | Harburg |

### Cavalry:

| # | Unit: | Strength: | | Quarter: |
|---|---|---|---|---|
| | | Coys: | Men: | |
| bcc-i | Trabanten Garde | 1 | ? | Lüneburg |
| BcC-1 | Nassau-Saarbrücken | 4 | 420 | |
| BcC-2 | Leibregiment | 4 | 420 | Celle |
| BcC-3 | Krosigk | 6 | ? | |
| BcC-4 | Villier | ? | ? | |

Source: Sichart, *Geschichte der königlich-hannoverschen Armee*, vol. I, pp.143–144.

## The Field Army for the campaign of Alsace in 1674

### Infantry:

| # | Unit: | Strength: | | |
|---|---|---|---|---|
| | | Companies: | Officers and NCOs: | Men: |
| BcI-1 | Ende | 10 | 100 | 900 |
| BcI-2 | Mollesson | 10 | 100 | 900 |
| BcI-3 | Jocquet | 10 | 100 | 900 |
| BcI-4 | *Melleville* (former militia battalion) | 5 | 50 | 450 |
| BcI-5 | Linstrow | 10 | ? | ? |

## Cavalry:

| # | Unit: | Strength: | | |
|---|---|---|---|---|
| | | Companies: | Officers and NCOs: | Men: |
| bci-i | Garde du Corps | 1 | 10 | 122 |
| BcC-6 | Haxthausen (Leibregiment) | 6 | 60 | 414 |
| BcC-5 | Feige | 6 | 60 | 414 |
| BcC-1 | Chauvet | 6 | 60 | 414 |
| BcC-7 | Mellinger | 6 | 60 | 414 |

## Dragoons

| # | Unit: | Strength: | | |
|---|---|---|---|---|
| | | Companies: | Officers and NCOs: | Men: |
| bcd-i | Leibdragoner | 1 | 10 | 106 |
| bcd-ii | Henning | 1 | 10 | 100 |

Artillery: 2 cannons of 24lb; 3 cannons of 12lb; 4 cannons of 8lb; 17 cannons of 3lb.

Source: Sichart, *Geschichte der königlich-hannoverschen Armee*, vol. I, pp.149–150.

# Brunswick-Lüneburg Calenberg (Hanover)

## The Standing Army in 1665

### Infantry:

| # | Unit: | Strength: | | Quarter: |
|---|---|---|---|---|
| | | Companies: | Men: | |
| Bhl-1 | Goertz (rothe Regiment) | 4 | 864 | |
| Bhl-2 | Mücheln (blaue Regiment) | 4 | 864 | |
| Bhl-3 | Öffener (gelbe Regiment) | 4 | 864 | |
| - | Schloss-Compagnie Fischer | 1 | 216 | Calenberg |
| - | Schloss-Compagnie Bülow | 1 | 216 | Hanover |
| - | Frey-Compagnie Wiedemann | 1 | 216 | |
| - | Frey-Compagnie Harling | 1 | 216 | |
| - | Frey-Compagnie Hesse | 1 | 216 | |
| - | Frey-Compagnie Bremer | 1 | 216 | |
| Total: | | 18 | 3,024 | |

## ORDERS OF BATTLE AND TABULAR DATA

### Cavalry and Dragoons:

| # | Unit: | Strength: | |
| --- | --- | --- | --- |
| | | Companies: | Men: |
| bhc-i | Leibgarde | 1 | 109 |
| BhC-1 | Rauchhaupt | 6 | 600 |
| BhC-2 | Öffener | 6 | 600 |
| bhd-i | Leibdragoner | 1 | 125 |
| Total: | | 14 | 1,434 |

Source: Robert Wilhelm Georg von Sichart, *Geschichte der königlich-hannoverschen Armee*, vol. I (Hannover, 1866), pp.127–128.

# Infantry Garrisons in 1675

| # | Unit: | Strength: | | Quarter: |
| --- | --- | --- | --- | --- |
| | | Coys: | Men: | |
| bhi-i | Leib-Schloss-Compagnie | 1 | 200 | Hanover |
| BhI-1 | *Podewils (alt-rothe Regiment)* | 12 | 1,500 | Hanover |
| BhI-2 | *Lippe-Detmold (alt-blaue Regiment)* | 12 | 1,500 | Hameln |
| BhI-3 | *Prinz von Modena (alt-gelbe Regiment)* | 12 | 1,500 | Neustadt, Wunstorf, Pattensen, Rehburg, Springe, Münder, Eldagsen |
| BhI-5 | *Wiedemann (graue-Regiment)* | 12 | 1,500 | Münden, Northeim, Hardegsen, Moringen, Uslar |
| BhI-6 | *Bolalto (weisse-Regiment)* | 12 | 1,500 | Einbeck, Ostterode |
| BhI-7 | *Mücheln (neue-blaue Regiment)* | 12 | 1,500 | Göttingen |
| - | Frey-Compagnie Öffener | 1 | 200 | Hameln |
| - | Frey-Compagnie Fischer | 1 | 179 | Einbeck |
| - | Kreiscompagnie Bisewang | 1 | 252 | Salzhemmendorf |

Source: Sichart, *Geschichte der königlich-hannoverschen Armee*, vol. I, p.133.

# The Professional Army in 1676

## Infantry:

| # | Unit: | Strength: | |
|---|---|---|---|
| | | Companies: | Men: |
| bhi-i | Leib-Schloss-Compagnie Floramonth | 1 | 200 |
| - | Schloss Artillerie Frey-Compagnie | 1 | 160 |
| BhI-1 | Podewils | 12 | 1,506 |
| BhI-2 | Flemming | 12 | 1,506 |
| BhI-3 | Modena | 12 | 1,506 |
| BhI-5 | Wiedemann | 12 | 1,506 |
| BhI-6 | Ilten | 12 | 1,506 |
| BhI-7 | Öffener | 12 | 1,506 |
| - | Frey-Compagnie Öffener | 1 | 200 |
| - | Frey-Compagnie Vitry | 1 | 200 |
| - | Kreiscompagnie Bisewang | 1 | 169 |
| - | Kreiscompagnie Rotzenberg | 1 | 160 |
| - | Frey-Compagnie Scharzfeld | 1 | 15 |

## Cavalry and Dragoons:

| # | Unit: | Strength: | |
|---|---|---|---|
| | | Companies: | Men: |
| bhc-i | Leibgarde zu Ross | 1 | 109 |
| BhC-1 | Rauchhaupt | 8 | 712 |
| BhC-2 | Öffener | 8 | 712 |
| BhC-3 | Löwen | 8 | 712 |
| BhC-4 | Massenbach | 8 | 712 |
| BhD-1 | Sozenau | 10 | 966 |

Artillery Corps:    89

Total: 15,342 men.

Source: Sichart, *Geschichte der königlich-hannoverschen Armee*, vol. I, p.137.

# Standing Troops in 1683.

## Infantry:

| #      | Unit:            | Strength: Companies: | Men:  |
|--------|------------------|----------------------|-------|
| bhi-i  | Leibgarde zu Fuss| 2                    | 215   |
| BhI-1  | Podewils         | 12                   | 1,215 |
| BhI-2  | Du Mont          | 12                   | 1,215 |
| BhI-3  | Bernholz         | 12                   | 1,215 |
| BhI-5  | Wiedemann        | 10                   | 1,015 |
| BhI-8  | Ohr              | ?                    | ?     |
| BhI-9  | Siegelberg       | ?                    | ?     |
| BhI-10 | Röbbig           | 12                   | 1,215 |
| BhI-11 | Pallandt         | 12*                  | 1,215 |

* 4 companies join the *Leibgarde zu Fuss* to form a field-battalion.

## Cavalry and Dragoons:

| #      | Unit:               | Strength: Companies: | Men: |
|--------|---------------------|----------------------|------|
| bhc-i  | Leibgarde zu Ross   | 1                    | 150  |
| BhC-1  | Rauchhaupt          | 6                    | 432  |
| BhC-6  | Offen               | 6                    | 432  |
| BhC-7  | Gordon              | 6                    | 432  |
| BhC-8  | Prinz Georg Ludwig  | 6                    | 432  |
| BhC-9  | Raugraf zur Pfalz   | 12                   | 864  |
| BhD-2  | Vitry               | 6                    | ?    |
| BhD-3  | Sommerfeld          | 6                    | ?    |

Source: Sichart, *Geschichte der königlich-hannoverschen Armee*, vol. I, pp.179–180.

# Auxiliary Troops for Hungary, May 1685

Commander-in-Chief: Prince Georg Ludwig of Hanover
*General Lieutenant* Chauvet (Celle), *General Mayor* Offener, Du Mont (Hanover), Boisdavid (Celle); von der Lippe (Wolfenbüttel).

## Infantry:

| # | Unit: | Nationality: | Strenght: |
|---|---|---|---|
| BhI-3 | Marteaux | Hanover | 8 coy |
| BhI-9 | Siegelberg | Hanover | 8 coy |
| BhI-10 | Röbbig | Hanover | 8 coy |
| ? | Sommerfeld | Hanover | 8 coy |
| BhI-2 | Du Mont | Hanover | 8 coy |
| BcI-1 | Nettelhorst | Celle | 7 coy |
| BcI-3 | Boisdavid | Celle | 7 coy |
| BcI-2 | La Motte | Celle | 7 coy |
| BcI-4 | Linstrow | Celle | 7 coy |
| BwI-5 | Holle | Wolfenbüttel | 7 coy |
| BwI-6 | Bernstorff | Wolfenbüttel | 7 coy |

## Cavalry:

| # | Unit: | Nationality: | Strenght: |
|---|---|---|---|
| BhC-8 | Erbprinz | Hanover | 6 coy |
| BhC-1 | Őffener | Hanover | 6 coy |
| BhC-6 | Offen | Hanover | 6 coy |
| BhC-7 | Gordon | Hanover | 6 coy |
| BhC-9 | Raugraf | Hanover | 6 coy |
| BcC-5 | Beauregard | Celle | 6 coy |
| BcC-1 | Chauvet | Celle | 6 coy |

## Dragoons:

| # | Unit: | Nationality: | Strenght: |
|---|---|---|---|
| BhD-2 | Vitry | Hanover | 6 coy |
| bcd-1 | Dragoner Garde | Celle | 2 coy |
| BcD-1 | Franke | Celle | 6 coy |

Hanover: 5,405 foot and horse; Celle: 4,900 foot and horse; Wolfenbüttel: 1,510 foot.

Source: Sichart, *Geschichte der königlich-hannoverschen Armee*, vol. I, pp.450-451.

# Hessen-Kassel

## Permanent Troops in December 1679

### Household troops:

| # | Companies: | Strength: |
|---|---|---|
| hci-i | Leibgarde zu Fuss | ? |
| hcc-i | Leibguardia zu Pferd | 63 |

### Infantry:

| # | Companies: | Strength: |
|---|---|---|
| - | Ufm Keller | 170 |
| - | Lippe | 288 |
| - | Prinz Philipp | 222 |
| - | Moss | 229 |
| - | Wartensleben | 209 |
| - | Braun | 187 |

### Cavalry:

| # | Companies: | Strength: |
|---|---|---|
| - | Urff | 75 |
| - | Baumbach | 75 |

### Dragoons:

| # | Companies: | Strength: |
|---|---|---|
| - | Friesenhausen | 115 |

Source: Carl von Stamford, *Die Feldzüge der Regimenter Ufm Keller und von Hornumb von Hessen-Kassel in dem Reichskriege gegen Schweden, auf Schonen und auf Rügen; 1677 und 1678* (Kassel, 1862), p.185.

## Standing Regiments, March 1683

### Infantry:

| # | Unit: | Strength: Companies: | Men: |
|---|---|---|---|
| HcI-4 | Ufm Keller | 11 | 1,200 |
| HcI-5 | Lippe | 8 | 1,000 |
| HcI-6 | Prinz Philipp | 8 | 1,000 |

### Cavalry and Dragoons:

| # | Unit: | Strength: Companies: | Men: |
|---|---|---|---|
| hcc-i | Leibgarde zu Pferd | 2 | 150 |
| HcD-1 | Prinz Philipp Dragoner | 5 | 500 |

Source: Strieder, *Grundlage zur Militär-Geschichte des Landgräflich Hessischen Corps* (Berlin, 1798), pp.9–10.

# The Palatinate

## Infantry Garrisons in 1663

| Location: | Privates and NCOs: |
|---|---|
| Heidelberg: | 200 |
| Ladenburg: | 200 |
| Frankenthal: | 424 |
| Friedrichsburg: | 553 |
| Sicholsheim: | 7 |
| Borberg: | 21 |
| Otzberg: | 28 |
| Zwingenberg: | 11 |
| Gutenfels: | 85 |
| Pfalzgrafenstein: | 22 |
| Landstron: | 18 |
| Friedelsheim: | 1 |
| Atzen: | 90 |
| Bacharach: | 28 |
| Germersheim: | 3 |
| Lindenfels: | 2 |
| Bretten: | 35 |

Source: Oskar Bezzel, *Geschichte des kurpfälzischen Heeres von seinen Anfängen bis zur Vereinigung von Kurpfalz und Kurbayern*, vol. I (Munich, 1925), p.90.

# ORDERS OF BATTLE AND TABULAR DATA

# The Professional Army, 3 July 1670

## Infantry:

| # | Unit: | Strength: Companies: | Men: | Garrison: |
|---|---|---|---|---|
| kpi-i | Leibgarde zu Fuss | 1 | 297 | Heidelberg and Friedrichsburg |
| kpi-ii | Kurprinz Leibcompagnie | 1 | 116 | |
| - | Menges | 1 | 85 | Heidelberg |
| - | Wilder | 1 | 90 | Friedrichsburg |
| - | Ploetz | 1 | 88 | |
| - | Wattewyl | 1 | 67 | |
| - | Toudorf | 1 | 65 | |
| - | Rebmacher | 1 | 68 | |
| - | Sando | 1 | 82 | |
| - | Diesbach | 1 | 78 | |
| - | Wolff | 1 | 66 | |
| - | Lucarfowsky | 1 | 73 | |
| - | Sparr | 1 | 75 | Frankenthal |
| - | Hoffmann | 1 | 88 | |
| - | Cellarius | 1 | 70 | |
| - | Herdt | 1 | 68 | |
| - | Schulz | 1 | 79 | |
| - | Dürbach | 1 | 84 | |
| - | Strupp | 1 | 69 | |
| - | Schenkel | 1 | 70 | Neustadt |
| - | Wilderholt | 1 | 80 | Germersheim |
| - | Vodelten | 1 | 80 | Setz and Hagenbach |
| - | van Dyle | 1 | 69 | Kaiserslautern |
| - | Dolne | 1 | 69 | |
| - | Stahl | 1 | 70 | |
| - | Scaab | 1 | 82 | |
| - | Jacquet | 1 | 72 | |
| - | Hennoy | 1 | 75 | Oppenheim |
| - | Beck | 1 | 81 | Bacharach |
| - | Krug | 1 | 80 | |
| - | detachments | - | 284 | (minor posts) |

Total: 30    2,820

## Cavalry:

| # | Unit: | Strength: Companies: | Men: | Garrison: |
|---|---|---|---|---|
| kci-i | Leibgarde zu Ross | 1 | 76 | Heidelberg |
| kci-ii | Kurprinz Leibcompagnie | 1 | 37 | Friedrichsburg |
| - | Leiningen | 1 | 40 | Kaiserslautern |

Total:   3     153

Source: Bezzel, *Geschichte des kurpfälzischen Heeres*, p.103-104.

# Standing Troops, 1683–1685

# Infantry in 1683:

| # | Unit: | Grenadier Companies | Ordinary Companies | Hauptleuten | Lieutenants | Ensigns | Reformed Officers | NCOs | Surgeons | Corporals | Musicians | *Gefreiten* | Privates | TOTAL |
|---|---|---|---|---|---|---|---|---|---|---|---|---|---|---|
| Kpl-3 | Leibregiment | 2 | 10 | 6 | 11 | 10 | 5 | 55 | 5 | 30 | 37 | 175 | 729 | 1,063* |
| Kpl-2 | Wittgenstein | - | 7 | 4 | 7 | 7 | 1 | 39 | 5 | 19 | 24 | 123 | 511 | 740 |
| Kpl-4 | Frays | - | 5 | 2 | 5 | 5 | - | 25 | 1 | 15 | 15 | 81 | 351 | 500 |
| Kpl-5 | Cattaneo | - | 6 | 3 | 6 | 6 | 1 | 31 | 6 | 18 | 16 | 108 | 455 | 649 |

* The figure does not include 245 grenadiers.

Source: Bezzel, *Geschichte des kurpfälzischen Heeres*, pp.116-117. Muster of 11 June 1683

# Cavalry and Dragoons in 1684:

| # | Unit: | Companies | strength |
|---|---|---|---|
| kpi-i | *Leibgarde zu Ross* | 1 | ? |
| KpD-1 | *Leib-Dragoner* | 6 | 410 |

Source: Bezzel, *Geschichte des kurpfälzischen Heeres*, p.117.

## Artillery in 1685

1 *Stückobristleutnant*; 2 *Stückhauptleute*; 4 *Stückleutnante*; 3 *Stückjunker*; 1 *Zeugwart*; 1 *Zeugschreiber*; 1 *Zimmermeister*; 2 *Zeugwagner*; 2 *Zeugschlosser*, 1 *Schiffbauer*; 2 *Feuerwerker*; 1 *Sergeant*; 9 *Korporale*; 56 *Konstabler*; 30 *Handlanger*.

## *Pionerbataillon* in 1685:

| Company | strenght |
|---|---|
| *Obristwachtmeister* de la Brasserie | 34 |
| *Hauptmann* Wolf | 41 |
| *Hauptmann* Ulmann | 39 |

Source: Bezzel, *Geschichte des kurpfälzischen Heeres*, p.117. Muster of 31 May 1685.

# Mecklenburg-Güstrow

## Professional Troops, December 1679:

### Cavalry:

*Garde zu Ross:* 90

### Infantry:

*Leibgarde zu Fuss:* 220
In Rostock: 90

Artillery and Specialists: 11

# Mecklenburg-Schwerin

## Professional Troops, December 1679:

### Cavalry:

*Leibcompagnie zu Pferde:* 61
*Kreiscompagnie:* 61

### Infantry:

in Schwerin: 149
in Dömitz: 161
in Rostock: 81

Sources: Klaus-Ulrich Keubke, *Kleine Militärgeschichte Mecklenburgs* (Schwerin: Stock & Stein, 1995), p.8; Georg Tessin, 'Mecklenburgisches Militär in Türken und Franzosenkriegen 1648–1718' in *Mitteldeutsche Forschungen*, Vol. 42 (Cologne: Böhlau, 1966), p.85.

# Osnabrück

## Professional Troops (22 August 1679).

### Infantry:

| # | Unit: | Strength: | |
| --- | --- | --- | --- |
| | | Companies: | Men: |
| OsI-1 | Leibregiment | 6 | 634 |
| OsI-2 | Siegelberg | 6 | 634 |
| OsI-3 | Röbbig | 6 | 634 |

### Cavalry and Dragoons:

| # | Unit: | Strength: | |
| --- | --- | --- | --- |
| | | Companies: | Men: |
| osc-i | Leibgarde zu Pferde | 1 | 113 |
| OsC-1 | Offen | 2 | 151 |
| OsC-3 | Prinzen | 2 | 151 |
| OsC-4 | Gordon | 2 | 151 |

## ORDERS OF BATTLE AND TABULAR DATA

| OsC-5 | Löwen | 2 | 151 |
|---|---|---|---|
| osd-i | Dragoner Garde | 1 | 106 |
| OsD-1 | Louvigny | 2 | 153 |

Artillery: 2 *Feuerwerker*, 1 *Zeugschmied*, 4 *Constabler*.

Total: 2,893 men.

Source: Sichart, *Geschichte der königlich-hannoverschen Armee*, vol. I, pp.168-170.

# Pfalz-Neuburg

## Professional Troops in 1672

### Infantry:

| # | Unit: | Strength: | |
|---|---|---|---|
| | | Companies: | Men: |
| PnI-3 | Waldbott | 6 | ? |
| - | Virmund | 1 | |
| - | Palant | 1 | |
| - | Hochstätten | 1 | |
| - | Spee | 1 | |
| - | Bock | 1 | |
| - | Couche | 1 | 2,276 |
| - | Linden | 1 | |
| - | Wilhelm von der Horst | 1 | |
| - | Hauptmann von der Horst | 1 | |
| - | Goltstein | 1 | |
| - | Schlimmer | 1 | |

### Cavalry:

| # | Unit: | Strength: | |
|---|---|---|---|
| | | Companies: | Men: |
| pnc-i | Leibgarden zu Pferd | 3 | 161 |
| - | Virmund | 1 | 140 |
| - | Belbrück | 1 | 140 |
| - | Landsberg | 1 | 140 |

| -   | Franckenberg | 1 | 140 |
| --- | --- | --- | --- |
| -   | Nagel | 1 | 140 |
| -   | Hasselrade | 1 | 140 |

Source: Oskar Bezzel, *Geschichte des kurpfälzischen Heeres von seinen Anfängen bis zur Vereinigung von Kurpfalz und Kurbayern*, vol. I (Munich, 1925), p.158.

## Auxiliary Troops in Dutch-Spanish Service, August 1676

### Infantry:

| #   | Unit: | Strength: | |
| --- | --- | --- | --- |
|     |       | Companies: | Men: |
| PnI-8 | Saint-Paul | 10 | 863 |
| PnI-9 | Waldenberg | 10 | 928 |
| PnI-6 | Boisbernard | 8 | 928 |
| PnI-5 | Spee | 10 | ? |

### Cavalry and Dragoons:

| #   | Unit: | Strength: | |
| --- | --- | --- | --- |
|     |       | Companies: | Men: |
| PnC-4 | Schellart zu Pferd | 6 | 503 |
| PnD-1 | Manderscheid Dragoner | 6 | 464 |

Source: Bezzel, *Geschichte des kurpfälzischen Heeres*, p.163.

# Württemberg

## *Landesdefensionsvölker* (territorial militia) in 1655

| #   | Unit (mixed regiments): | Companies | | Quarters: |
| --- | --- | --- | --- | --- |
|     |       | Infantry: | Cavalry: |     |
| -   | Leibregiment | 8 | 5 | Stuttgart, Waiblingen, Göppingen, Schorndorf, Plieningen, Cannstatt, Lorch, Heidenheim. |
| -   | Herzog Johann Friederich | 8 | 4 | Herrenberg, Calm, Dornstadt, Sulz, Böblingen, Nagold, Neuenbürg, Hornberg. |

| # | | | | |
|---|---|---|---|---|
| - | Wiederhold | 8 | 5 | Urach, Kirchheim, Tübingen, Balingen, Bebenhausen, Pfullingen, Blaubeuren, Nürtingen. |
| - | Pslaumer | 10 | 3 | Marbach, Vaihingen, Weinsberg, Lauffen, Asperg, Leonberg, Brackenheim, Maulbronn, Güglingen, Wildberg. |

Source: Leo Ignaz Stadlinger, *Geschichte des Württembergischen Kriegswesens von der frühesten bis zur neuesten Zeit* (Stuttgart, 1856), p.311.

## Professional Troops and Militia (12 February 1674)

*Trabanten*: 24 men.

### Infantry:

*Cronhiorst Zu Fuss* (Wül-1): 10 companies including the *Leibwache*: 1,000 foot.

### Cavalry;

*Regiment zu Pferde*: 4 companies including the *Leibgarde des Herzogs*: 100;
*Leigarde des Erbrinzen*: 80;
2 companies: 160: 340 horse.

Artillery: with 20 guns: 100 men.

### *Landwehr*:

Infantry: 4 regiments: 4,000 foot.
Cavalry: 3 regiments (one of 600 horse, the others of 580): 1,760 horse.
TOTAL: 7,224 men.

Source: Stadlinger, *Geschichte des Württembergischen Kriegswesens*, p.321.

# Lorraine

## Standing Army (11 December 1655)

### Guards' Squadron:

| # | Unit: |
|---|---|
| loc-i | Gardes du Corps |
| loc-ii | Chevaux-Légers |

Total 244 men.

## Infantry:

| # | Unit: |
|---|---|
| LoI-1 | Massey |
| LoI-2 | *Des Marais* (German) |
| LoI-4 | Tornielle |
| LoI-5 | *Cascar* (German) |
| LoI-6 | *O'Connor* (Irish) |
| LoI-7 | *Cusack* (Irish) |

Total: 1,625 men

## Cavalry:

| # | Unit: |
|---|---|
| LoC-1 | Hauracourt |
| LoC-2 | Bassompierre |
| LoC-3 | Lenoncourt |
| LoC-4 | *Nicolas-François de Vaudemont* (German) |
| LoC-5 | Mercy |
| LoC-6 | *Ferdinand de Vaudemont* (German) |
| LoC-7 | *Allamont* (German) |
| LoC-8 | *Delouze* (German) |
| LoC-9 | *Braquy* (German) |
| LoC-10 | *Du Châtelet* (German) |
| LoC-11 | *Fournier* (German) |
| LoC-12 | Ligniville |
| LoC-13 | *Du Plessy* (German) |
| LoC-14 | *Speltz* (mixed German-Lorraine) |
| LoC-15 | *Trastorff* (German) |

Total: 2,025 men.

Source: Jean-Charles Fulaine, *Le Duc Charles IV de Lorraine et son Armée* (Metz: Editions Serpenoise, 1997), pp.168–169.

# Battle Orders

## Relief of Bremen, 15 November 1666

Main Army: Commander in Chief: duke Georg Wilhelm of Braunschweig-Lüneburg Celle
General Adjutant: count Josias von Waldeck

## ORDERS OF BATTLE AND TABULAR DATA

| # | Unit: | Nationality: | Strenght: |
|---|---|---|---|
| bci-i | Leibgarde zu Fuss | Celle | 1 coy |
| bcc-i | Leibgarde zu Pferd | Celle | 1 coy |

### Right Wing (Cavalry):

| # | Unit: | Nationality: | Strenght: |
|---|---|---|---|
| BcC-2 | Leibregiment | Celle | 420 |
| BcC-4 | Villier | Celle | 420 |
| BcC-3 | Krosigt | Celle | 420 |
| OsC-1 | Alt-Ziegeler | Osnabrück | 420 |
| BwC-1 | Waldeck | Wolfenbüttel | 420 |

### Centre (Infantry):

| # | Unit: | Nationality: | Strenght: |
|---|---|---|---|
| ? | Kurcölnische Regiment | Electoral Cologne | 1,000 |
| BwI-1 | *Staufen* (*Schönberg*) | Wolfenbüttel | 1,000 |
| BcI-1 | Waldeck | Celle | 1,000 |
| BcI-2 | Flüte | Celle | 1,000 |
| BcI-3 | Rasfeldt | Celle | 1,000 |
| OsI-1 | Uffeln | Osnabrück | 1,000 |
| WaI-1 | Degenfeld | Waldeck | 800 |

### Left Wing (Cavalry):

| # | Unit: | Nationality: | Strenght: |
|---|---|---|---|
| BcI-1 | Nassau-Saarbrück | Celle | 420 |
| OsC-2 | Jung-Ziegeler | Osnabrück | 420 |
| KkC-3 | Waldeck | Electoral Cologne? | 420 |

Artillery: 20 *Halbe Karthaunen*; 22 *Viertel Karthaune*; 40 light fieldguns; 5 mortars.

## Reserve Corps: General Georg Friedrich von Waldeck

### Cavalry:

| # | Unit: | Nationality: | Strenght: |
|---|---|---|---|
| bhd-i | Leibdragoner | Hanover | 150 |
| BhC-1 | Rauchhaupt | Hanover | 600 |
| BhC-2 | Öffener | Hanover | 600 |
| ? | ? | Wolfenbüttel | 500 |

| KkC-4 | Helle | Electoral Cologne | 400 |
| BrC-31 | Kannenberg | Brandenburg | 460 |
| BrC-34 | Ellern | Brandenburg | 440 |
| - | ? | Brandenburg | 400 |

Infantry:

| # | Unit: | Nationality: | Strenght: |
|---|---|---|---|
| BhI-1 | Görtz | Hanover | 600 |
| BhI-3 | Öffener | Hanover | 600 |
| BhI-2 | Mücheln | Hanover | 600 |
| - | ? | Brandenburg | 1,000 |

Source: Sichart, *Geschichte der königlich-hannoverschen Armee*, vol. I, pp.351–354.

# Celle-Wolfenbüttel Auxiliary Corps in Alsace, July-August 1674

Infantry:

| # | Unit: | Nationality: | Strenght: |
|---|---|---|---|
| BcI-1 | Ende | Celle | 1,000 |
| BcI-2 | Mollesson | Celle | 1,000 |
| BcI-3 | Joquet | Celle | 1,000 |
| BcI-4 | *Melleville* (militia) | Celle | 1,000 |
| BwI-3 | Holsten-Ploen | Wolfenbüttel | 1,000 |
| BwI-2 | Reuss | Wolfenbüttel | 1,000 |
| BwI-4 | Roth | Wolfenbüttel | 1,000 |

Cavalry:

| # | Unit: | Nationality: | Strenght: |
|---|---|---|---|
| BcC-6 | Haxthausen | Celle | 474 |
| BcC-1 | Chauvet | Celle | 474 |
| BcC-5 | Feige | Celle | 474 |
| BcC-7 | Mellinger | Celle | 474 |
| BwC-7 | Reuss | Wolfenbüttel | 474 |
| BwC-6 | Ziegel | Wolfenbüttel | 474 |
| BwC-3 | Wilcken | Wolfenbüttel | 474 |
| BwC-8 | Lobach | Wolfenbüttel | 474 |

## Dragoons:

| # | Unit: | Nationality: | Strenght: |
|---|---|---|---|
| BcD-1 | Franke | Celle | 1,000 |

Artillery: 2 for 24lb; 3 for 12lb; 4 for 8lb; 17 for 3lb.

Source: Sichart, *Geschichte der königlich-hannoverschen Armee*, vol. I. pp.369–370.

# Battle of Conzer Brücke, 11 August 1675

*Feldmarschall* duke Johann Adolph von Holstein-Ploen
*General Lieutenant* Jeremias de Chauvet, *General Mayor* Ende, Offen, von der Lippe.

## Infantry:

| | Sichart: | Janke: | |
|---|---|---|---|
| Nationality: | Conzer Brücke | Conzer Brücke | Trier and Karthaus |
| Celle | 3,500 | 3 bat. | 1 bat. |
| Osnabrück | 2,000 | 2 bat. | 1 bat. |
| Münster | 3,000 | 2 bat. | 1 bat. |
| Spain | 2,000 | 2 bat. | - |
| Trier | 3,000 | 2 bat. | 1 bat. |
| Imperialists | 1,300 | - | 3 bat. |
| Mainz | 3,000 | - | - |
| Wolfenbüttel | 2,000 | - | - |

## Cavalry:

| | Sichart: | Janke: | |
|---|---|---|---|
| Nationality: | Conzer Brücke | Conzer Brücke | Trier and Karthaus |
| Celle | 1,500 | 11.5 sqn. | 3 sqn. |
| Osnabrück | 1,000 | 6.5 sqn. | 1 sqn. |
| Imperialists | 1,000 | 8 sqn. | - |
| Lorraine | 6,000 | 16 sqn. | 1 sqn. |
| Wolfenbüttel | 1,000 | - | - |

Source: Sichart, *Geschichte der königlich-hannoverschen Armee*, vol. I, pp.385–386; Arthur Janke *Die Belagerungen der Stadt Trier in den Jahren 1673 bis 1675 und die Schlacht an der Conzer Brücke am 11. August 1675* (Trier, 1890), pp.103–105.

# Empire's Contingents

## *Miles Perpetuus*: Circle's Contingent Repartition (in *Simplum*), 1681:

| Circle: | Infantry | Cavalry* | Total: |
|---|---|---|---|
| Austria | 5,507 | 2,522 | 8,029 |
| Burgundy | 2,708 | 1,322 | 4,030 |
| Westphalia | 2,708 | 1,321 | 4,029 |
| Lower Saxony | 2,707 | 1,322 | 4,029 |
| Upper Saxony | 2,707 | 1,322 | 4,029 |
| Swabia | 2,707 | 1,321 | 4,028 |
| Franconia | 1,902 | 980 | 2,882 |
| Bavaria | 1,494 | 800 | 2,294 |
| Upper Rhine | 2,853 | 491 | 3,344 |
| Electoral Rhine | 2,707 | 600 | 3,307 |
| Total: | 28,000 | 12,001 | 40,001 |

* including 2,000 dragoons.

Source: *Matrikel in der Reichsdefensionalordnung von 1681.*

## *Oberrheinische Kreiscontingent* (1685):

### Infantry Regiment *Nassau-Saarbrücken*:

| State: | Companies: |
|---|---|
| Hessen-Kassel | 4 |
| Hessen-Darmstadt | 2 |
| Frankfurt am Main | 1 |
| Fulda | 1 |
| Nassau – Saarbrück | 1 |
| Waldeck / Leiningen | 1 |
| Ysenburg / Friedberg / Solms / Wetzlar | 1 |

## Cavalry Regiment *Rau zu Holzhausen*:

| State: | Companies: |
|---|---|
| Hessen-Kassel | 3 |
| Hessen-Darmstadt | 2 |
| Fulda | 1 |
| Hessen-Hanau | 1 |
| Nassau-Idstein | |
| Solms | 1 |
| Wittgenstein | |

Source: Stamford, *Die Feldzüge der Regimenter Ufm Keller und von Hornumb*, p.194.

# Imperial Circles' Troops for the League of Augsburg:

| *Circle*: | 1689 | 1690 |
|---|---|---|
| Franconia | 7,023 | 9,000 |
| Lower Saxony* | 7,754 | 1,112 |
| Upper Rhine** | 4,720 | 4,720 |
| Swabia | 4,000 | 5,500 |
| Upper Saxony | 2,648 | 2,648 |
| Westphalia | 2,400 | 2,400 |
| Bavaria | 1,450 | 1,450 |
| Electoral Rhine | - | - |
| Austria | - | - |
| Total: | 29,995 | 26,830 |

* Contingents from Hanover, Celle and Wolfenbüttel assigned to the *Reichsarmee* but outside the formal circles' military organisation.
** Hessen-Kassel and Hessen-Darmstadt troops in Dutch service are not included.

Appendix II

# German Regiments, Squadrons and Companies – 1657–1690

## Ansbach-Bayreuth (Brandenburg-Onolzpach-Bayreuth)

### Infantry Regiment:

| Id. | Year: | Colonel Proprietor – Denomination: | Campaigns-Engagements: | History: | Uniforms: |
|---|---|---|---|---|---|
| AnI-1 | 1661 | Sargan, 1667 Onolzpach | Crete (1661–1668) | in Venetian service from 1661 to 1668 | |

## Baden-Baden

### Infantry Regiment:

| Id. | Year: | Colonel Proprietor – Denomination: | Campaigns-Engagements: | History: | Uniforms: |
|---|---|---|---|---|---|
| Bal-1 | 1674 | Anton Montfort; 1676 Maximilian Franz zu Fürstenberg | Trier (1675), Philippsburg (1676) | to the Swabian circle, disbanded in 1677 | (1675)[1] Private: dark grey coat with scarlet stockings. |

# Brandenburg-Bayreuth (Brandenburg-Bayreuth-Culmbach)

## Infantry Regiment:

| Id. | Year: | Colonel Proprietor - Denomination: | Campaigns-Engagements: | History: | Uniforms: |
|---|---|---|---|---|---|
| Bbl-1 | 1687 | Carl Sparre von Kronenbergh | Greece and Dalmatia | in Venetian service in 1687; disbanded in 1688 | (1687)[2] Private: black headgear with red ribbon; light grey coat with red cuffs and lining; natural leather breeches; grey stockings. |
| Bbl-2 | 1687 | Erbprinz Georg Wilhelm or Venediger | Greece and Dalmatia: | in Venetian service in 1687; disbanded in 1690 | (1687)[3] Private: black headgear with blue ribbon; light grey coat with blue cuffs and lining; natural leather breeches; light grey stockings. |

## Cavalry Companies

| Id. | Year: | Colonel Proprietor - Denomination: | Campaigns-Engagements: | History: | Uniforms: |
|---|---|---|---|---|---|
| bbc-i | 1672 | Leibgarde zu Ross | | to Brandenburg in 1673 | |

## Dragon Regiment:

| Id. | Year | Colonel Proprietor or Denomination | Campaigns-Engagements: | History: | Uniforms: |
|---|---|---|---|---|---|
| BbD-1 | 1687 | Christian Ernst von Brandenburg-Bayreuth | | to Austria in 1688 | (1689-1690)[4] Private: black headgear with white edging; white cravat; medium blue coat with red cuffs, aiguillettes and breeches; tin buttons; red saddle cover with yellow trim. |

# Brunswick-Lüneburg Celle

## Infantry Companies:

| Id. | Year: | Colonel Proprietor - Denomination: | Campaigns-Engagements: | History: | Uniforms: |
|---|---|---|---|---|---|
| bci-i | 1594 | Garde zu Fuss | Bremen (1666) | | (1690)[5] Private: black headgear with yellow edging; white cravat; scarlet red coat with black cuffs and lining; scarlet red waistcoat, breeches and stockings; brass buttons. |

# WARS AND SOLDIERS IN THE EARLY REIGN OF LOUIS XIV – VOLUME 7 PART 3

## Infantry Regiments:

| | | | | | |
|---|---|---|---|---|---|
| Bcl-1 | 1665 | Leibregiment; Josias von Waldeck; 1670 Ende; 1683 Nettelhorst; 1691 Dalberg | Bremen (1666); Crete (1668–1669); Entzheim, Mulhouse (1674); Türkheim, Conzer Brücke, Trier (1675); Stade (1676); Stettin (1677); Érsekúivár, Gran (1685); Buda (1686); Mohács (1687), | in Venetian service from 1668 to 1670; in Spanish service in 1688; disbanded in 1803 as Alt-Scheither Infanterie | (1665)[6] Private: red coat with green cuffs and lining, brass buttons. (late 1660s)[7] Private: black headgear; white cravat; scarlet red coat with green cuffs and lining; natural leather breeches; green stockings; brass buttons. (1674)[8] Private: red coat with dark green cuffs and lining, tin buttons. |
| Bcl-2 | 1665 | Flüte; 1666 Mollesson; 1676 Jäger; 1677 Carmaillon; 1683 La Motte | Bremen (1666); Crete (1668–1669); Entzheim, Mulhouse (1674); Türkheim, Trier (1675); Stade (1676); Stettin (1677); Érsekúivár, Gran (1685); Buda (1686); Mohács (1687), | in Venetian service from 1668 to 1670; disbanded in 1803 as Steding Infanterie | (1672)[9] Private: black headgear; white cravat; green coat with red cuffs; natural leather breeches; green stockings; brass buttons. (1674)[10] Private: black headgear; white cravat; green coat and cuffs; natural leather breeches; green stockings; brass buttons. (1676)[11] Private: green coat with tin buttons. (1680s)[12] Private: grey-white coat with dark blue cuffs and lining; dark blue waistcoat, breeches and stockings; tin buttons. (1692)[13] Private: red coat with grey-white cuffs and lining; grey-white waistcoat, tin buttons |
| Bcl-3 | 1665 | Rasfeld; 1671 Jocquet; 1675 Malortie; 1684 Boisdavid | Bremen (1666); Crete (1668–1669); Entzheim, Mulhouse (1674); Türkheim, Conzer Brücke, Trier 1675); Stade (1676); Stettin (1677); Érsekúivár, Gran (1685); Buda (1686); Mohács (1687), | in Venetian service from 1668 to 1670; disbanded in 1803 as Prinz Friedrich Infanterie | (1676)[14] Private: green coat, tin buttons (1680)[15] Private: light grey coat, green cuffs and lining, natural leather waistcoat; brass buttons (1690s)[16] Private: black headgear with yellow edging; white cravat; scarlet red coat with deep yellow cuffs and lining; deep yellow waistcoat, natural leather breeches; grey stockings; brass buttons (1690s)[17] Private: black headgear; black cravat; grey-white coat with dark green cuffs and lining; deep yellow waistcoat, breeches and stockings; brass buttons |
| Bcl-4 | 1671 | Friesen; 1673 Melleville; 1674 Mellin; 1684 Linstrow; 1691 Rantzow | Entzheim, Mulhouse (1674); Türkheim, Conzer Brücke, Trier (1675); Stade (1676); Stettin (1677); Érsekúivár, Gran (1685); Bergedorf (1686) | Ausschuss Regiment (militia); disbanded in 1776 as Linsingen Infanterie | (1675)[18] Private: scarlet red coat with dark blue cuffs and lining; natural leather breeches; dark blue stockings; brass buttons. |
| Bcl-5 | 1674 | Linstrow | Entzheim, Mulhouse (1674); Türkheim (1675); Hamburg (1685–1686) | disbanded in 1675 | |
| Bcl-6 | 1691 | Bibrach | | disbanded in 1769 as Otten Infanterie | |

## GERMAN REGIMENTS, SQUADRONS AND COMPANIES – 1657–1690

### Cavalry Companies and Squadrons:

| Id. | Year: | Denomination: | Campaigns-Engagements: | History: | Uniforms: |
|---|---|---|---|---|---|
| bcc-i | 1644 | Trabanten Garde, 1672 Garde zu Pferd | Conzer Brücke, Trier (1675), Maastricht (1676); Charleroi (1677); Saint-Denis (1678) | disbanded in 1705 | (1660s)[19] Trooper: sleeveless buff coat; red coats with black facings; silver buttons. (1668)[20] Trooper: buff coat, (1680)[21] Trooper: red coat with black velvet facings; silver lacing; black breeches; carbine belts with silver lace. |

### Cavalry Regiments:

| Id. | Year: | Colonel Proprietor - Denomination: | Campaigns-Engagements: | History: | Uniforms: |
|---|---|---|---|---|---|
| BcC-1 | 1657 | Nassau-Saarbrücken, 1669 Haxthausen; 1670 Jeremias de Chauvet | Bremen (1666); Entzheim, Mulhouse (1674), Türkheim, Conzer Brücke, Trier (1675), Saint-Denis (1678); Érsekújvár, Gran (1685); Buda (1686); Mohács (1687), | disbanded in 1775 as Hodenberg Cavallerie | (1674)[22] Trooper: pale coloured broad-brimmed hat; light grey coat with red cuffs and lining; natural leather breeches, brass buttons. (1690s)[23] Trooper: pale straw-yellow headgear; grey-white coat; red cuffs; tin buttons; red saddle cover. |
| BcC-2 | 1665 | Leibregiment, Haxthausen | Bremen (1666) | disbanded in 1669 | |
| BcC-3 | 1665 | Krosigk, Wilm | Bremen (1666); Brunswick (1671) | in Dutch service in 1667–1668; disbanded in 1671 | |
| BcC-4 | 1665 | Villiers | Bremen (1666) | disbanded in 1669 | |
| BcC-5 | 1670 | Villers; 1671 Feige; 1674 Beauregard; 1690 Brennecke | Entzheim, Mulhouse (1674), Türkheim, Conzer Brücke, Trier (1675), Saint-Denis (1678); Érsekújvár, Gran (1685); Buda (1686); Mohács (1687), | disbanded in 1775 as Bülow Cavallerie | (1674)[24] Trooper: pale coloured broad-brimmed hat; light grey coat with azure cuffs and lining; natural leather breeches, tin buttons. (1690s)[25] Trooper: grey-white coat; azure cuffs and lining; lemon yellow waistcoat and breeches; tin buttons. |
| BcC-6 | 1671 | Leibregiment (Haxthausen) | Entzheim, Mulhouse (1674), Türkheim, Conzer Brücke, Trier (1675), Saint-Denis (1678) | disbanded in 1679 | (1674)[26] Trooper: red coat laced of silver |
| BcC-7 | 1674 | Mellinger | Entzheim, Mulhouse (1674), Türkheim, Conzer Brücke, Trier (1675), Saint-Denis (1678) | disbanded in 1679 | |
| BcC-8 | 1678 | Lippe | Saint-Denis (1678); Hamburg (1686) | disbanded in 1697 | |

# WARS AND SOLDIERS IN THE EARLY REIGN OF LOUIS XIV – VOLUME 7 PART 3

## Dragoon Companies and Squadrons:

| Id. | Year: | Colonel Proprietor – Denomination: | Campaigns-Engagements: | History: | Uniforms: |
|---|---|---|---|---|---|
| bcd-i | 1672 | Leibdragoner or Dragoner-Garde | Entzheim, Mulhouse (1674), Türkheim Conzer Brücke, Trier (1675) | disbanded in 1705 | |
| bcd-ii | 1672 | Henning | Entzheim, Mulhouse (1674), Türkheim (1675) | disbanded in 1675 | |

## Dragoon Regiments:

| Id. | Year | Colonel Proprietor – Denomination: | Campaigns-Engagements: | History: | Uniforms: |
|---|---|---|---|---|---|
| BcD-1 | 1671 | Franke | Conzer Brücke, Trier (1675); Érsekúivár, Gran (1685), Bergedorf (1686) | former Electoral Cologne regiment; in Spanish service in 1689; disbanded in 1803 as Bremer Dragoner | (1671)[27] Private: light grey coat with carmine red cuffs and lining; tin buttons; bearskin cap for the Leibcompagnie.<br>(1674)[28] Private: pale coloured broad-brimmed hat, light grey coat with red cuffs, collar and lining, natural leather breeches; tin buttons.<br>(1690)[29] Private: black headgear; light grey coat, dark blue cuffs and lining; tin buttons |
| BcD-2 | 1689 | Horn; 1690 Bothmer | | disbanded in 1803 as Hattorf Cavallerie | (1688)[30] Private: bearskin cap; dark blue coat, white buttonholes, tin buttons.<br>(1689)[31] Private: grey-white coat; blue cuffs and lining; brass buttons. |

## Brunswick-Lüneburg Hanover (Calenberg)

### Infantry Companies:

| Id. | Year: | Colonel Proprietor - Denomination: | Campaigns-Engagements: | History: | Uniforms: |
|---|---|---|---|---|---|
| bhI-i | 1648 | Leibwache; 1675 Leib-Schloss-Compagnie; 1683 Leibgarde zu Fuss | Buda (1686) | Garde zu Fuss in 1690 | (1676)[32] Private: black headgear; red coat, golden lace; brass buttons (1679)[33] Private: black headgear; red coat with red cuffs and lining; brass buttons |

### Infantry Regiments:

| Id. | Year: | Colonel Proprietor - Denomination: | Campaigns-Engagements: | History: | Uniforms: |
|---|---|---|---|---|---|
| BhI-1 | 1650 | Görtz or Das Rothe Regiment, 1670 Heinrich von Podewils | Bremen (1666); Brunswick (1671); Greece (1684-1688) | disbanded in 1803 as Hammerstein Infanterie | (1662)[34] Private: red coat with red cuffs and lining; tin buttons (1660s)[35] Private: scarlet red coat with blue cuffs and lining; natural leather breeches; blue stockings; tin buttons. (1667)[36] Private: black headgear, white cravat; scarlet red coat with dark blue cuffs and lining; natural leather breeches; grey stockings; tin buttons. (1684)[37] Private: red coat with medium blue cuffs and lining; tin buttons |
| BhI-2 | 1650 | Sparr or Das Blaue Regiment; 1665 Mücheln; 1673 Lippe-Detmold; 1676 Flemming; 1685 Du Mont. | Érsekúivár, Gran (1685); Buda (1686); Mohács (1687) | disbanded in 1768 as La Chavallerie Infanterie | (1665)[38] Private: blue coat. (1672)[39] Private: blue coat with red lining. (1675)[40] Private: black headgear; white cravat; red scarlet coat with dark blue cuffs and lining; natural leather breeches; red stockings; brass buttons. (1690s)[41] Private: black headgear with yellow ribbon, white cravat; scarlet red coat, cuffs and lining; natural leather breeches; red stockings; brass buttons. |
| BhI-3 | 1650 | (1663) Öffener or Das Gelbe Regiment; 1673 Rinaldo d'Este, Prinz von Modena; 1679 Bernholz; 1685 Marteux | Bremen (1666); Érsekúivár, Gran (1685); Buda (1686); Mohács (1687) | disbanded in 1803 as Hassel Infanterie | (1665)[42] Private: yellow coat. (1675)[43] Private: scarlet red coat with apple green cuffs and lining; natural leather breeches; apple green stockings; tin buttons. |
| BhI-4 | 1663 | Mücheln | Hungary (1663-1664) | disbanded in 1664 | |

| | | | | | |
|---|---|---|---|---|---|
| Bhl-5 | 1668 | Pallandt, or Das Graue-Regiment; 1670 Wiedemann; 1687 Bremer | Crete (1668-1669) | in Venetian service in 1668-1670; in 1675 becomes das Grüne-Regiment; disbanded in 1689 | (1673)[44] Private: grey coat, tin buttons (1675)[45] Private: green coat, cuffs and lining. |
| Bhl-6 | 1673 | Bolalto (Volalto) or Das Weisse-Regiment); 1675 Ilten | | disbanded in 1679 | (1673)[46] Private: black headgear; light grey coat with green lining; natural leather breeches; tin buttons. (1675)[47] Private: red coat, light green cuffs and lining; tin buttons. |
| Bhl-7 | 1673 | Mücheln or Das Neue-blaue Regiment; 1676 Öffener | | disbanded in 1679 | (1673)[48] Private: black headgear; light blue coat with red lining; natural leather breeches; tin buttons. (1680)[49] Private: scarlet red coat with blue cuffs and lining; tin buttons. |
| Bhl-8 | 1679 | Hermann Philipp von Ohr | Greece (1684-1688); Mainz (1689) | former Osnabrück (Osl-1); in Venetian service from 1684 to 1688; disbanded in 1803 as Prinz Adolph Infanterie | (1687)[50] Private black headgear; red coat with blue lining, blue stockings. (1688)[51] Private black headgear; red coat with black lining, red stocking; red overcoat lined black. |
| Bhl-9 | 1679 | Siegelberg; 1689 Schotte de Weber; 1691 Königsmarck | Érsekúivár, Gran (1685); Buda (1686); Mohács (1687) | former Osnabrück (Osl-2); disbanded in 1773 as Zastrow Infanterie | (1682)[52] Private: scarlet red coat grey-white cuffs and lining; red stockings, tin buttons. (1688)[53] Private: black headgear; scarlet red coat with apple green cuffs and lining; natural leather breeches; apple green stockings; brass buttons. |
| Bhl-10 | 1679 | Röbbig; 1685 Sommerfeld | Érsekúivár, Gran (1685); Buda (1686); Mohács (1687) | former Osnabrück (Osl-3); disbanded in 1803 as Wenen Infanterie | (1679)[54] Private: black headgear; white cravat; scarlet red coat with medium green cuffs and lining; natural leather breeches; medium green stockings; tin buttons. |
| Bhl-11 | 1680 | Öffener; 1683 Pallandt; 1684 Bernholz | Kahlenberg (1683) | with the Lower Saxony circle in 1683; disbanded in 1686 | |
| Bhl-12 | 1684 | Prinz Maximilian Wilhelm | Greece (1684-1687) | in Venetian service from 1684 to 1687; disbanded in 1687 | |
| Bhl-13 | 1684 | Raugraf; 1688 Bremer | Greece (1685-1688) | disbanded in 1764 as Block Infanterie | (1680s)[55] Private: grey coat, cuffs and lining; natural leather breeches; grey stockings; tin buttons. |
| Bhl-14 | 1687 | Prinz Maximilian Wilhelm; 1689 Harleville | Greece (1687-1688) | disbanded in 1764 as Du Plat Infanterie | (1680s)[56] Private: scarlet red coat with dark blue cuffs and lining; natural leather breeches; dark blue stockings; tin buttons. |
| Bhl-15 | 1688 | Gordon | | disbanded in 1697 as Cinqvilles zu Fuss | |
| Bhl-16 | 1689 | Batticourt; 1691 Vitry | | ceded to Austria in 1694 | |

# GERMAN REGIMENTS, SQUADRONS AND COMPANIES – 1657–1690

## Cavalry Company:

| Id. | Year: | Colonel Proprietor – Denomination: | Campaigns-Engagements: | History: | Uniforms: |
|---|---|---|---|---|---|
| bhc-i | 1631 | Leibgarde, 1671 Garde du Corps, 1679 Leibgarde zu Pferd | Érsekúivár, Gran (1685); Buda (1686); Mohács (1687) | disbanded in 1803 | (1660s)[57] Trooper: scarlet red coat and lining, black cuffs; pale yellow (natural leather) waistcoat and breeches; tin buttons. (1676)[58] black headgear; red coat with silver lace; brass buttons (1690)[59] Trooper: scarlet red coat, cuffs and lining; deep yellow waistcoat and breeches; tin buttons. |

## Cavalry Regiment:

| Id. | Year: | Colonel Proprietor – Denomination: | Campaigns-Engagements: | History: | Uniforms: |
|---|---|---|---|---|---|
| BhC-1 | 1663 | Rauchhaupt; 1684 Öffener | Hungary (1663–1664); Bremen (1666); Brunswick (1671); Érsekúivár, Gran (1685); Buda (1686); Mohács (1687) | to the circle of Lower Saxony in 1664; in Spanish service in 1689; disbanded in 1776 as Alt- Sprengel Cavallerie | (1665)[60] Trooper: grey-white coat and lining, dark green cuffs; brass buttons. |
| BhC-2 | 1665 | Öffener | | disbanded in 1679 | |
| BhC-3 | 1670 | Löwen | | disbanded in 1679 | |
| BhC-4 | 1673 | Massenbach | | disbanded in 1679 | |
| BhC-6 | 1679 | Offen; 1691 Noyelles | Érsekúivár, Gran (1685); Buda (1686); Mohács (1687) | from Osnabrück (OsC-1); disbanded in 1803 as Garde Cavallerie | |
| BhC-7 | 1679 | Gordon; 1686 Voigt | Érsekúivár, Gran (1685); Buda (1686); Mohács (1687) | from Osnabrück (OsC-2); in Spanish service in 1689; disbanded in 1803 as Schulten Cavallerie | (1690s)[61] Trooper: pale straw-yellow headgear; black cravat; grey-white coat; dark blue cuffs; brass buttons; dark blue saddle cover. |
| BhC-8 | 1683 | Erbprinz Georg Ludwig;; 1689 Benningsen | Érsekúivár, Gran (1685); Buda (1686); Mohács (1687) | in Spanish service in 1689; disbanded in 1803 as Jonquières Cavallerie | (1680s)[62] Trooper; grey-white coat with deep yellow cuffs and lining; natural leather breeches; tin buttons. (1690s)[63] Trooper: grey-white coat; royal blue cuffs and lining; tin buttons. |
| BhC-9 | 1683 | Raugraf zur Pfalz; 1685 Montigny | Érsekúivár, Gran (1685); Buda (1686); Mohács (1687) | disbanded in 1698 | (1690s)[64] Trooper: pale straw-yellow headgear; white cravat; grey-white coat; medium blue cuffs; tin buttons; medium blue saddle cover. |
| BhC-10 | 1683 | Öffener | | disbanded in 1683 | |
| BhC-11 | 1683 | Podewils | | disbanded in 1683 | |
| BhC-12 | 1683 | Hammerstein | | disbanded in 1683 | |

# WARS AND SOLDIERS IN THE EARLY REIGN OF LOUIS XIV – VOLUME 7 PART 3

| Id. | Year | Denomination | | History | Uniforms |
|---|---|---|---|---|---|
| BhC-13 | 1683 | Berlepach | | disbanded in 1683 | |
| BhC-14 | 1684 | Prinz Friedrich August | | ceded to Austria in 1684 | |
| BhC-15 | 1688 | Breidenbach | | in Spanish service in 1689; disbanded in 1803 as Pflueg Cavallerie | (1680s)[65] Trooper: grey-white coat; carmine red cuffs and lining; brass buttons. (1688)[66] Trooper: grey-white coat with blue cuffs and lining. (1690s)[67] Trooper: grey-white coat; scarlet red cuffs and lining; tin buttons. |
| BhC-16 | 1688 | Ferdinand von Ohr; 1691 Schulenburg | | disbanded in 1697 | |
| BhC-17 | 1688 | Hammerstein | | disbanded in 1697 | (1688)[68] Trooper: grey-white coat with red cuffs and lining. |

## Dragoon Company:

| Id. | Year: | Colonel Proprietor - Denomination: | Campaigns- Engagements: | History: | Uniforms: |
|---|---|---|---|---|---|
| bhd-i | 1664 | Leibdragoner | Bremen (1666) | disbanded in 1665 | |

## Dragoon Regiments:

| Id. | Year: | Colonel Proprietor - Denomination: | Campaigns- Engagements: | History: | Uniforms: |
|---|---|---|---|---|---|
| BhD-1 | 1673 | Sozenau | | disbanded in 1679 | |
| BhD-2 | 1680 | Vitry | Érsekúivár (1685); Buda (1686); Mohács (1687) | ceded to Austria in 1691 | |
| BhD-3 | 1683 | Sommerfeld | | disbanded in 1684 | |
| BhD-4 | 1688 | Bülow | | disbanded in 1803 as Oeynhausen Dragoner | (1690s)[69] Private: pale straw-yellow headgear; black cravat; grey-white coat with azure blue cuffs and lining; natural leather waistcoat and breeches; brass buttons; azure blue saddle cover. |

# GERMAN REGIMENTS, SQUADRONS AND COMPANIES – 1657–1690

# Brunswick-Wolfenbüttel

## Infantry Companies:

| Id. | Year: | Colonel Proprietor – Denomination: | Campaigns-Engagements: | History: | Uniforms: |
|---|---|---|---|---|---|
| bwI-i | 1642 | Leibgarde zu Fuss or Trabanten | | disbanded in 1704 and merged with the Leibregiment (BwI-2) | (1675)[70] Trabant: yellow coat with blue facing. |

## Infantry Regiments:

| Id. | Year: | Colonel Proprietor – Denomination: | Campaigns-Engagements: | History: | Uniforms: |
|---|---|---|---|---|---|
| BwI-1 | 1642 | (1657) Schönberg; 1675 Wallwitz or Leibregiment Rudolph August | Bremen (1666) | disbanded in 1680 | (1675)[71] Private: dark blue coat with yellow facings. |
| BwI-2 | 1666 | Stauffeln; 1674 Reuss; 1675 Schmiedberg; 1689 Druchtleben or Leibregiment Anton Ulrich | Entzheim (1674); Türkheim, Trier (1675); Bonn (1689) | disbanded in 1714 as Leibregiment | (1675)[72] Private: dark blue coat with red facings. (1689)[73] Private: grey coat with blue facings. (1690s)[74] Private: black headgear with yellow edging; white cravat; grey coat with dark blue cuffs and lining; dark blue breeches and stockings; brass buttons. |
| BwI-3 | 1670 | Brüggen; 1674 1Johann Adolph von Holstein-Ploen,; 1675 Wrede | Entzheim (1674); Türkheim, Trier (1675); Stettin (1677) | disbanded in 1680 | |
| BwI-4 | 1674 | Roth; 1675 Rumor; 1676 Schack; 1681 Prinz August Wilhelm; 1686 Lippe | Entzheim (1674); Türkheim, Trier (1675); Stettin (1677) | disbanded in 1697 | (1689)[75] Private: dark blue coat with red facings. |
| BwI-5 | 1682 | Holle | Érsekújvár, Gran (1685) | disbanded in 1697 | (1689)[76] Private: black headgear with white edging; dark blue coat with pink cuffs and lining; dark blue waistcoat; pink stockings; tin buttons. |
| BwI-6 | 1682 | Bernstorff | Érsekújvár, Gran (1685) | disbanded in 1736 as Niepage Infanterie | (1690s)[77] Private: black headgear with yellow edging and carmine red ribbon; red cravat; dark blue coat with carmine red cuffs; natural leather breeches; carmine red stockings; brass buttons. |
| BwI-7 | 1687 | Zanthier; 1689 Kragen | Dalmatia and Greece | in Venetian service from 1687 to 1690; disbanded 1754 as Kniestedt Infanterie | |

169

## Cavalry Companies:

| Id. | Year: | Colonel Proprietor – Denomination: | Campaigns-Engagements: | History: | Uniforms: |
|---|---|---|---|---|---|
| bwc-i | 1668 | Anton Ulrich Garde zu Pferde | | disbanded in 1714 | (1675)[78] Trooper: light grey coat.<br>(1690)[79] Trooper: light grey coat with dark blue cuffs. |

## Cavalry Regiments:

| Id. | Year: | Colonel Proprietor – Denomination: | Campaigns-Engagements: | History: | Uniforms: |
|---|---|---|---|---|---|
| BwC-1 | 1666 | Waldeck | Bremen (1666) | disbanded in 1666 | |
| BwC-2 | 1666 | Siegel | | disbanded in 1666 | |
| BwC-3 | 1671 | Leibregiment; 1674 Wilcken | | disbanded in 1675 | (1675)[80] Trooper: yellow coat. |
| BwC-4 | 1671 | Siegel | | disbanded in 1673 | |
| BwC-5 | 1671 | Ilten | | disbanded in 1672 | |
| BwC-6 | 1674 | Siegel; 1676 Lippe | | disbanded in 1686 | |
| BwC-7 | 1674 | Reuss; 1675 Kottwitz | | disbanded in 1679 | |
| BwC-8 | 1674 | Lobach | Entzheim (1674) | disbanded in 1675 | |
| BwC-9 | 1688 | Prinz Ludwig Rudolf or Wolfenbüttel, | | disbanded in 1697 | |
| BwC-10 | 1688 | Leibregiment; Sachsen-Merseburg;<br>1690 Öst-Friesland | | disbanded in 1697 | |
| BwC-11 | 1690 | Leibgarde | | disbanded in 1697 | |

## Dragoon Regiments:

| Id. | Year: | Colonel Proprietor – Denomination: | Campaigns-Engagements: | History: | Uniforms: |
|---|---|---|---|---|---|
| BwD-1 | 1671 | Ditharding | | disbanded in 1672 | |
| BwD-2 | 1674 | Prinz Ludwig Rudolph, 1676 Schack; 1682 Cramm | | disbanded in 1685 | (1675)[81] Private: red coat. |
| BwD-3 | 1688 | Lippe | | disbanded in 1803 as Klösterlein Dragoner | |

# GERMAN REGIMENTS, SQUADRONS AND COMPANIES – 1657–1690

# Electorate of Cologne (Kur-Köln)

## Infantry Regiments:

| Id. | Year: | Colonel Proprietor – Denomination: | Campaigns-Engagements: | History: | Uniforms: |
|---|---|---|---|---|---|
| KkI-1 | 1657 | Landsberg | | disbanded in 1657 | |
| KkI-2 | 1660 | Roist | Hungary and Transylvania (1661) | disbanded in 1662 | |
| KkI-3 | 1663 | Waldeck | Hungary (1664) | with the Deutsche Allianz in 1663–1664; disbanded in 1664 | |
| KkI-4 | 1672 | Leibregiment; Fürstenberg | | to France in 1674 | (1674)[82] Private: blue coat with red facings. |
| KkI-5 | 1672 | Enschering | | disbanded in 1674 | |
| KkI-6 | 1672 | Sachsen | | disbanded in 1674 | |
| KkI-7 | 1672 | Bellerose | | former Lorraine regiment; disbanded in 1674 | |
| KkI-8 | 1672 | Frens | | disbanded in 1683 | |
| KkI-9 | 1672 | Viancourt | | disbanded in 1674 | |
| KkI-10 | 1673 | Landsberg | | disbanded in 1674 | |
| KkI-11 | 1673 | Siegfried von Bibow | | from Mecklenburg ; disbanded in 1674 | |
| KkI-12 | 1674 | Esch | | disbanded in 1674 | |
| KkI-13 | 1676 | Norprath | | disbanded in 1676 | |
| KkI-14 | 1684 | Fürstenberg | | to Austria in 1684 | |
| KkI-15 | 1688 | Leibregiment | | disbanded in 1761 | |

## Cavalry Regiments:

| Id. | Year: | Colonel Proprietor – Denomination: | Campaigns-Engagements: | History: | Uniforms: |
|---|---|---|---|---|---|
| KkC-1 | 1660 | Labrique | | disbanded in 1661 | |
| KkC-2 | 1664 | Richelieu | Hungary (1664) | with the Deutsche Allianz in 1663–1664; disbanded in 1664 | |
| KkC-3 | 1666 | Waldeck | Bremen (1666) | disbanded in 1666 | |
| KkC-4 | 1666 | Helle | Bremen (1666) | disbanded in 1666 | |
| KkC-5 | 1672 | Homburg; 1673 Renelle | | disbanded in 1674 | |
| KkC-6 | 1672 | Lippe | | former Lorraine regiment; disbanded in 1674 | |
| KkC-7 | 1672 | Salins | | former Lorraine regiment; disbanded in 1674 | |

| Id. | Year | | | | |
|---|---|---|---|---|---|
| KkC-8 | 1672 | Halberstadt | | hired from Mecklenburg, disbanded in 1673 | |
| KkC-9 | 1672 | Courcelle | | former Münster regiment; disbanded in 1674 | |
| KkC-10 | 1672 | Sachsen | | disbanded in 1674 | |
| KkC-11 | 1672 | Helen; 1674 Mellinger | | disbanded in 1674 | |
| KkC-12 | 1672 | Gordon | | disbanded in 1674 | |

## Dragons

| Id. | Year: | Colonel Proprietor – Denomination: | Campaigns-Engagements: | History: | Uniforms: |
|---|---|---|---|---|---|
| KkD-1 | 1672 | Martiny | | disbanded in 1674 | |
| KkD-2 | 1672 | Weichs | | disbanded in 1674 | |
| KkD-3 | 1685 | Hoitersleben | | disbanded in 1685 | |

# Cologne (Imperial City)

## Infantry Regiments:

| Id. | Year: | Colonel Proprietor – Denomination: | Campaigns-Engagements: | History: | Uniforms: |
|---|---|---|---|---|---|
| Kol-1 | 1672 | Johann Emmanuel Waldbott von Bassenheim | | to the Westphalian circle in 1673; disbanded in 1679. | |
| Kol-2 | 1679 | 1679 d'Avila; 1680 Körberin | | disbanded in 1685 | |

# Frankfurt am Main

## Infantry Regiment:

| Id. | Year | Colonel Proprietor – Denomination: | Campaigns-Engagements: | History: | Uniforms: |
|---|---|---|---|---|---|
| Frl-1 | 1619 | (1633) Debitzen; 1656 Runckel; 1669 Kieser; 1673 Schaub; 1679 Volcker | | disbanded in 1806 | (1690s)[83] Private: white cravat; dark blue coat with red cuffs and lining, grey stockings: brass buttons. |

# GERMAN REGIMENTS, SQUADRONS AND COMPANIES – 1657–1690

# Hamburg

### Infantry Regiments:

| Id. | Year: | Colonel Proprietor – Denomination: | Campaigns-Engagements: | History: | Uniforms: |
|---|---|---|---|---|---|
| Hal-1 | 1616 | (1651) Wischaert; 1656 Schack; 1658 Copey; 1676 Delwig; 1679 Jobst Moritz von Uffeln | | also known as Leibregiment; disbanded in 1811 | (1686)[84] Private: scarlet coat with blue cuffs and lining. |
| Hal-2 | 1686 | Scheiter; 1687 Borch | | disbanded in 1695 | (1686)[85] Private: scarlet coat with green cuffs and lining. |

# Hessen-Darmstadt

### Infantry Companies:

| Id. | Year: | Denomination: | Campaigns-Engagements: | History: | Uniforms: |
|---|---|---|---|---|---|
| hdi-i | 1621 | Leib Compagnie, 1672 Leibgarde zu Fuss | | became Leibgarde Battalion in 1677 | |

### Infantry regiment:

| Id. | Year: | Colonel Proprietor – Denomination: | Campaigns-Engagements: | History: | Uniforms: |
|---|---|---|---|---|---|
| HdI-1 | 1677 | Leibgarde zu Fuss; 1685 Ludwig Balthasar von Weitolhausen-Schrautenbach | Rhine* (1677) | Leibgarde Infanterie in 1806 | (1678)[86] Private: dark blue coat with red cuffs and lining; red stockings; white buttonholes; tin buttons. |

### Cavalry Companies:

| Id. | Year: | Denomination: | Campaigns-Engagements: | History: | Uniforms: |
|---|---|---|---|---|---|
| hdc-i | 1648 | Leib Compagnie zu Ross, | | merged in the Erbprinz regiment in 1702. | (1668)[87] Trooper: dark blue casaque lined of red, white-red-blue laces. |

### Cavalry Regiment:

| Id. | Year: | Colonel Proprietor – Denomination: | Campaigns-Engagements: | History: | Uniforms: |
|---|---|---|---|---|---|
| HdC-1 | 1677 | Riedesel von Eisenbach | Upper-Rhine (1677) | disbanded in 1678 | (1677)[88] Trooper: dark blue coat with grey-white cuffs and lining. |

# Hessen-Kassel

## Infantry Companies:

| Id. | Year: | Denomination: | Campaigns-Engagements: | History: | Uniforms: |
|---|---|---|---|---|---|
| hki-i | 1648 | Leibgarde zu Fuss | | became Leibregiment in 1683 | (1660s)[89] private: black headgear, white cravat; dark blue coat with red facings and stockings; dark blue breeches; tin buttons. |

## Infantry Regiments:

| Id. | Year: | Colonel Proprietor - Denomination: | Campaigns-Engagements: | History: | Uniforms: |
|---|---|---|---|---|---|
| HkI-1 | 1663 | Zobel | | disbanded in 1664 | |
| HkI-2 | 1666 | Rabenhaupt | | disbanded in 1666 | |
| HkI-3 | 1676 | Johann zur Brüggen; 1677 Ufm-Keller | Philippsburg (1676), Landskrona, Rügen (1677), Warskow (1678) | in Danish service in 1677; disbanded in 1679 | (1676)[90] Private: white cravat; dark blue coat, cuffs and lining; natural leather breeches; grey-white stockings; tin buttons. |
| HkI-4 | 1683 | Ufm-Keller; 1690 Sames | | disbanded in 1703 | |
| HkI-5 | 1683 | August zur Lippe-Brake; 1684 Landgraf Carl von Hessen-Kassel or Leibregiment | Hungary (1685–1688); Mainz (1689) | becomes the second battalion of the Garde Regiment in 1788 | (1675)[91] Private: white cravat; dark blue coat with grey-white cuffs and lining; white-grey breeches; tin buttons. |
| HkI-6 | 1683 | Prinz Philipp von Hessen-Kassel; 1685 Wartensleben; 1690 Rotarius | Hungary (1685–1688) | disbanded in 1806 as Erbprinz Infanterie | |
| HkI-7 | 1684 | Dietrich von Hanstein; 1690 Prinz Wilhelm von Hessen-Kassel | | disbanded in 1789 as Knyphausen Infanterie | |
| HkI-8 | 1684 | Leiningen | | disbanded in 1685 | |
| HkI-9 | 1687 | Prinz Carl von Hessen-Kassel | Athens (1687), Negroponte (1688) | in Venetian service from 1687 to 1688; disbanded in 1806 as Kurprinz Infanterie | (1687)[92] Private: white cravat; dark blue coat and cuffs; red breeches and stockings; brass buttons. |
| HkI-10 | 1688 | Friedrich Erbprinz von Hessen-Kassel | Hungary (1685–1688) | With the Upper-Rhenish circle from 1685 to 1688; disbanded in 1789 as Leibregiment | (1690)[93] Private: white cravat; dark blue coat with red cuffs; red breeches, white stockings; brass buttons. |
| HkI-11 | 1688 | Stockhausen | | disbanded in 1688 | |
| HkI-12 | 1689 | Derenthak | | disbanded in 1693 | |

# GERMAN REGIMENTS, SQUADRONS AND COMPANIES – 1657–1690

## Cavalry Companies and Squadrons:

| Id. | Year: | Denomination: | Campaigns-Engagements: | History: | Uniforms: |
|---|---|---|---|---|---|
| hkc-i | 1648 | Leib Compagnie zu Pferd, 1652 Leibguarde zu Pferd | | Garde du Corps in 1716 | |
| hkc-ii | 1672 | Wilhelm von Hörnumb | Philippsburg (1676) | became regiment Hörnumb in 1676 | |

## Cavalry Regiments:

| Id. | Year: | Colonel Proprietor – Denomination: | Campaigns-Engagements: | History: | Uniforms: |
|---|---|---|---|---|---|
| HkC-1 | 1676 | Hörnumb | Landskrona, Rügen (1677); Warskow (1678) | in Danish service in 1677; disbanded in 1678 | (1678)[94] Trooper: black polished breastplate; light grey coat and cuffs, natural leather breeches; brass buttons; light grey cloak. |
| HkC-2 | 1683 | Otto Rudolph Rau zu Holzhausen; 1685 Wilhelm von Spiegel | Pécs, Siklós (1686), Harsány (1687), Dervent (1688) | to the Upper-Rhenish circle from 1685 to 1688; disbanded in 1765 as Erbprinz zu Pferde | (1687)[95] Trooper: light grey coat with dark blue cuffs and lining (1691)[96] Trooper: black headgear with white piping, white cravat; grey coat, dark pink cuffs, lining and waistcoat, natural leather breeches, tin buttons. |
| HkC-3 | 1684 | Leibregiment or Gensdarmes | | disbanded in 1806 as Gensdarmes | (1678)[97] Trooper: black cravat; light grey coat with red cuffs and lining, natural leather breeches; tin buttons; red saddle cover edged of white. |
| HkC-4 | 1686 | Johann Ernst von Nassau-Weilburg | | disbanded in 1697 as Lippe-Brake zu Pferde | |
| HkC-5 | 1687 | Prinz Wilhelm von Hessen-Homburg | | disbanded in 1688 | |
| HkC-6 | 1688 | Leibgarde (Garde du Corps) | | disbanded in 1730 | (1678)[98] Trooper: dark blue coat. |

## Dragoons:

| Id. | Year: | Colonel Proprietor – Denomination: | Campaigns-Engagements: | History: | Uniforms: |
|---|---|---|---|---|---|
| HkD-1 | 1683 | August von der Lippe-Brake; 1684 Prinz Philipp von Hessen-Kassel | Kahlenberg (1683) | disbanded in 1697 | (1684)[99] Private: red coat. |
| HkD-2 | 1688 | Nassau-Weilburg; 1689 Lippe-Brake | | disbanded in 1806 as Prinz Friedrich Dragoner | (1688)[100] Private: yellow coat. |
| HkD-3 | 1688 | Alexander Hermann von Wartensleben; 1690 Ernst Quirin von Grâffendorff | | disbanded in 1806 as Leibregiment Dragoner | (1688)[101] Private: dark blue coat with red cuffs and lining; natural leather breeches. |

# Hildesheim

### Infantry Regiments:

| Id. | Year: | Colonel Proprietor – Denomination: | Campaigns-Engagements: | History: | Uniforms: |
|---|---|---|---|---|---|
| HiI-1 | 1685 | Fartsch | | disbanded in 1685 | |
| HiI-2 | 1689 | Byland | | to Brunswick-Wolfenbüttel in 1692 as Kerberin zu Fuss | |

### Cavalry Regiment:

| Id. | Year: | Colonel Proprietor – Denomination: | Campaigns-Engagements: | History: | Uniforms: |
|---|---|---|---|---|---|
| HiC-1 | 1685 | Hildesheim | Hungary (1685) | disbanded in 1685 | |

### Dragoon Regimant:

| Id. | Year: | Colonel Proprietor – Denomination: | Campaigns-Engagements: | History: | Uniforms: |
|---|---|---|---|---|---|
| HiI-3 | 1689 | Schorlemmer | | disbanded in 1691 | |

# Hohenlohe

### Infantry Regiment:

| Id. | Year: | Colonel Proprietor – Denomination: | Campaigns-Engagements: | History: | Uniforms: |
|---|---|---|---|---|---|
| HhI-1 | 1690 | Johann Friedrich I von Hohenlohe-Öhringen | Greece (1690–1695) | in Venetian service from 1690 to 1695; disbanded in 1696 | (1690)[102] Private: black headgear with white piping; black cravat; medium grey coat with yellow cuffs and lining; grey waistcoat and stockings; brass buttons. |

# Holstein-Gottorf

### Infantry Company

| Id. | Year: | Colonel Proprietor – Denomination: | Campaigns-Engagements: | History: | Uniforms: |
|---|---|---|---|---|---|
| hgi-i | 1658 | Leibgarde zu Fuss | | disbanded in 1675 | (1664)[103] red coat |

# GERMAN REGIMENTS, SQUADRONS AND COMPANIES – 1657–1690

## Infantry Regiments:

| Id. | Year: | Colonel Proprietor – Denomination: | Campaigns-Engagements: | History: | Uniforms: |
|---|---|---|---|---|---|
| HgI-1 | 1658 | Brockdorff | | to Sweden in 1658 | |
| HgI-2 | 1658 | Plettenberg | | to Sweden in 1658 | |
| HgI-3 | 1672 | Wieck; 1675 Walter | | disbanded in 1675 | |
| HgI-4 | 1689 | Leibregiment | | to Sweden in 1714 | (1690s)[104] Private: black headgear with yellow piping; white cravat; scarlet red coat with medium blue cuffs and lining; yellow buttonholes, scarlet red waistcoat, white stockings; brass buttons. |
| HgI-5 | 1690 | Bülow | | to Sweden in 1714 | (1690s)[105] Private: black headgear with white piping; white cravat; scarlet red coat with medium blue cuffs and lining; scarlet red waistcoat, white stockings; white buttons. |

## Cavalry Company

| Id. | Year: | Colonel Proprietor – Denomination: | Campaigns-Engagements: | History: | Uniforms: |
|---|---|---|---|---|---|
| hgc-i | 1679 | Leibgarde zu Ross | | disbanded in 1682 | |

## Cavalry Regiment:

| Id. | Year: | Colonel Proprietor – Denomination: | Campaigns-Engagements: | History: | Uniforms: |
|---|---|---|---|---|---|
| HgC-1 | 1658 | Osten | | to Sweden in 1658 | |

# Liège

## Infantry Regiments:

| Id. | Year: | Colonel Proprietor – Denomination: | Campaigns-Engagements: | History: | Uniforms: |
|---|---|---|---|---|---|
| LiI-1 | 1687 | Cleuter | Greece (1687-1688) | in Venetian service from 1687 to 1688; disbanded in 1689 | |

## Dragoon Regiments:

| Id. | Year: | Colonel Proprietor – Denomination: | Campaigns-Engagements: | History: | Uniforms: |
|---|---|---|---|---|---|
| LiD-1 | 1670 | Johan Ludwig von Eldern | | to Celle in 1671 | |

# Lorraine

## Infantry Regiments:

| Id. | Year | Colonel Proprietor – Denomination: | Campaigns-Engagements: | History: | Uniforms: |
|---|---|---|---|---|---|
| Lol-1 | 1643? | (1655) Mussy (or Massey) | | disbanded in 1659? | |
| Lol-2 | 1645? | (1655) Des Marais; 1668 Bellerose | Oudenarde, Scarpe, Armentières, Lille, Alost, Mons (1667) | German; disbanded in 1669 | |
| Lol-3 | 1646? | (1655) Beaufort; 1658? Berrier | | disbanded in 1658 | |
| Lol-4 | 1648? | (1655) Tornielle | Oudenarde, Scarpe, Armentières, Lille, Alost, Mons (1667) | disbanded in 1669 | |
| Lol-5 | 1655? | Cascar | | German; disbanded in 1659? | |
| Lol-6 | 1655? | O'Connor | | Irish; disbanded in 1659? | |
| Lol-7 | 1655? | Cusack | | Irish; disbanded in 1659? | |
| Lol-8 | 1655? | Bellerose | | disbanded in 1659? | |
| Lol-9 | 1656? | Dominique Lhuillier; 1659 Des Pilliers; 1669 Charles-Henry de Vaudemont | Oudenarde, Scarpe, Armentières, Lille, Alost, Mons (1667) | disbanded in 1669 | |
| Lol-10 | 1656? | Jean de Grondeur (or Cronders) | | disbanded in 1659? | |
| Lol-11 | 1656? | Des Pilliers | | disbanded in 1659? | |
| Lol-12 | 1667 | Mauleon | Oudenarde, Scarpe, Armentières, Lille; Alost, Mons (1667) | disbanded in 1669 | |
| Lol-13 | 1667 | Eltz, 1668 La Mothe | Landstuhl (1668) | disbanded in 1669 | |
| Lol-14 | 1668 | Lippe | | German; disbanded in 1671? | |
| Lol-15 | 1668 | Jorman | | German; disbanded in 1669 | |
| Lol-16 | 1668 | Raincourt | | German; disbanded in 1669 | |
| Lol-17 | 1668 | Harcourt | Crete (1669) | French; in Venetian service in 1669; disbanded in 1669 | |
| Lol-18 | 1668 | Des Marais | | In Spanish service from 1668 to 1672; disbanded in 1673 | |
| Lol-19 | 1669 | Lippe | | disbanded in 1671 | |
| Lol-20 | 1669 | Bellerose | | ceded to the Electorate Cologne in 1672 | |

# GERMAN REGIMENTS, SQUADRONS AND COMPANIES – 1657–1690

## Cavalry Squadrons or Companies:

| Id. | Year: | Colonel Proprietor – Denomination: | Campaigns-Engagements: | History: | Uniforms: |
|---|---|---|---|---|---|
| Ioc-i | 1624 | Gardes du Corps | Geimersheim (1666); Bingen (1668); Conzer Brücke, Trier (1675) | disbanded in 1675 | (1670)[106] Trooper: red coat with yellow facings, golden buttons (?) |
| Ioc-ii | 1627 | Chavaux-Legers | Geimersheim (1666); Bingen (1668); Conzer Brücke; Trier (1675) | disbanded in 1675 | (1670)[107] Trooper: red coat with yellow facings, silver buttons (?) |
| Ioc-iii | 1664? | Mousquetaires de la Garde | Bingen (1668) | disbanded in 1669 | (1660)[108] Private: red casaque laced of gold; red coat with yellow facings, silver buttons. |

## Cavalry Regiments:

| Id. | Year: | Colonel Proprietor – Denomination: | Campaigns-Engagements: | History: | Uniforms: |
|---|---|---|---|---|---|
| LoC-1 | 1631? | (1655) Haraucourt | Oudenarde, Scarpe, Armentières, Lille, Alost, Mons (1667) | disbanded in 1669 | |
| LoC-2 | 1631? | (1655) Bassompierre | Oudenarde, Scarpe, Armentières, Lille, Alost, Mons (1667) | disbanded in 1669 | |
| LoC-3 | 1635? | (1655) Lenoncourt; 1668? La Chaussée | Oudenarde, Scarpe, Armentières, Lille, Alost, Mons (1667) | disbanded in 1669 | |
| LoC-4 | 1645? | (1655) Nicolas-François de Lorraine-Vaudemont; | Oudenarde, Scarpe, Armentières, Lille, Alost, Mons (1667) | disbanded in 1669 | |
| LoC-5 | 1645? | (1655) Mercy (1664) Charles-Henry de Lorraine-Vaudemont | Erfurt (1664) Oudenarde, Scarpe, Armentières, Lille, Alost, Mons (1667) | disbanded in 1669 | |
| LoC-6 | 1655? | Ferdinand de Vaudemont; 1658? Jean-Philippe de Savigny | | German; disbanded in 1665? | |
| LoC-7 | 1655? | Vervienne (?); 1663 Florimond d'Allamont; (1675) Housse | Sinsheim, Entzheim, Mulhouse (1674); Türkheim (1675) | In Spanish service from 1668 to 1672; disbanded in 1675 | |
| LoC-8 | 1655? | Delouz; 1661 Silly | | disbanded in 1663? | |
| LoC-9 | 1655? | Braquy | | disbanded in 1668 | |
| LoC-10 | 1655? | Du Châtelet, 1668 Faulquemont | | disbanded in 1669 | |
| LoC-11 | 1655? | Fournier; 1667? Michel de Salins | | disbanded in 1668 | |
| LoC-12 | 1655? | Ligniville; 1662 Bellerose | Oudenarde, Scarpe, Armentières, Lille, Alost, Mons (1667) | disbanded in 1669 | |
| LoC-13 | 1655? | Du Plessy | | mixed German-Lorraine; disbanded in 1659? | |
| LoC-14 | 1655? | Speltz; 1662? Lippe | Oudenarde, Scarpe, Armentières, Lille, Alost, Mons (1667) | German; disbanded in 1668 | |

# WARS AND SOLDIERS IN THE EARLY REIGN OF LOUIS XIV – VOLUME 7 PART 3

| LoC-15 | 1656? | Trastorff; 1663? Welzander | Oudenarde, Scarpe, Armentières, Lille, Alost, Mons (1667) | German; disbanded in 1668 | |
|---|---|---|---|---|---|
| LoC-16 | 1656? | Baudricourt; 1667 Viange | | disbanded in 1668 | |
| LoC-17 | 1656? | Dufour, 1668 Gerbevillier | | disbanded in 1669 | |
| LoC-18 | 1656? | Valdenbourgh | | disbanded in 1659? | |
| LoC-19 | 1656? | Ourches; 1663 Du Puy | | disbanded in 1668 | |
| LoC-20 | 1668 | Couvonge | | disbanded in 1669 | |
| LoC-21 | 1668 | Boudonville | | disbanded in 1669 | |
| LoC-22 | 1668 | Daucourt | | disbanded in 1669 | |
| LoC-23 | 1668 | Arnolet | | disbanded in 1669 | |
| LoC-24 | 1668 | Paul Heinrich von Raab | | German; disbanded in 1669 | |
| LoC-25 | 1668 | Berrier | | In Spanish service from 1668 to 1673; disbanded in 1675 | |
| LoC-26 | 1668 | Créhange | Sinsheim, Entzheim, Mulhouse (1674); Türkheim (1675) | In Spanish service from 1668 to 1673; disbanded in 1675 | |
| LoC-27 | 1668 | Igny de Fontenoy; (1675) Mitry de Facouncourt | Sinsheim, Entzheim, Mulhouse (1674); Türkheim (1675) | In Spanish service from 1668 to 1673; disbanded in 1675 | |
| LoC-28 | 1668 | Rheingraf; (1675) Trichâteau | Sinsheim, Entzheim, Bénéménil, Mulhouse (1674); Türkheim (1675), | In Spanish service from 1668 to 1673; disbanded in 1675 | |
| LoC-29 | 1669 | François-Marie de Lillebonne | | ceded to France in 1669 | |
| LoC-30 | 1669 | Charles-Henry de Vaudemont | Sinsheim, Entzheim, Mulhouse (1674); Türkheim, Conzer Brücke, Trier (1675) | in Spanish service from 1668 to 1673; disbanded in 1675 | |
| LoC-31 | 1669 | Lippe | | ceded to Electoral Cologne in 1672 | |
| LoC-32 | 1669 | Sötern; 1670 Salin | | in Spanish service from 1668 to 1672; ceded to Electoral Cologne in 1672 | |
| LoC-33 | 1669 | Funck | | disbanded in 1671 | |
| LoC-34 | 1669 | Weibenom | | disbanded in 1671 | |
| LoC-35 | 1669 | Haraucourt | | German; disbanded in 1671 | |

## GERMAN REGIMENTS, SQUADRONS AND COMPANIES – 1657–1690

| Id. | Year | Colonel Proprietor - Denomination | Campaigns-Engagements | History | Uniforms |
|---|---|---|---|---|---|
| LoC-36 | 1669 | Wulffen | | German; disbanded in 1671 | |
| LoC-37 | 1669 | Ludwig Christian von Wittgenstein | | German; disbanded in 1671 | |
| LoC-38 | 1672 | Leiningen | | disbanded in 1672 | |
| LoC-39 | 1672 | Öttingen | | disbanded in 1673 | |
| LoC-40 | 1674 | Du Puy | Sinsheim, Entzheim, Bénemènil, Mulhouse (1674) Türkheim; Conzer Brücke, Trier (1675) | disbanded in 1675 | |
| LoC-41 | 1674 | Thouvenin | Sinsheim, Entzheim, Mulhouse (1674); Türkheim, Conzer Brücke, Trier (1675) | disbanded in 1675 | |
| LoC-42 | 1674 | Pierre Ernest de Mercy | Sinsheim, Entzheim, Bénemènil, Mulhouse (1674); Türkheim, Conzer Brücke, Trier (1675) | disbanded in 1675 | |
| LoC-43 | 1675 | Du Houx | Conzer Brücke, Trier (1675) | disbanded in 1675 | |
| LoC-44 | 1675 | Mortal | Conzer Brücke, Trier (1675) | disbanded in 1675 | |
| LoC-45 | 1675 | Rosieres | Conzer Brücke, Trier (1675) | disbanded in 1675 | |
| LoC-46 | 1675 | Ruchemfeld | | German; disbanded in 1675 | |
| LoC-47 | 1675 | Welden | | German; disbanded in 1675 | |

## Dragoon Regiments:

| Id. | Year: | Colonel Proprietor - Denomination: | Campaigns-Engagements: | History: | Uniforms: |
|---|---|---|---|---|---|
| LoD-1 | 1674 | Silbach; (1675) Salin | Sinsheim, Entzheim, Bénemènil, Mulhouse (1674); Türkheim, Conzer Brücke, Trier (1675) | German; disbanded in 1675 | |
| LoD-2 | 1675 | Ranfaing | Trier (1675) | disbanded in 1675 | |

# Electorate of Mainz (Kur-Mainz)

## Infantry Regiments:

| Id. | Year: | Colonel Proprietor - Denomination: | Campaigns-Engagements: | History: | Uniforms: |
|---|---|---|---|---|---|
| Kml-1 | 1657 | Lucas Spieckh | | disbanded in 1657 | |
| Kml-2 | 1661 | Kuno von der Leyen | | ceded to Austria in 1661 | |
| Kml-3 | 1662 | Köth; 1672 Heddersdorff; 1675 Schönborn; 1685 Langwerth; 1689 Solingen | Erfurt (1664) | disbanded in 1691 | |
| Kml-4 | 1663 | Leyen | Szentgotthárd (1664) | mixed Mainz-Würzburg; disbanded in 1664 | |
| Kml-5 | 1689 | Thüngen | | disbanded in 1697 | |
| Kml-6 | 1689 | Leyen | | disbanded in 1803 as Gymnich Infanterie | (1690s)[109] Private: grey coat, red cuffs and stockings |

## Dragoons Regiments:

| Id. | Year: | Colonel Proprietor - Denomination: | Campaigns-Engagements: | History: | Uniforms: |
|---|---|---|---|---|---|
| KmD-I | 1689 | Langwerth; 1690 Leiningen | | disbanded in 1695 | |

# Mecklenburg (Schwerin and Güstrow)

## Infantry Companies:

| Id. | Year: | Colonel Proprietor - Denomination: | Campaigns-Engagements: | History: | Uniforms: |
|---|---|---|---|---|---|
| mei-i | 1672? | Leibgarde zu Fuss (Güstrow) | | disbanded in 1695 | (1664) Private: red coat* |

## Infantry Regiments:

| Id. | Year: | Colonel Proprietor - Denomination: | Campaigns-Engagements: | History: | Uniforms: |
|---|---|---|---|---|---|
| Mel-1 | 1672 | Siegfried von Bibow (Schwerin) | | ceded to Electoral Cologne in 1673 | |
| Mel-2 | 1687 | Österling (Güstrow) | Hungary (1688-1689) | disbanded in 1689 | |

# GERMAN REGIMENTS, SQUADRONS AND COMPANIES – 1657–1690

## Cavalry Companies:

| Id. | Year: | Colonel Proprietor - Denomination: | Campaigns-Engagements: | History: | Uniforms: |
|---|---|---|---|---|---|
| mec-ii | 1664 | Garde zu Ross (Güstrow) | | disbanded in 1695 | |
| mec-ii | 1672 | Leibkompagnie zu Pferde (Schwerin) | | disbanded in 1698 | |
| mec-iii | 1687 | Jordan (Güstrow) | | disbanded in 1689 | |

## Cavalry Regiments:

| Id. | Year: | Colonel Proprietor - Denomination: | Campaigns-Engagements: | History: | Uniforms: |
|---|---|---|---|---|---|
| MeC-1 | 1672 | Halberstadt (Schwerin) | Groningen (1672) | ceded to France and Cologne in 1673 | |
| MeC-2 | 1672 | Örtzen (Schwerin) | | ceded to Denmark in 1672 | |

# Nuremberg

## Infantry:

| Id. | Year: | Colonel Proprietor - Denomination: | Campaigns-Engagements: | History: | Uniforms: |
|---|---|---|---|---|---|
| NuI-1 | 1618 | (1654) Harsdörfer; 1600 Haller; 1670 Paumgärtner; 1676 Volkamer; 1679 Rirter; 1689 Fürer | | disbanded in 1803 | (1686)[110] Private: black headgear, red cravat; grey coat with red cuffs and lining, red stockings; grey buttons. |

# Osnabrück

## Infantry:

| Id. | Year: | Colonel Proprietor - Denomination: | Campaigns-Engagements: | History: | Uniforms: |
|---|---|---|---|---|---|
| OsI-1 | 1662 | Johan Georg von Uffeln; 1678 Hermann Philipp von Ohr (Leibregiment in 1677) | Brunswick (1671) Conzer Brücke, Trier (1675); Zweibrücken, Maastricht (1676); Charleroi (1677); Saint-Denis (1678) | in Dutch service in 1668; to Hanover in 1679 | (1676)[111] Trooper: yellow coat. |

| Id. | Year | Colonel Proprietor - Denomination | Campaigns-Engagements | History | Uniforms |
|---|---|---|---|---|---|
| OsI-2 | 1665 | Verckel, 1675 Hülsen | Conzer Brücke, Trier (1675); Maastricht (1676); Saint-Denis (1678) | to Hanover in 1679 | |
| OsI-3 | 1671 | Borch | Brunswick (1671); Trier (1675); Maastricht (1676); Charleroi (1677); Saint-Denis (1678) | to Hanover in 1679 | |
| OsI-4 | 1671 | Degenfeld | | disbanded in 1671 | |
| OsI-5 | 1676 | Derenthal | Charleroi (1677) | disbanded in 1678 | |
| OsI-6 | 1678 | Kawan | | disbanded in 1679 | |

## Cavalry Companies:

| Id. | Year: | Colonel Proprietor - Denomination: | Campaigns-Engagements: | History: | Uniforms: |
|---|---|---|---|---|---|
| osc-i | 1661 | Leib Ross | | to Hanover in 1679 | (1668)[112] Trooper: red coat with black velvet facing laced of gold. |

## Cavalry Regiments:

| Id. | Year: | Colonel Proprietor - Denomination: | Campaigns-Engagements: | History: | Uniforms: |
|---|---|---|---|---|---|
| OsC-1 | 1665 | Leibregiment (Alt Ziegler, 1676 Offen) | Bremen (1666); Conzer Brücke, Trier (1675); Maastricht (1676); Saint-Denis (1678) | in Dutch service in 1668; to Hanover in 1679 | |
| OsC-2 | 1666 | Ziegler (Jung Ziegler) | Bremen (1666) | disbanded in 1666 | |
| OsC-3 | 1673 or 1675 | Offen; 1676 Prinzen | Conzer Brücke, Trier (1675); Maastricht (1676); Saint-Denis (1678) | disbanded in 1679 | (1675)[113] Trooper: deep yellow coat and cuffs; brass buttons. |
| OsC-4 | 1675 | Hitzfeld; 1678 Gordon | Conzer Brücke, Trier (1675); Maastricht (1676); Saint-Denis (1678) | to Hanover in 1679 | (1675)[114] Trooper: grey-white coat; dark blue cuffs and lining; brass buttons. |
| OsC-5 | 1676 | Lippe; 1679 Löwen | | disbanded in 1679 | |

## Dragons Squadrons and Companies:

| Id. | Year: | Colonel Proprietor - Denomination: | Campaigns-Engagements: | History: | Uniforms: |
|---|---|---|---|---|---|
| osd-i | 1675 | Garde Dragoner | | regiment in 1677 (OsD-1) | |
| osd-ii | 1676 | Jean-Charles de Louvigny | Conzer Brücke (1675); Saint-Denis (1678) | Walloons, joined to regiment OsD-1 in 1677 | |

# GERMAN REGIMENTS, SQUADRONS AND COMPANIES – 1657–1690

### Dragons:

| Id. | Year: | Colonel Proprietor – Denomination: | Campaigns-Engagements: | History: | Uniforms: |
|---|---|---|---|---|---|
| OsD-1 | 1677 | Louvigny | | disbanded in 1679 | |

## Paderborn

### Infantry:

| Id. | Year: | Colonel Proprietor – Denomination: | Campaigns-Engagements: | History: | Uniforms: |
|---|---|---|---|---|---|
| PaI-1 | 1676 | Plettenberg | Saint-Denis (1678) | disbanded in 1678 | |
| PaI-1 | 1690 | Lippe | | disbanded in 1697 | |

### Dragons:

| Id. | Year: | Colonel Proprietor – Denomination: | Campaigns-Engagements: | History: | Uniforms: |
|---|---|---|---|---|---|
| PaD-1 | 1676 | Spiegel | | disbanded in 1678 | |

## The Palatinate (Kur-Pfalz)

### Infantry Companies:

| Id. | Year: | Colonel Proprietor – Denomination: | Campaigns-Engagements: | History: | Uniforms: |
|---|---|---|---|---|---|
| kpi-i | 1665 | Kurfürstliche Leibcompagnie | Bingen (1668) | disbanded in 1680 | (1665)[115] Private: dark blue coat. |
| kpi-ii | 1670 | Kurprinz Leibcompagnie | | disbanded in 1680 | |

### Infantry Regiments:

| Id. | Year: | Colonel Proprietor – Denomination: | Campaigns-Engagements: | History: | Uniforms: |
|---|---|---|---|---|---|
| KpI-1 | 1666 | Wilder | Bingen (1668) | disbanded in 1680 | (1664)[116] Private: dark blue coat and breeches. |
| KpI-2 | 1674 | Sparr; 1679 Degenfeld; 1683 Wittgenstein | | disbanded in 1688 | |
| KpI-3 | 1683 | Leibregiment | | disbanded in 1686 | |
| KpI-4 | 1683 | Frays | | disbanded in 1686 | |
| KpI-5 | 1683 | Cattaneo | | disbanded in 1686 | |

| Id. | Year | Colonel Proprietor - Denomination | Campaigns-Engagements | History | Uniforms |
|---|---|---|---|---|---|
| KpI-6 | 1685 | Kurprinz | | from Pfalz-Neuburg; disbanded in 1798 as Bavarian Kinkel Füsilieren | |
| KpI-7 | 1685 | Avila; 1687 Lybeck | | from Pfalz-Neuburg; reformed in 1806. | |
| KpI-8 | 1685 | Bernsau; 1688 Efferen | | disbanded in 1799 as Bavarian Hohenhausen Infanterie | |
| KpI-9 | 1688 | Sulzbach; 1690 Ernst Ludwig von Sachsen-Meiningen | | disbanded in 1798 as Bavarian Isenburg Füsilieren | (1690s)[117] Private: carmine red coat with green cuffs, waistcoat and lining; scarlet breeches, grey stockings; white metal buttons. |

## Cavalry Companies:

| Id. | Year: | Colonel Proprietor - Denomination: | Campaigns-Engagements: | History: | Uniforms: |
|---|---|---|---|---|---|
| kpc-i | 1650 | Kurfürstliche Leibgarde zu Ross | Sinsheim (1674) | reformed in 1734 as Leibagrde zu Pferd | (1650s)[118] Private: broad-brimmed hat with blue plumes; dark blue coat with silver lace. |
| kpc-ii | 1670 | Kurprinz Leibgarde | | disbanded in 1680 | |

## Cavalry Regiments:

| Id. | Year: | Colonel Proprietor - Denomination: | Campaigns-Engagements: | History: | Uniforms: |
|---|---|---|---|---|---|
| KpC-1 | 1668 | Chauvet | | mixed cavalry-dragons: disbanded in 1668 | |
| KpC-2 | 1685 | Leibregiment zu Pferd | | from Pfalz-Neuburg; disbanded in 1745 as Kurfürstin Cavallerie | (1690s)[119] Trooper: dark blue coat with carmine red cuffs and lining |
| KpC-3 | 1689 | Franckenberg | | Bavarian Kurfürst Chevaux-Legers in 1806. | (1690s)[120] Trooper: ash grey coat with medium blue cuffs and lining. |

## Dragons:

| Id. | Year: | Colonel Proprietor - Denomination: | Campaigns-Engagements: | History: | Uniforms: |
|---|---|---|---|---|---|
| KpD-1 | 1684 | Leib-Dragoner; 1690 Jungheim | | disbanded in 1745 as Kurfürstin Dragoner | |
| KpD-2 | 1687 | Kurprinz (Vehlen); 1690 Leibregiment | | disbanded in 1803 as Bavarian Dragoner Regt. Nr. 1 | |

# Pfalz-Neuburg

## Infantry

| Id. | Year: | Colonel Proprietor – Denomination: | Campaigns-Engagements: | History: | Uniforms: |
|---|---|---|---|---|---|
| PnI-1 | 1657 | Goltstein; Spielberg | Münster (1660–1661) | to Münster in 1661 | |
| PnI-2 | 1663 | Gerhard Wilhelm von Hochstätten | Hungary (1663–1664) | disbanded in 1664 | |
| PnI-3 | 1671 | Johann Emmanuel Waldbott von Bassenheim | | disbanded in 1672 and reduced to a single company | (1672)[121] Private: grey coat with deep yellow cuffs and lining. |
| PnI-4 | 1676 | Franz von Schellart; 1677 Leibregiment des Erbprinzen | Saint-Denis (1678) | to Kur-Pfalz in 1685 | (1679)[122] Private: black broad-brimmed hat with red band; dark blue coat with red cuffs, lining; breeches and stockings; tin buttons. Officer: dark blue coat with red cuffs and lining laced of silver or gold. |
| PnI-5 | 1676 | Friedrich Christian von Spee; 1677 Franz Jacob von Avila | Saint-Denis (1678) | to Kur-Pfalz in 1685 | |
| PnI-6 | 1676 | Saint-Paul de Fange | Maastricht (1676) | disbanded in 1679 | |
| PnI-7 | 1676 | Otto Ludwig von Manderscheid | | disbanded in 1679 | |
| PnI-8 | 1676 | Waldenberg | Maastricht (1676) | disbanded in 1678 | |
| PnI-9 | 1676 | Elss de Boisbernard | Maastricht (1676) | disbanded in 1679 | |
| PnI-10 | 1676 | Neuland | Maastricht (1676) | disbanded in 1677 | |
| PnI-11 | 1683 | Bernsau; 1685 Jung d'Avila | | to Kur-Pfalz in 1685 | |

## Cavalry Companies:

| Id. | Year: | Colonel Proprietor – Denomination: | Campaigns-Engagements: | History: | Uniforms: |
|---|---|---|---|---|---|
| pnc-i | 1651 | Leibgarden zu Ross | | to regiment Schellart (PnC-4) in 1676. | |
| pnc-ii | 1679 | Leibgarde zu Pferd | | to the Leibregiment (PnC-6) in 1682 | |

# WARS AND SOLDIERS IN THE EARLY REIGN OF LOUIS XIV – VOLUME 7 PART 3

## Cavalry:

| Id. | Year: | Colonel Proprietor – Denomination: | Campaigns-Engagements: | History: | Uniforms: |
|---|---|---|---|---|---|
| PnC-1 | 1671 | Velbrück | | disbanded in 1671 | |
| PnC-2 | 1671 | Landsberg | | disbanded in 1671 | |
| PnC-3 | 1674 | Johann Friedrich von Frankenberg | Fehrbellin (1675); Saint-Denis (1678) | in Brandenburg service in 1675–1676; disbanded in 1679 | |
| PnC-4 | 1676 | Schellart | Saint-Denis (1678) | disbanded in 1679 | |
| PnC-5 | 1682 | Erbprinz, Burgsdorff | | to Kur-Pfalz in 1685 | |
| PnC-6 | 1682 | Leibregiment | | to Kur-Pfalz in 1685 | (1682)[123] Trooper: dark blue coat with carmine red cuffs and lining. |

## Dragons:

| Id. | Year: | Colonel Proprietor – Denomination: | Campaigns-Engagements: | History: | Uniforms: |
|---|---|---|---|---|---|
| PnD-1 | 1676 | Otto Ludwig von Manderscheid | Maastricht (1676); Saint-Denis (1678) | disbanded in 1679 | |
| PnD-2 | 1679 | Steindorff | | from Würzburg, disbanded in 1679 | |

# Reuss

## Infantry

| Id. | Year: | Colonel Proprietor – Denomination: | Campaigns-Engagements: | History: | Uniforms: |
|---|---|---|---|---|---|
| ReI-1 | 1673 | Heinrich von Reuss | Upper-Rhine | passed into the Imperial army in 1674 | |

# Saxe-Eisenach

| Id. | Year: | Colonel Proprietor – Denomination: | Campaigns-Engagements: | History: | Uniforms: |
|---|---|---|---|---|---|
| SeI-1 | 1674 | Herzog Johann Georg | Upper-Rhine | to Saxe-Gotha in 1676 | |

# Saxe-Coburg

## Infantry

| Id. | Year: | Colonel Proprietor - Denomination: | Campaigns-Engagements: | History: | Uniforms: |
|---|---|---|---|---|---|
| ScI-1 | 1688 | Albrecht III von Sachsen-Coburg | Mainz (1689) | ceded to Austria in 1689 | Private (1689)[124] black headgear with white piping, pearl grey coat, black cuffs, pearl grey waistcoat and breeches, black stockings, brass buttons, white cravat.. |

# Saxe-Gotha

## Infantry

| Id. | Year: | Colonel Proprietor - Denomination: | Campaigns-Engagements: | History: | Uniforms: |
|---|---|---|---|---|---|
| SgI-1 | 1676 | Herzog Friedrich | Upper-Rhine | disbanded in 1679 | |
| SgI-2 | 1676 | Erbprinz Friedrich | Upper-Rhine | disbanded in 1679 | |
| SgI-3 | 1676 | Saxe-Eisenach (Prinz Johann Georg) | Upper-Rhine | disbanded in 1679 | |
| SgI-4 | 1683 | Prinz Ernst | | disbanded in 1685 | |
| SgI-5 | 1690 | Neuhof | | Prinz Friedrich Infanterie in 1785 | |

## Cavalry:

| Id. | Year: | Colonel Proprietor - Denomination: | Campaigns-Engagements: | History: | Uniforms: |
|---|---|---|---|---|---|
| SgC-1 | 1689 | Saxe-Gotha, 1690 Butler | | Kirchbach Dragoner in 1806 | |

# Salzburg

## Infantry

| Id. | Year: | Colonel Proprietor - Denomination: | Campaigns-Engagements: | History: | Uniforms: |
|---|---|---|---|---|---|
| SzI-1 | 1664 | Plettinger | Zrínyivár (1664) | disbanded in 1664 | |
| SzI-2 | 1674 | Freising | | disbanded in 1679 | |
| SzI-3 | 1683 | Steindorf; 1686 Grimming | Kahlenberg (1683) | disbanded in 1699 | |

# Electorate of Trier (Kur-Trier)

## Infantry

| Id. | Year: | Colonel Proprietor – Denomination: | Campaigns-Engagements: | History: | Uniforms: |
|---|---|---|---|---|---|
| KtI-1 | 1658 | Wolframsdorf | | ceded to Austria in 1661 | |
| KtI-2 | 1662 | Leyen; 1675 Eltern; 1680 d'Autel | Hungary (1663–1664); Conzer Brücke, Trier (1675) | disbanded in 1699 | |

# Waldeck-Pyrmont

## Infantry

| Id. | Year: | Colonel Proprietor – Denomination: | Campaigns-Engagements: | History: | Uniforms: |
|---|---|---|---|---|---|
| Wal-1 | 1666 | Degenfeld | Bremen (1666) | disbanded in 1666 | |
| Wal-2 | 1688 | Georg Ludwig zu Waldeck | | in Venetian service from 1688 to 1690; disbanded in 1690 | |

## Cavalry:

| Id. | Year: | Colonel Proprietor – Denomination: | Campaigns-Engagements: | History: | Uniforms: |
|---|---|---|---|---|---|
| WaC-1 | 1672 | Georg Ludwig zu Waldeck | | in Brandenburg service from 1672 to 1673; disbanded in 1673 | |

# Württemberg

## Infantry companies:

| Id. | Year: | Colonel Proprietor – Denomination: | Campaigns-Engagements: | History: | Uniforms: |
|---|---|---|---|---|---|
| wüi-i | 1651 | Leibwache | | becomes the Leibcompagnie of regiment Cronhjorst in 1674; | |

# GERMAN REGIMENTS, SQUADRONS AND COMPANIES – 1657–1690

## Infantry Regiments:

| Id. | Year: | Colonel Proprietor - Denomination: | Campaigns-Engagements: | History: | Uniforms: |
|---|---|---|---|---|---|
| Wül-1 | 1673 | Cronhjorst | | disbanded in 1675 | (1674)[25] Private: yellow coat with company facing of different colours.. |
| Wül-2 | 1687 | Carl Rudolph von Württemberg-Neuenstadt (Alt-Württemberg) | Greece: Patras, Athen (1687); Negroponte (1688) | in Venetian service from 1687 to 1689; in Austrian service in 1689. | (1690s)[26] Private: ash grey coat with yellow cuffs. |
| Wül-3 | 1687 | Prinz Heinrich Friedrich (Jung-Württemberg) | Greece, | in Venetian service from 1688 to 1689; into the Spanish army in 1690 | |
| Wül-4 | 1687 | Plissen, 1688 Ramstätt | Negroponte (1688) | in Venetian service from 1687 to 1689; into the Spanish army in 1690 | |
| Wül-5 | 1687 | Riedesel | Negroponte (1688) | in Venetian service from 1688 to 1689; into the Spanish army in 1690 | |
| Wül-6 | 1688 | Prinz Georg von Hessen-Darmstadt | Greece, | in Venetian service from 1688 to 1689; disbanded in 1690. | |
| Wül-7 | 1689 | Leibregiment (Horn) or Gelb-Württemberg | | disbanded in 1739 | (1689)[27] Private: yellow coat |
| Wül-8 | 1689 | Sauerbrei or Rot-Württemberg | | disbanded in 1693 | (1689)[28] Private: scarlet red coat |
| Wül-9 | 1689 | Eyb or Grün-Württemberg | | disbanded in 1693 | (1689)[29] Private: green coat |

## Cavalry Companies:

| Id. | Year: | Colonel Proprietor - Denomination: | Campaigns-Engagements: | History: | Uniforms: |
|---|---|---|---|---|---|
| wüc-i | 1660 | Leibwache zu Pferd; (1671) Leibgarde des Herzogs | | merged with regiment Truchsess (WüC-1) in 1688. | (1660)[130] Trooper: white metal helm and breastplate, yellow coat with black cuffs and lining; natural leather breeches, golden buttons; black saddle cover edged of yellow. Officer: black saddle cover edged of gold. |
| wüc-ii | 1664 | Leibgarde des Erbprinzen | | disbanded in 1679. | (1674)[131] Trooper: black polished metal helm and breastplate, yellow coat with black cuffs and lining; leather breeches, silver buttons black saddle cover edged of white. Officer: black saddle cover edged of silver. |

## Cavalry Regiments:

| Id. | Year: | Colonel Proprietor – Denomination: | Campaigns-Engagements: | History: | Uniforms: |
|---|---|---|---|---|---|
| WüC-1 | 1688 | Johann Eitel Truchsess von Wetzhausen; 1689 Hessen-Darmstadt | | ceded to the Dutch Republic in 1697 | |
| WüC-3 | 1688 | Prinz Friedrich Carl von Württemberg | | ceded to the Dutch Republic in 1697 | |
| WüC-3 | 1688 | Erffa, 1690 Saxe-Hildburghausen | | ceded to the Dutch Republic in 1697 | |
| WüC-4 | 1689 | Freudenberg or Württemberg Reiter | | Leibdragoner in 1701; disbanded in 1736 as Prinz Louis Dragoner | |

## Dragoon Regiments:

| Id. | Year: | Colonel Proprietor – Denomination: | Campaigns-Engagements: | History: | Uniforms: |
|---|---|---|---|---|---|
| WüD-1 | 1689 | Carlin or Württemberg Dragoner | | disbanded in 1701 | |

# Würzburg

## Infantry Regiments:

| Id. | Year: | Colonel Proprietor – Denomination: | Campaigns-Engagements: | History: | Uniforms: |
|---|---|---|---|---|---|
| WzI-1 | 1661 | Fuchs | | ceded to Austria in 1661 | |
| WzI-2 | 1674 | Kuno von der Leyen, 1684 Copp | | disbanded in 1688 | (1675)[32] Private: dark blue coat, white facings |
| WzI-3 | 1675 | Johann Carl von Thüngen | | disbanded in 1685 | (1675)[33] Private: dark blue coat and facings. |
| WzI-4 | 1688 | Johann Carl von Thüngen or Würzburg | | in Venetian service from 1688 to 1689; disbanded in 1747 as Draxdorf Infanterie | (1688)[34] Private: grey coat with red cuffs and linings; red breeches and stockings; brass buttons. |

# GERMAN REGIMENTS, SQUADRONS AND COMPANIES – 1657–1690

## Cavalry:

| Id. | Year: | Colonel Proprietor – Denomination: | Campaigns-Engagements: | History: | Uniforms: |
|---|---|---|---|---|---|
| WzC-1 | 1675 | Würzburg Cuirassieren | | disbanded in 1679 | (1675)[135] Trooper: buff coat and black polished metal breast armour. |
| WzC-2 | 1675 | Johann Eitel Truchsess von Wetzhausen Cuirassieren | | ceded to Austria in 1685 | (1685)[136] Trooper: buff coat with black cuffs, black polished metal breast armour, white cravat, tin buttons, red saddle cover. |

## Dragoons:

| Id. | Year: | Colonel Proprietor – Denomination: | Campaigns-Engagements: | History: | Uniforms: |
|---|---|---|---|---|---|
| WzD-1 | 1675 | Müller or Würzburg Dragoner | Phippsburg (1676) | to Pfalz-Neuburg in 1679 | (1675)[137] Private: dark blue coat with red facings. |
| WzD-2 | 1683 | Hedesdorff | | disbanded in 1685 | |
| WzD-3 | 1688 | Münster, 1690 Truchsess | Kahlenberg (1683) | Bubenhofen Dragoner in 1792 | |

## Appendix II Notes

1. Archivio di Stato di Napoli (ASNa): 'Museo' vol. 994146 (Antonio Carafa di Stigliano), c. 13, *Stato delle Truppe Cesaree in Germania, il mese di Ottobre, l'anno 1675*.
2. *Capitolation 16. Februar 1687*, in Jochen Koch, *Johann Philipp Winheim: Kriegskommissair der Bayreuther Regimenter im 'Grossen Türkenkrieg' (1687–1695) und späterer Reichspostmeister in Coburg (1698–1717)* (Regensburg, Roderer, 1998), pp.129–130.
3. *Capitolation 16. Februar 1687*, pp.129–130.
4. Rudolph Donath, *Die Kaiserliche und Kaiserlich und Königliche Österreichische Armee 1618 – 1918* (Manuscript, Vienna, 1970).
5. Belaubre-Goldberg, *Les Armées qui combattirent Louis XIV – Les 3 Brunswick*, p. II, plate 10.
6. Robert Wilhelm Georg von Sichart, *Geschichte der königlich-hannoverschen Armee* (Hanover, 1866), Vol. I, p 298.
7. Belaubre-Goldberg, *Les Armées qui Combattirent Louis XIV – Les 3 Brunswick*, p. II, plate 10.
8. Friedrich Schirmer, 'Die Schlacht bei Entzheim, 24. 9. 1674,' in *Alte und Neue Zinnfiguren* (1971), Heft 9, p.178.
9. Belaubre-Goldberg, *Les Armées qui Combattirent Louis XIV – Les 3 Brunswick*, p. II, plate 11.
10. Belaubre-Goldberg, *Les Armées qui Combattirent Louis XIV – Les 3 Brunswick*, p. II, plate 11.
11. Sichart, *Geschichte der Königlich-Hannoverschen Armee*, vol. I, p 298.
12. Belaubre-Goldberg, *Les Armées qui Combattirent Louis XIV – Les 3 Brunswick*, p. II, plate 11, and Sichart, *Geschichte der königlich-hannoverschen Armee*, vol. I, p 298.
13. Sichart, *Geschichte der Königlich-Hannoverschen Armee*, vol. I, p.299.
14. Sichart, *Geschichte der Königlich-Hannoverschen Armee*, vol. I, p 298.
15. Sichart, *Geschichte der Königlich-Hannoverschen Armee*, vol. I, p 298.
16. Belaubre-Goldberg, *Les Armées qui Combattirent Louis XIV – Les 3 Brunswick*, p. II, plate 10.
17. Belaubre-Goldberg, *Les Armées qui Combattirent Louis XIV – Les 3 Brunswick*, p. II, plate 24.
18. Belaubre-Goldberg, *Les Armées qui Combattirent Louis XIV – Les 3 Brunswick*, p. II, plate 12.
19. Felix Schütz von Brandis, *Übersicht der Geschichte der Hannoversche Armee von 1617 bis 1866* (Hanover-Leipzig, 1903), p.110.
20. Sichart, *Geschichte der Königlich-Hannoverschen Armee*, vol. I, p 298.
21. Sichart, *Geschichte der Königlich-Hannoverschen Armee*, vol. I, p 298.
22. Schirmer, 'Die Schlacht bei Entzheim, 24. 9. 1674', p.178.
23. Belaubre, *Les Triomphes du Louis XIV*, p.172.
24. Schirmer, 'Die Schlacht bei Entzheim, 24. 9. 1674', p.178.
25. Belaubre-Goldberg, *Les Armées qui Combattirent Louis XIV – Les 3 Brunswick*, p. II, plate 16.
26. Schirmer, 'Die Schlacht bei Entzheim, 24. 9. 1674', p.178.
27. Belaubre-Goldberg, *Les Armées qui Combattirent Louis XIV – Les 3 Brunswick*, p. II, plate 19.
28. Schirmer, 'Die Schlacht bei Entzheim, 24. 9. 1674', p.178.
29. Brandis, *Übersicht der Geschichte der Hannoversche Armee*, p.75.
30. Brandis, *Übersicht der Geschichte der Hannoversche Armee*, p.76.
31. Belaubre-Goldberg, *Les Armées qui Combattirent Louis XIV – Les 3 Brunswick*, p. II, plate 19.
32. Richard & Herbert Knötel, *Mittheilungen* (Rathenow, 1909); Band 15, Beilage 5, p.19.
33. Brandis, *Übersicht der Geschichte der Hannoversche Armee*, p.75.
34. Sichart, *Geschichte der Königlich-Hannoverschen Armee*, vol. I, p.297.
35. Jean Belaubre & Klaus Peter Goldberg, *Les Armées qui combattirent Louis XIV – Les 3 Brunswick* (Paris: self-published, 1976–1977), p. II, plate 12.
36. Belaubre-Goldberg, *Les Armées qui Combattirent Louis XIV – Les 3 Brunswick*, p. II, plate 24.

## GERMAN REGIMENTS, SQUADRONS AND COMPANIES – 1657–1690

37  Johann von Reitzenstein, *Die Uniformbilder in der Armee-Ehrenhalle des Vaterländischen Museum in Celle* (Celle, 1914), Plate 4.
38  Robert Wilhelm Georg von Sichart, *Geschichte der Königlich-Hannoverschen Armee*, vol. I (Hannover, 1866), pp.127–128.
39  Niedersachsen Hauptstaatsarchiv Hannover (NSHa), *Fürstentum Calemberg*, Cal. 16, Nr. 844, p.144: *Capitulation 27.May.1672*.
40  Belaubre-Goldberg, *Les Armées qui Combattirent Louis XIV – Les 3 Brunswick*, p. II, plate 24, and Sichart, *Geschichte der königlich-hannoverschen Armee*, vol. I, p.297.
41  Belaubre-Goldberg, *Les Armées qui Combattirent Louis XIV – Les 3 Brunswick*, p. II, plate 15.
42  Sichart, *Geschichte der Königlich-Hannoverschen Armee*, vol. I, pp.127–128.
43  Sichart, *Geschichte der Königlich-Hannoverschen Armee*, vol. I, p.297, and Belaubre-Goldberg, *Les Armées qui combattirent Louis XIV – Les 3 Brunswick*, p. II, plate 12.
44  Sichart, *Geschichte der Königlich-Hannoverschen Armee*, vol. I, pp.127–128, and p.297.
45  NSHa, Cal. 16, Nr. 844, pp.34–36,.and Sichart, *Geschichte der Königlich-Hannoverschen Armee*, vol. I, p.297.
46  NSHa, Hann. 47 - I, Nr. 50.
47  Sichart, *Geschichte der Königlich-Hannoverschen Armee*, vol. I, p.297.
48  NSHa, Hann. 47 – I, Nr. 92.
49  Sichart, *Geschichte der königlich-hannoverschen Armee*, vol. I, p.297.
50  NSHa, Cal Br 16 Nr 956, *Auswärtige Lieferanten*.
51  NSHa, Cal Br 16 Nr 956, *Auswärtige Lieferanten*.
52  NSHa, Cal Br 16 Nr 956 *Auswärtige Lieferanten*.
53  Belaubre-Goldberg, *Les Armées qui Combattirent Louis XIV – Les 3 Brunswick*, p. II, plate 15.
54  Belaubre-Goldberg, *Les Armées qui Combattirent Louis XIV – Les 3 Brunswick*, p. II, plate 15.
55  Belaubre-Goldberg, *Les Armées qui Combattirent Louis XIV – Les 3 Brunswick*, p. II, plate 14.
56  Belaubre-Goldberg, *Les Armées qui Combattirent Louis XIV – Les 3 Brunswick*, p. II, plate 13.
57  Belaubre-Goldberg, *Les Armées qui Combattirent Louis XIV – Les 3 Brunswick*, p. II, plate 16.
58  Sichart, *Geschichte der Königlich-Hannoverschen Armee*, vol. I, p.205..
59  Belaubre-Goldberg, *Les Armées qui Combattirent Louis XIV – Les 3 Brunswick*, p. II, plate 16.
60  Belaubre-Goldberg, *Les Armées qui Combattirent Louis XIV* – Les 3 Brunswick, p. II, plate 17
61  Belaubre-Goldberg, *Les Armées qui Combattirent Louis XIV* – Les 3 Brunswick, p. II, plate 9.
62  Belaubre-Goldberg, *Les Armées qui Combattirent Louis XIV* – Les 3 Brunswick, p. II, plate 17.
63  Belaubre-Goldberg, *Les Armées qui Combattirent Louis XIV* – Les 3 Brunswick, p. II, plate 17.
64  Belaubre, *Les Triomphes du Louis XIV*, p.172.
65  Belaubre-Goldberg, *Les Armées qui Combattirent Louis XIV* – Les 3 Brunswick, p. II, plate 18.
66  Sichart, *Geschichte der Königlich-Hannoverschen Armee*, vol. I, p.205.
67  Belaubre-Goldberg, *Les Armées qui Combattirent Louis XIV* – Les 3 Brunswick, p. II, plate 18.
68  Sichart, *Geschichte der Königlich-Hannoverschen Armee*, vol. I, p.205.
69  Belaubre-Goldberg, *Les Armées qui Combattirent Louis XIV* – Les 3 Brunswick, p. II, plate 9.
70  Carl Venturini, *Umriss Einer Pragmatischen Geschichte des Kriegswesens im Herzogtum Braunschweig* (Magdeburg, 1837-Mv-Miliray Verlag, 2020), p.22.
71  Carl Venturini, *Umriss Einer Pragmatischen Geschichte des Kriegswesens im Herzogtum Braunschweig*, p.22.
72  Carl Venturini, *Umriss Einer Pragmatischen Geschichte des Kriegswesens im Herzogtum Braunschweig*, p.22.

73 'A List of our Army as it was drawn up at Tillroy Camp (July-August.1689) by an unkown British officer,' in *Journal of the Society for Army Historical Research*, Vol. 20, No. 79 (Autumn, 1941), p.177.
74 Belaubre-Goldberg, *Les Armées qui Combattirent Louis XIV – Les 3 Brunswick*, p. I, plate 1.
75 'A List of our Army as it was drawn up at Tillroy Camp (July-August.1689) by an unkown British officer,' in *Journal of the Society for Army Historical Research*, Vol. 20, No. 79 (Autumn, 1941), p.177.
76 'A List of our Army as it was drawn up at Tillroy Camp (July-August.1689) by an unkown British officer,' in *Journal of the Society for Army Historical Research*, Vol. 20, No. 79 (Autumn, 1941), p.177.
77 Belaubre, *Les Triomphes du Louis XIV*, p.81.
78 Carl Venturini, *Umriss Einer Pragmatischen Geschichte des Kriegswesens im Herzogtum Braunschweig*, p.22.
79 Otto Elster, *Geschichte der Stehenden Truppen im Herzogtum Braunschweig-Wolfenbüttel, 1600–1806*, vol. II (Leipzig, 1899–1901), p.134.
80 Carl Venturini, *Umriss Einer Pragmatischen Geschichte des Kriegswesens im Herzogtum Braunschweig*, p.22.
81 Venturini, *Umriss Einer Pragmatischen Geschichte des Kriegswesens im Herzogtum Braunschweig*, p.22.
82 *Gazette de France*, 1674, p.775.
83 Belaubre, *Les Triomphes du Louis XIV*, p.151.
84 Thomas Muhsfeldt, 'Tracht Einiges über Hamburger Stadtsoldaten' in Richard Knötel, *Mittheilungen zur Geschichte der militärischen Tracht* (Rathenow, 1896), Nr. 8.
85 Muhsfeldt, 'Tracht Einiges über Hamburger Stadtsoldaten', Nr. 8.
86 Christian Röder von Diersburg, *Geschichte des 1. Großherzoglich Hessischen Infanterie (Leibgarde) Regiments Nr. 115, 1621–1899* (Berlion, 1899), p.14.
87 Galeazzo Gualdo-Priorato, *Relatione delle Corti e Stati delli Serenissimi Landgravii d'Hassia in Cassel e Darmstadt* (Leyden, 1668), p.21.
88 Friedrich Hild, *Militärchronik des Großherzogthums Hessen von Anfang des Regierenden Hauses bis auf die neueste Zeit – Teil 1 - 1567–1790*, p.22.
89 Lezius, Martin, *Die Entwicklung des Deutschen Heeres von Seinen Frühesten Anfängen bis unsere Tage in Uniformtafeln* (Berlin, 1936), plate 1.
90 (Various Authors): *Stamm-und-Rang-Liste des Kurfürstlich Hessischen Armee Corps von 16ten Jahrhundert bis 1866* (Kassel, 1866), p.6.
91 (Various Authors): *Stamm-und-Rang-Liste des Kurfürstlich Hessischen Armee Corps von 16ten Jahrhundert bis 1866* (Kassel, 1866), p.6.
92 (Various Authors): *Stamm-und-Rang-Liste des Kurfürstlich Hessischen Armee Corps von 16ten Jahrhundert bis 1866* (Kassel, 1866), p.6.
93 (Various Authors): *Stamm-und-Rang-Liste des Kurfürstlich Hessischen Armee Corps von 16ten Jahrhundert bis 1866* (Kassel, 1866), p.6.
94 Carl von Stamford, *Das Stehende Hessische Heer von 1670–1866* (Kassel, 1900), p.122.
95 Stamford, *Das Stehende Hessische Heer*, p.122.
96 Jean Belaubre- & Klaus Peter Goldberg, *Les Armées qui combattirent Louis XIV : Oberrhein* (Paris: private publishing, 1974).
97 Stamford, *Das stehende hessische Heer*, p.122.
98 (Various Authors): *Stamm-und-Rang-Liste des Kurfürstlich Hessischen Armee Corps von 16ten Jahrhundert bis 1866* (Kassel, 1866), p.6.
99 (Various Authors): *Stamm-und-Rang-Liste des Kurfürstlich Hessischen Armee Corps*, p.7.
100 (Various Authors): *Stamm-und-Rang-Liste des Kurfürstlich Hessischen Armee Corps*, p.6.
101 Hessische Staatsarchiv Marburg, *Hessen-Kassel*, 5/2028.
102 Archivio di Stato di Venezia, *Inquisitori*, f. 601 (1691).
103 Günter Knüppel, *Das Heerwesen der Fürstentums Schleswig-Holstein-Gottorf, 1600–1715* (Neumünster, Karl Wachholtz, 1972), p.170.
104 Jean Belaubre & Klaus Peter Goldberg : *Les Armées qui Combattirent Louis XIV – Holstein-Gottorp* (Paris : privately published, 1973), p.44.

105 Belaubre-Goldberg : Les *Armées qui Combattirent Louis XIV – Holstein-Gottorp*, p.44.
106 *Gazette de France*, 1670, p.443.
107 *Gazette de France*, 1670, p.443.
108 Jean-Charles Fulaine, *Le Duc Charles IV de Lorraine et son Armée* (Metz: Editions Serpenoise, 1997), p.37.
109 Belaubre, *Les Triomphes du Louis XIV*, p.160.
110 *Nürnbergische Kleider Arten* (Nuremberg, 1686), plate 17.
111 Robert Wilhelm Georg von Sichart, *Geschichte der königlich-hannoverschen Armee* (Hanover, 1866), Vol. I, p.155.
112 Galeazzo Gualdo-Priorato, *Relatione delle Corti e Stati (…) e del Vescovato e Principato di Osnabruch* (Leyden, 1668), pp.125–126.
113 Belaubre-Goldberg, *Les Armées quiCcombattirent Louis XIV – Les 3 Brunswick*, p. II, plate 9.
114 Belaubre-Goldberg, *Les Armées qui Combattirent Louis XIV – Les 3 Brunswick*, p. II, plate 9.
115 Oskar Bezzel, *Geschichte des Kurpfälzischen Heeres, von Seinen Anfängen bis zur Vereinigung von Kurpfalz und Kurbayern*, vol. I (Munich, 1925), p.90.
116 Bezzel, *Geschichte des Kurpfälzischen Heeres*, p.91.
117 Belaubre, *Les Triomphes du Louis XIV*, p.148.
118 Bezzel, *Geschichte des Kurpfälzischen Heeres, von Seinen Anfängen bis zur Vereinigung von Kurpfalz und Kurbayern*, vol. I (Munich, 1925), p.90.
119 Bezzel, *Geschichte des Kurpfälzischen Heeres*, p.172.
120 Belaubre, *Les Triomphes du Louis XIV*, p.148.
121 Bezzel, *Geschichte des Kurpfälzischen Heeres*, p.158.
122 Bezzel, *Geschichte des Kurpfälzischen Heeres*, pp.172–173.
123 Bezzel, *Geschichte des Kurpfälzischen Heeres*, p.172.
124 Rudolph Donath, *Die Kaiserliche und Kaiserlich und Königliche Österreichische Armee 1618–1918* (Simbach/Inn: privately published, 1965–1971).
125 Leo Ignaz Stadlinger, *Geschichte des Württembergischen Kriegswesens von der Frühesten bis zur Neuesten Zeit* (Stuttgart, 1856), p.322.
126 Stadlinger, *Geschichte des Württembergischen Kriegswesens*, p.359..
127 Stadlinger, *Geschichte des Württembergischen Kriegswesens*, p.347.
128 Stadlinger, *Geschichte des Württembergischen Kriegswesens*, p.347.
129 Stadlinger, *Geschichte des Württembergischen Kriegswesens*, p.347.
130 Stadlinger, *Geschichte des Württembergischen Kriegswesens*, p.322.
131 Stadlinger, *Geschichte des Württembergischen Kriegswesens*, p.322.
132 (ASNa): 'Museo' vol. 994146 (Antonio Carafa di Stigliano), c. 13, *Stato delle Truppe Cesaree in Germania, il mese di Ottobre, l'anno 1675*.
133 (ASNa): 'Museo' vol. 994146 (Antonio Carafa di Stigliano), c. 13, *Stato delle Truppe Cesaree in Germania, il mese di Ottobre, l'anno 1675*.
134 Belaubre, *Les Triomphes du Louis XIV*, p.67.
135 (Anonymous), *Ausführliche Lista der Kayserl. Kriegs-Volcker* (1675), p.7.
136 Belaubre, *Les Triomphes de Louis XIV*, p.66.
137 Anonymous, *Ausführliche Lista der Kayserl. Kriegs-Volcker* (1675), p.7.

## About the author

Bruno Mugnai was born in Florence in 1962 and still lives there with his partner Silvia. Active for years as a historical researcher and illustrator, he is the author of several titles published by, among others, the Historical Office of the Italian Army and Helion & Co. His books focus on the historical periods and geographical areas of his interest – the ancient Italian states, Central and Eastern Europe in the sixteenth, seventeenth, and eighteenth centuries, and South America after the conquest. He is a member of 'La Sabretache', the Society for Military History Studies, and of the Italian Society of Military History. As an illustrator, he collaborates with important Italian and foreign specialists, and with the Stibbert Museum of Florence. Bruno is a Rugby Football Union enthusiast, who still believes in an Italian Grand Slam in the Six Nations Tournament.

# Other titles in the Century of the Soldier series

No 38 **Wars and Soldiers in the Early Reign of Louis XIV:** Volume 1 - The Army of the United Provinces of the Netherlands, 1660–1687

No 39 **In The Emperor's Service:** Wallenstein's Army, 1625–1634

No 40 **Charles XI's War:** The Scanian War Between Sweden and Denmark, 1675–1679

No 41 **The Armies and Wars of The Sun King 1643-1715:** Volume 1: The Guard of Louis XIV

No 42 **The Armies Of Philip IV Of Spain 1621–1665:** The Fight For European Supremacy

No 43 **Marlborough's Other Army:** The British Army and the Campaigns of the First Peninsular War, 1702–1712

No 44 **The Last Spanish Armada:** Britain And The War Of The Quadruple Alliance, 1718–1720

No 45 **Essential Agony:** The Battle of Dunbar 1650

No 46 **The Campaigns of Sir William Waller**

No 47 **Wars and Soldiers in the Early Reign of Louis XIV:** Volume 2 - The Imperial Army, 1660–1689

No 48 **The Saxon Mars and His Force:** The Saxon Army During The Reign Of John George III 1680–1691

No 49 **The King's Irish:** The Royalist Anglo-Irish Foot of the English Civil War

No 50 **The Armies and Wars of the Sun King 1643-1715:** Volume 2: The Infantry of Louis XIV

No 51 **More Like Lions Than Men:** Sir William Brereton and the Cheshire Army of Parliament, 1642–46

No 52 **I Am Minded to Rise:** The Clothing, Weapons and Accoutrements of the Jacobites from 1689 to 1719

No 53 **The Perfection of Military Discipline:** The Plug Bayonet and the English Army 1660–1705

No 54 **The Lion From the North:** The Swedish Army During the Thirty Years War: Volume 1, 1618–1632

No 55 **Wars and Soldiers in the Early Reign of Louis XIV:** Volume 3 - The Armies of the Ottoman Empire 1645–1718

No 56 **St. Ruth's Fatal Gamble:** The Battle of Aughrim 1691 and the Fall Of Jacobite Ireland

No 57 **Fighting for Liberty:** Argyll & Monmouth's Military Campaigns against the Government of King James, 1685

No 58 **The Armies and Wars of the Sun King 1643-1715:** Volume 3: The Cavalry of Louis XIV

No 59 **The Lion From the North:** The Swedish Army During the Thirty Years War: Volume 2, 1632–1648

No 60 **By Defeating My Enemies:** Charles XII of Sweden and the Great Northern War 1682–1721

No 61 **Despite Destruction, Misery and Privations..:** The Polish Army in Prussia during the war against Sweden 1626–1629

No 62 **The Armies of Sir Ralph Hopton:** The Royalist Armies of the West 1642–46

No 63 **Italy, Piedmont, and the War of the Spanish Succession 1701–1712**

No 64 **'Cannon played from the great fort':** Sieges in the Severn Valley during the English Civil War 1642–1646

No 65 **Carl Gustav Armfelt and the Struggle for Finland During the Great Northern War**

No 66 **In the Midst of the Kingdom:** The Royalist War Effort in the North Midlands 1642–1646

No 67 **The Anglo-Spanish War 1655–1660:** Volume 1: The War in the West Indies

No 68 **For a Parliament Freely Chosen:** The Rebellion of Sir George Booth, 1659

No 69 **The Bavarian Army During the Thirty Years War 1618–1648:** The Backbone of the Catholic League (revised second edition)

No 70 **The Armies and Wars of the Sun King 1643-1715:** Volume 4: The War of the Spanish Succession, Artillery, Engineers and Militias

No 71 **No Armour But Courage:** Colonel Sir George Lisle, 1615–1648 (Paperback reprint)

No 72 **The New Knights:** The Development of Cavalry in Western Europe, 1562–1700

No 73 **Cavalier Capital:** Oxford in the English Civil War 1642-1646 (Paperback reprint)

No 74 **The Anglo-Spanish War 1655-1660:** Volume 2: War in Jamaica

No 75 **The Perfect Militia:** The Stuart Trained Bands of England and Wales 1603–1642

No 76 **Wars and Soldiers in the Early Reign of Louis XIV:** Volume 4 - The Armies of Spain 1659–1688

No 77 **The Battle of Nördlingen 1634:** The Bloody Fight Between Tercios and Brigades

No 78 **Wars and Soldiers in the Early Reign of Louis XIV:** Volume 5 - The Portuguese Army 1659–1690

No 79 **We Came, We Saw, God Conquered:** The Polish-Lithuanian Commonwealth's military effort in the relief of Vienna, 1683

No 80 **Charles X's Wars:** Volume 1 - Armies of the Swedish Deluge, 1655–1660

No 81 **Cromwell's Buffoon:** The Life and Career of the Regicide, Thomas Pride (Paperback reprint)

No 82 **The Colonial Ironsides:** English Expeditions under the Commonwealth and Protectorate, 1650–1660

No 83 **The English Garrison of Tangier:** Charles II's Colonial Venture in the Mediterranean, 1661–1684

No 84 **The Second Battle of Preston, 1715:** The Last Battle on English Soil

No 85 **To Settle the Crown:** Waging Civil War in Shropshire, 1642–1648 (Paperback reprint)

No 86 **A Very Gallant Gentleman:** Colonel Francis Thornhagh (1617–1648) and the Nottinghamshire Horse

No 87 **Charles X's Wars:** Volume 2 - The Wars in the East, 1655–1657

No 88 **The Shōgun's Soldiers:** The Daily Life of Samurai and Soldiers in Edo Period Japan, 1603–1721 Volume 1

No 89 **Campaigns of the Eastern Association:** The Rise of Oliver Cromwell, 1642–1645

No 90 **The Army of Occupation in Ireland 1603–42:** Defending the Protestant Hegemony

No 91 **The Armies and Wars of the Sun King 1643-1715:** Volume 5: Buccaneers and Soldiers in the Americas

No 92 **New Worlds, Old Wars:** The Anglo-American Indian Wars 1607–1678

No 93 **Against the Deluge:** Polish and Lithuanian Armies During the War Against Sweden 1655–1660

No 94 **The Battle of Rocroi:** The Battle, the Myth and the Success of Propaganda

No 95 **The Shōgun's Soldiers:** The Daily Life of Samurai and Soldiers in Edo Period Japan, 1603–1721 Volume 2

No 96 **Science of Arms: the Art of War in the Century of the Soldier 1672-1699:** Volume 1: Preparation for War and the Infantry

No 97 **Charles X's Wars:** Volume 3 - The Danish Wars 1657–1660

No 98 **Wars and Soldiers in the Early Reign of Louis XIV:** Volume 6 - Armies of the Italian States 1660–1690 Part 1

No 99 **Dragoons and Dragoon Operations in the British Civil Wars, 1638–1653**

No 100 **Wars and Soldiers in the Early Reign of Louis XIV:** Volume 6 - Armies of the Italian States 1660–1690 Part 2

No 101 **1648 and All That:** The Scottish Invasions of England, 1648 and 1651: Proceedings of the 2022 Helion and Company 'Century of the Soldier' Conference

No 102 **John Hampden and the Battle of Chalgrove:** The Political and Military Life of Hampden and his Legacy

No 103 **The City Horse:** London's militia cavalry during the English Civil War, 1642–1660

No 104 **The Battle of Lützen 1632:** A Reassessment

No 105 **Monmouth's First Rebellion:** The Later Covenanter Risings, 1660–1685

No 106 **Raw Generals and Green Soldiers:** Catholic Armies in Ireland 1641–1643

Polish, Lithuanian and Cossack armies versus the might of the Ottoman Empire

No 108 **Soldiers and Civilians, Transport and Provisions:** Early Modern Military Logistics and Supply Systems During The British Civil Wars, 1638-1653

No 109 **Batter their walls, gates and Forts:** The Proceedings of the 2022 English Civil War Fortress Symposium

No 110 **The Town Well Fortified:** The Fortresses of the Civil Wars in Britain, 1639-1660

No 111 **Crucible of the Jacobite '15:** The Battle of Sheriffmuir 1715

No 112 **Charles XII's Karoliners Volume 2 -** The Swedish Cavalry of the Great Northern War 1700-1721

No 113 **Wars and Soldiers in the Early Reign of Louis XIV:** Volume 7 - Armies of the German States 1655–1690 Part 1

No 114 **The First British Army 1624-1628:** The Army of the Duke Of Buckingham (Revised edition)

No 115 **The Army of Transylvania (1613–1690):** War and military organization from the 'golden age' of the Principality to the Habsburg conquest

No 116 **The Army of the Manchu Empire:** The Conquest Army and the Imperial Army of Qing China, 1600–1727

No 117 **French Armies of the Thirty Years' War 1618-48**

No 118 **Soldiers' Clothing of the early 17th century:** Britain and Western Europe 1618–1660

No 119 **Novelty and Change:** New research, ideas, thoughts and interpretation on the British Civil Wars and the military history of the 17th century

No 120 **Peter the Great's Disastrous Defeat:** The Swedish Victory at Narva, 1700

No 121 **Royalist Newark, 1642–1646:** Sieges and Siege Works

No 122 **The Battle of Fribourg 1644:** Enghien and Turenne at War

No 123 **Science of Arms:** The Art of War in the Century of the Soldier, 1672 to 1699: Volume 2: Cavalry, Artillery & the Conduct of War

No 124 **Supplying the New Model Army:** Logistics, arms, ammunition, clothing, victuals and the matériel of war, 1645–1646

No 125 **Wars and Soldiers in the Early Reign of Louis XIV:** Volume 7 - Armies of the German States 1655–1690 Part 2

No 126 **Wars and Soldiers in the Early Reign of Louis XIV:** Volume 7 - Armies of the German States 1655–1690 Part 3

## SERIES SPECIALS:

No 1 **Charles XII's Karoliners:** Volume 1: The Swedish Infantry & Artillery of the Great Northern War 1700–1721

For the complete range of Century of the Soldier titles please go to
www.helion.co.uk/series/century-of-the-soldier-1618-1721.php